D1572311

Global Migration and Social Change series

Series Editors: **Nando Sigona**, University of Birmingham, UK and **Alan Gamlen**, Monash University, Australia

The Global Migration and Social Change series showcases original research that looks at the nexus between migration, citizenship and social change.

Forthcoming in the series:

Mediterranean Migration:
Reception, Governance and Industry
Alessio D'Angelo and **Nicola Montagna**

Out now in the series:

Negotiating Migration in the Context of Climate Change:
International Policy and Discourse
Sarah Louise Nash

Belonging in Translation:
Solidarity and Migrant Activism in Japan
Reiko Shindo

Borders, Migration and Class in an Age of Crisis:
Producing Workers and Immigrants
Tom Vickers

Time, Migration and Forced Immobility:
Sub-Saharan African Migrants in Morocco
Inka Stock

Find out more at

bristoluniversitypress.co.uk/global-migration-and-social-change

Global Migration and Social Change series

Series Editors: **Nando Sigona**, University of Birmingham, UK and **Alan Gamlen**, Monash University, Australia

---

International advisory board:

Find out more at
bristoluniversitypress.co.uk/global-migration-and-social-change

TEMPORALITY IN MOBILE LIVES

Contemporary Asia–Australia Migration and Everyday Time

Shanthi Robertson

BRISTOL
UNIVERSITY
PRESS

First published in Great Britain in 2021 by

Bristol University Press
University of Bristol
1-9 Old Park Hill
Bristol
BS2 8BB
UK
t: +44 (0)117 954 5940
e: bup-info@bristol.ac.uk

Details of international sales and distribution partners are available at bristoluniversitypress.co.uk

British Library Cataloguing in Publication Data
A catalogue record for this book is available from the British Library

ISBN 978-1-5292-1151-1 hardcover
ISBN 978-1-5292-1154-2 ePub
ISBN 978-1-5292-1153-5 ePdf

Cover design: Andrew Corbett
Front cover image: © Andy Lawrence www.andylawrencephotography.com
Bristol University Press uses environmentally responsible print partners.
Printed in Great Britain by CPI Group (UK) Ltd, Croydon, CR0 4YY

FSC
www.fsc.org
MIX
Paper from
responsible sources
FSC® C013604

Contents

List of Figures

Acknowledgements

The writing of this book interwove with the brutally sudden deaths, in quick succession, of my dad and my brother. So while convention dictates tucking a spouse at the end of a long list of intellectual influences, I must acknowledge mine, Tristan Masters, foremost, because he provided the emotional bedrock for the book to be completed during an extraordinarily difficult period. He is, always, hearth, heart, home, and unshakeable believer in me.

I am very grateful to have received Australian Research Council funding for the project that underpins this book, and to the research participants who gave their time and stories with such generosity. And I am thankful for the Institute for Culture and Society (ICS) at Western Sydney University, which was my home over the life of this project, especially, for Ien Ang's leadership and valuable feedback on the initial project proposal, and very, very especially for my mentor Greg Noble's generous insight on drafts and unfailing support at every turn. Stephen Healy, Emma Power, Malini Sur and Megan Watkins each provided solidarity and encouragement at critical moments. Karen Soldatić has been an outstanding role model, sounding board and friend. Very special thanks are owed to the ICS running group for the biweekly reminder that some things are in fact harder and more painful than writing a book. In particular, I am indebted to Liam Magee, a most singular ally across the many travails of both running and academic life, for always pushing me forward during the tougher intervals.

This book first began to take form during a visiting research fellowship at the Asia Research Institute (ARI) at the National University of Singapore. ARI provided me with the great gift of time immersed within a dynamic research culture on Asian migration, and my ARI friends gave indispensable feedback on my early thinking on migration and time. My particular thanks go to Brenda Yeoh, Michiel Baas, Elaine Lynn-Ee Ho, Denise Spitzer and Rhacel Salazar Parreñas for their contributions and their kindness during my time in Singapore.

I have been lucky to present and develop this work in a variety of welcoming and stimulating spaces. My thanks to the Centre for Educational Research at Lancaster University; the Alfred Deakin Institute at Deakin University; the Creative People, Products and Places research concentration at the University of South Australia (UniSA), and the CaDDANZ research programme at the University of Waikato and Massey University for the invitations to present during the final stages of the research. Special thanks to Kirsty Finn and Nicola Ingram at Lancaster and Rosie Roberts at UniSA for being such delightful hosts. I am also very grateful to Rachel Silvey, Danièle Bélanger and Hae Yeon Choo for inviting me to a very productive workshop on im/mobilities, migration and care at the University of Toronto, which allowed me to develop some of the early thinking for Chapter 5. I also thank Anita Harris and Loretta Baldassar for many productive discussions on youth and transnational mobility, and for teaching me through their example how to be an academic within a genuine ethics of care for ourselves and for each other.

The project benefitted from the input of a series of brilliant research assistants. Much gratitude to Harriet Westcott, Jennifer Cheng, Jen Sherman, Kate Naidu, Bjorn Rostron, Marina Khan and Yinghua Yu, all of whom brought important insights to the project at different stages and rose to the sometimes very significant challenge of keeping me organized. I also thank Shannon Kneis and the staff at Bristol University Press for their seamless support of the project, and the reviewers for critical and constructive feedback on the manuscript.

Much love and thanks to Rochelle Ransom, for bringing infinite care and patience both to our friendship and to checking and formatting my manuscripts, and to Ash Watson for the final and excellent proofread. I am grateful to Lucy and Andy Lawrence, who opened their home to me for a week in Penzance, Cornwall. It was there that I was able to restart the writing after a long stall due to my bereavements. Andy also provided the beautiful cover photograph. I also thank Lucy, along with Bree Davies and Jess Leefe, for being my own transnational circuit of care, for 'intention words'; for much-needed distractions; and for yelling at me over WhatsApp to keep writing.

Parts of Chapters 3 and 5 were originally published in Robertson, Shanthi (2019) 'Migrant, interrupted: the temporalities of "staggered" migration from Asia to Australia.' *Current Sociology* 67(2): 169–85 and Robertson, Shanthi (2020) 'Suspending, settling, sponsoring: the intimate chronomobilities of young Asian migrants in Australia.' *Global Networks*, doi: 10.1111/glob.12291.

Series Preface

Temporality in Mobile Lives: Contemporary Asia–Australia Migration and Everyday Time by Shanthi Robertson is a welcome addition to the Global Migration and Social Change series published by Bristol University Press. The aim of the series is to offer a platform for new scholarship in refugee and migration studies that is open to different disciplinary perspectives, theoretical frameworks and methodological approaches. Robertson's dissection of migrant biographies offers a unique perspective on the ambivalence, hybridity and uncertainty of migrant experience in contemporary societies. Through a fine-grained examination of everyday ruptures, transits, beginnings and endings in the lives of Asian migrants in Australia, Robertson portrays a vivid and layered series of unexpected contingencies and detours, and necessarily fluid aspirations and desires, all framed within a sense of unfinished and always precarious mobility.

Through the concept of chronomobility, Robertson's book contributes to an emerging body of scholarship in migration studies which brings the temporal both theoretically and empirically into focus in the analysis of migration and migrant experiences, casting light on the multiple and 'different time-space horizons guiding the lives of migrants and non-migrants' (Scott, 2006: 1119). How these multiple regimes and logics of time both produce and are produced by and in migration processes is a core concern of *Temporality in Mobile Lives*, in which young, middle class and aspirational Asian migrants, mainly from India, China, Taiwan, South Korea, Malaysia and the Philippines, have to reckon with the reality of migration regimes that can disrupt, delay, halt or accelerate their everyday lives out of their control.

Robertson's approach brings to the fore questions currently at the margin of migration scholarship, including the role of time in the governance of mobile bodies, not only when on the move but also in the process of settlement; the impact of multiple regimes and logics of time on migrant biographies and everyday lived experiences; the salience of timelines and timings to the structuring of migrants' social relations; and the ways migrant mobilities shape everyday temporal practices in their places of residence.

The lives of Robertson's informants offer a rich and compelling counter narrative to established understandings of the migration experience, particularly in settler societies, centred on the linearity of migrant trajectories, from arrival to settlement to integration. They also reveal how mobility and the migration regime that governs it, patterns the timings, timelines and tempo of working lives, of place attachments and of intimate relationships throughout migrants' life course and in terms of everyday embodied experiences of time.

But migrants also transform the temporality of their new societies, as a review of the cultural calendar of an Asia-Pacific migrant city like Sydney easily reveals. Annual festivities that initially at least travelled with migrants to their new places of residence are now part of the shared cultural repertoire of the city, 'emblematic', Robertson argues in the book, 'of the possibilities for wider social transformation that emerge from the everyday temporalities and mobilities of the individual lives that have knitted together new transnational networks between Asia and Australia over the last twenty years'.

Nando Sigona
Oxford
September 2020

Introduction

In 2004, as an undergraduate engineering student in South Korea, David came to Australia for six months on a one-year working holiday visa. His aim was to enjoy Australia and improve his English enough to be able to potentially apply for jobs internationally after he graduated. After a happy six months spent working odd jobs and completing an English course in sunny Brisbane, David returned to South Korea (hereafter, 'Korea'), completed his engineering studies, and married Carolyn, a nurse. Wanting to share his Australian experience with his new wife, David brought Carolyn to Australia for their honeymoon, arriving in the tropical city of Cairns – a major tourist gateway ringed by ocean and rainforest, over 1,000 kilometres north of Brisbane. They were both struck by the vastly different daily tempo of Cairns compared with their lives in Seoul, where it was common for David to work 18-hour days at his engineering firm, and for Carolyn to do long shifts as a surgical nurse in a busy hospital. When I first met Carolyn, she recalled their honeymoon visit fondly:

> 'I had a good impression of Australia because the thing is, the people in the park, the public park. I had seen the families, like parents and high school students with school uniforms. It was just half past three in the afternoon but in Korea that time there is no people, no family around. … In Cairns, it was a weekday and people were having picnics but in Korea there is not much time to spend with families at all so everyone has full time, even overtime is, well it's just almost every day for nurse. … There was no break or time off from the work.'

After their honeymoon, David and Carolyn began to read up on Australian migration policies, noting that nurses were an in-demand occupation for skilled migration. Although Carolyn would have to retrain to get an Australian nursing qualification, it seemed to the couple to be a clear pathway forward for them both to gain Australian permanent residency (PR). David would then be able to pursue graduate studies in Australia without having to pay the higher fees required of international students, and they could start a family in the relaxed and balanced pace of life they had witnessed on their honeymoon. While they weren't certain they would stay in Australia forever, it seemed the right decision for the next stage of their lives – after all, living and working in an English-speaking country, would, they thought, ultimately be good for their future job prospects if they returned to Korea, or if they decided to move on somewhere else. David thought an Australian master's degree could also be a stepping stone to a PhD programme in the US.

Carolyn easily secured a student visa, and they arrived in Australia in 2005. She spent one year, longer than they had initially thought she would need, studying English to prepare for her nursing course. David, meanwhile, worked in a Korean supermarket (where he was illegally underpaid), did unskilled work at a factory, and had short stints making coffee and preparing sushi. He estimated he had worked on nearly 100 applications for engineering jobs but had no success. Most employers were unwilling to even interview him without PR, although his dependent visa, attached to Carolyn's student visa, legally allowed him unrestricted work rights.

Carolyn studied intensely to complete her nursing qualification, spending hours on even minor assignments, checking her English over and over again. She felt constantly stressed, knowing that failing any courses would cost both time and money, and delay the plans she and David had agreed on. Carolyn told me:

> 'I lost maybe five kilos due to stress. I couldn't eat much because it was – truth is, quite expensive, almost three times [more] expensive than domestic students so I was under a bunch of pressure to pass. If I failed, we would pay again and visa has to be extended as well and health insurance I have to pay more … lots of things just going on if I can't pass. One [of] my friends they failed just one subject, one unit, they ha[d] to extend six months. And I worried about the time because I was thinking I had to pass on time, then my husband starts his study.'

Shortly before Carolyn graduated, the English language requirements for nursing licenses in Australia changed, increasing from an International English Language Testing System (IELTS) score of 6.5 to 7.0. Thus, although Carolyn secured her Australian nursing qualification when she graduated, she now needed this IELTS score to be formally accredited to practise and to be eligible to apply for PR. Their planned pathway to PR was now suspended, and David had to commence his master's degree as an international student and pay the higher level of fees. David became the primary student visa holder, while Carolyn switched to a dependent spouse visa. She spent the next 12 months working a series of part-time jobs in aged care homes, while studying for and sitting the IELTS test multiple times, always narrowly missing out on the 7.0 score. She also spent a period back in Korea at a specialist IELTS cram school, but her increasing anxiety seemed to hold her back whenever she sat the exam.

Although their plans for PR, and subsequently starting a family, were on hold, David received an offer for a coveted PhD scholarship with a national science agency at the end of his master's. This would give the couple another student visa for the duration of the PhD, as well as a living stipend, and, most crucially, more time to try to achieve PR. At the last minute, however, government funding cuts to both the science agency offering the scholarship and the state-funded nursing home where Carolyn was working meant the scholarship was withdrawn and Carolyn lost her job. This left them without an income and also without a visa to be able to stay. David returned to Korea, frantically seeking out new PhD opportunities online in the US and Canada as well as Australia, while Carolyn tried desperately to get a new student visa by enrolling in a cheap vocational course. After a stressful few months of not knowing where they would end up, David found a new PhD position in Brisbane, was granted a new visa and returned to Australia to commence his programme.

When I met Carolyn and David, now both in their mid-thirties, they had been living in Brisbane for over ten years. David and I met on his university campus as he took a break from his thesis work, while Carolyn met me a few days later at a café next to the Brisbane city library, on her way home from a morning shift at her new aged care home job. Carolyn had given up on achieving a 7.0 IELTS score and gaining full nursing accreditation – she said she had lost confidence in her ability, and no longer wished to pay the expensive fees to resit the test. Although she misses the challenges of surgical nursing, Carolyn said she enjoys her job as a nursing assistant in aged care and has also picked up some shifts in the mental health sector. Her English capability is seldom a problem in these roles, and she is popular with the other staff and patients. David and Carolyn love their rare days off together, when Carolyn told me they go to a local park with coffee, lie on the grass, look at the blue sky and listen to the kids playing – brief moments that reflect the kind of life they imagined a decade earlier on their honeymoon. They are sometimes hopeful about securing their future in Australia – David will be eligible for a four-year temporary graduate work visa after his PhD, and if he finds an employer to sponsor him, could also eventually be eligible for PR – but this remains a long and uncertain road.

David and Carolyn's lives retain a temporal uncertainty that has deep material and affective impacts. The longed-for baby, which they had planned to have in the first two years of their marriage, has been infinitely delayed, even now that their ten-year wedding anniversary has come and gone. They rely too much at present on Carolyn's income, and without PR, they do not have access to paid maternity leave or to subsidized healthcare, childcare or education. Carolyn in fact returned to Korea recently for dental surgery; it was cheaper to pay for the flights and have a family connection treat her in Korea than to pay as a private patient in Australia. The fact that PR might never materialize, and David and Carolyn might have to return to Korea or move on to somewhere else, remains a constant cloud on the horizon. With the sideways, and sometimes backwards, moves that both their careers have taken in Australia, David and Carolyn no longer think that their international experience will allow an easy reinsertion into the Korean labour market in their fields. Carolyn also thinks she could not get used to the intensities of Korean life again: the long work hours; the rigid workplace hierarchies; the filial duties she would have to fulfil every weekend as a daughter and daughter-in-law. Yet, when things get difficult in Australia, David and Carolyn also have moments when they desire to return or think about trying to migrate to Canada or the UK.

David and Carolyn's story reflects the fact that, for many of the young and middleclass in Asia, living, working and studying internationally – particularly in the Anglophone West – is generally understood as a process that engenders possibilities to craft global lifestyles and careers, and to experience different ways of life. In reality, however, these paths are seldom smooth, often involving the suspension of teleological progression through work or life goals. What emerges instead are a series of temporal contingencies, unexpected detours, and reimagined aspirations and desires, all framed within a sense of unfinished mobility and future uncertainty. The uncertainties and contingencies of this kind of migration affect daily, lived experiences of time as social, cultural and embodied, and construct new ways of being. For David and Carolyn, at times managing packed schedules of work and study made their days both fragmented and intense; at other points, there were frenzied and anxious rushes to find new means to stay. Yet they also found pockets, here and there, of the slow leisure time that had initially inspired them to migrate. A constant sense of waiting became deeply embedded in their everyday lives, with the pace of waiting varying – while the weeks often seemed to fly with a worrying rapidity towards visa expiry dates, the wait for the 'right time' to start their family seemed endless. The orientation towards flexibility required by these divergent lived temporalities engendered worry and instability, but also new senses of openness and possibility.

I begin with David and Carolyn's story, one of many similar stories that I heard during the course of my research, because it illustrates clearly this book's two central premises. The first is that migration, understood as a set of processes that are increasingly temporally heterogeneous and multidirectional, alters the way that time is lived. Complex relations between migration and the temporal – and the ways these relations shape migrants' lives – are my core concern throughout this book; in particular, how multiple regimes and logics of time both produce and are produced by migration processes. The second premise is that for the young, mobile and middleclass today, there is a sense of promise in being 'on the move'; a sense that as modern subjects, moving transnationally can create expanded possibilities for lives and lifestyles as well as livelihoods. However, for these 'middling' migrants, this promise is more likely to be borne out through experiences of unevenness and contingency than through upward mobility into a class of mobile elites who can move fluidly across borders to seek lifestyle and work opportunities.

Mobility pathways like David and Carolyn's are becoming the norm within Australia's migration landscape. There are now over 1.9 million temporary residents living and working in Australia (DIBP, 2016a), and migrant arrivals with temporary visas are now outstripping permanent visa entries. The majority hold working holiday, student, or skilled graduate work visas, and a smaller number hold temporary skilled work visas, bridging visas and dependent or spouse visas. Far from transient sojourners, however, many of these migrants, like David and Carolyn, stay on for extended periods, transitioning across different visa categories over time. Some eventually acquire PR; over 50% of permanent residencies are granted to migrants already living onshore on temporary visas. While such pathways often mean periods of 'long-term temporariness' (Mares, 2016) and little certainty of eventual outcomes for migrants, they also engender new types of circulation between Australia and other countries, as ongoing and flexible mobility is often the goal, rather than permanent settlement.

It is young and educated Asian migrants, like David and Carolyn, who are particularly prominent within these new patterns of temporally heterogeneous mobility. Of the more than six million Australian residents born overseas, nearly 40% now hail from Asian source countries (ABS, 2016). Asian migrants are statistically more likely to have non-linear and multistage migration pathways than migrants from non-Asian source countries, with greater propensity for temporary and permanent departures and onshore status 'switching' (Hugo, 2008). Asian migrants on temporary visas are also far more likely than permanent migrants to be mobile across different regions in Australia and across different jobs (Khoo et al, 2008; Rowe et al, 2013). Asian migrants, particularly Chinese and Indian, dominate the temporary categories such as student visas and temporary work visas that are often the entry point for multistep migration pathways. Indian, Chinese, Filipino and South Korean nationals also make up about 40% of skilled temporary work visas (DIBP, 2016b), while Taiwan and South Korea make up 30% of working holiday visa grants and China over 26% of 'work and holiday' grants[1] (DIBP, 2016c).

The migrant interlocutors I met in the course of my research for this book were mostly middle-class young people from India, China, Taiwan, South Korea, Malaysia and the Philippines living with uncertain temporal horizons in Australia. Despite the prevalence of these aforementioned forms of migration in Australia, as well as in other Anglophone 'settler' contexts globally such as the US, Canada and New Zealand, the mobilities, decisions, aspirations and social experiences of these migrants are difficult to place analytically within migration scholarship. There is little space for understanding their experiences within the existing vocabularies of migration studies globally, or within sociological research into migrant experience in traditionally settler contexts, which in Australia usually falls under the banner of migration, ethnicity and multiculturalism sociology. In the case of global migration studies, migrants are commonly categorized as either skilled or unskilled, temporary or permanent, sojourner or settler, privileged or marginalized. The spaces between and the journeys across these categories over time are less often explored. In the case of migration sociology in Anglophone settler contexts like Australia, Canada, the UK, the US and New Zealand, the focus historically has been on the settlement, integration, identity and belonging of permanent settler migrants and their second-generation children, often implicitly guided by ideas of migrant trajectories as linear progression from 'arrival' to 'belonging'. Assimilationist and integrationist approaches to belonging have given way, since the 1970s, to studies that foreground hybridity, multiple identities and transnationalism. Yet, migration as an 'event' with a clear-cut 'before' and 'after' often remains the foundational framing of sociological migration narratives. Before and after temporalities of 'migration-as-event' do not adequately reflect the fragmented and often open-ended trajectories experienced by contemporary migrants like David and Carolyn.

The migrants whose lives I explore in this book – young and mostly middle-class Asians who arrived in Australia during the first decades of the 21st century on temporary visas – also belong to a generation who have come of age in a global economy with a specific temporal orientation; namely, an economy where a 'logic of flexibility' (Scott, 2006: 1122) is hegemonic. As part of a burgeoning middle class from rapidly industrializing or recently industrialized nations in Asia, they are also part of a generation for whom 'global' life experience, often in the form of transient mobilities for study and work rather than classical settler migration, has become culturally normative. To live, work and study overseas is increasingly seen as a normal and desirable part of middle-class identities and life trajectories, rather than the domain of global elites (Scott, 2006; Gomes, 2016). David and Carolyn, as well as my other interlocutors, therefore fall into the broad category of middling migration experiences – they neither belong to an elite stratum of highly skilled and highly paid entrepreneurs or knowledge workers, nor migrate as unskilled labour to escape economic and social hardship. Middling migrants now comprise the majority of regular migration flows to post-industrial countries where migrants with skills and educational capital are increasingly prioritized over unskilled migrant workers (Mar, 2005). While this middle space is one of relative privilege compared with low-skilled and undocumented labour migrants globally, it is also a space, particularly for those who are young and navigating early career and life transitions, of decidedly uneven experiences. Middling migrants are often, as David and Carolyn's experiences attest, 'anxious subjects' (Mar, 2005: 367). Their migration trajectories involve: complex social and economic locations and relocations, as they combine skilled and unskilled work; periods of precarity as well as potential upward social mobility; and short-term sacrifices of middle-class lifestyles and incomes to achieve longer-term goals (Ho and Ley, 2014; Parutis, 2011). I seek to show in this book how aspirations and imaginaries of mobility play out in diverse and uneven outcomes in the unfolding of middling migrants' biographies over time, as well as in their everyday lived experiences of time in different places. I draw on the narratives of migrants like David and Carolyn to explore some of these complexities around middling migrants' temporal experiences in mobility – experiences that I understand through the concept of 'chronomobilities'.

David and Carolyn's migration journey, for example, moved them not only across space, but in between multiple and intersecting experiences of time. David's initial move to Australia was only ever intended to be transient – a youthful experiential sojourn to enable a future globalized career. But lifestyle desires for a slower pace of life and more time with family attracted David and Carolyn to consider a longer-term – although not necessarily permanent – move via skilled migration. Yet this linear plan was disrupted and suspended at various points in their journey, with policy changes and new circumstances sometimes suspending or rerouting their progress, and once, in the case of David's lost PhD opportunity, instantly evaporating their right to stay.

David spoke about how, when he had first come to Australia, he had "never worried about anything" and only thought about the future in terms of the positive outcomes his global experience would bring. Now he is in a different stage of life, and the stakes of leaving or staying have become, over time, much higher:

> 'Most working holiday visa is temporarily life in Australia. ... In my case, I just want to study English and to meet every, many friends from overseas and so on. But these days ... I have family and I have to [have] permanent work, permanent job I have to get ... and every situation is totally different. Just at that moment [when I was a working holiday maker] I just want to experience. But these days I need more stable things for our life, so it's totally different.'

After seeing their 'planful' (Clausen, 1993) and linear imagined migration trajectory break down step by step, David and Carolyn both feel they now have a different way of looking at their future, one that is cautiously hopeful, but ever-flexible. Carolyn feels that their long and rocky experience has changed not only her outlook on the future, but also her attitudes to life and her way of being in more intimate ways. She feels she used to be more rigid with her expectations of what she should do and what life should look like. Although still worried about how unsettled they remain, especially given their plans for a family, she values the openness and flexibility that she feels have become part of her identity:

'I'm more relaxed [now]. [In Korea] I had a certain – this one had to be this way and that way, you know, I'm much forced by my parents or my brother and all my friends, you have to do this and do this, like a bit bossy but it's now – I respect what they're thinking but I'm thinking [differently than] what they're expecting or what they hope, believe or expect. For me, [I want] a different life and [to know] different people. … [It has been a] good opportunity to get myself, get an open-mind and relax, balanced.'

Exploring these lived experiences of mobile temporality is, I argue, highly significant to migration studies, largely because these experiences reflect the broader spatio-temporal changes migration has undergone in our current era of globalized modernity. Papastergiadis (2000) evocatively described migration in the space-time of global modernity as 'turbulence' – an endless motion with multiple routes and uncertain consequences. At an individual level, contemporary migrations often involve multiple geographic trajectories and changing forms of status, encompassing an ongoing process of movement across time and space rather than a single movement from one place to another (Harney and Baldassar, 2007; Samers, 2010). Migrant mobilities are thus no longer about permanent and one-time ruptures, but transient and complex routes with multiple destinations (Yeoh, 2017). 'Push–pull' economic models and 'rational choice' behavioural models that explain migration as a preordained event that occurs at a specific moment in time (McHugh, 2000) clearly no longer hold in the context of these complex, transient and continuous mobilities. Yet, despite these inherently temporal changes to how migration is both understood sociologically and experienced in the everyday, time has only recently begun to seriously enter in to discussions of the heterogeneity of contemporary migration (Griffiths et al, 2013), previously often emerging theoretically only as implicit or subordinate in discussions of space and spatiality (May and Thrift, 2004).

Analysis of the mutually constitutive relationships between transforming migrant mobilities and transforming migrant temporalities – what I refer to as chronomobilities – is an important challenge for the sociology of contemporary migration experiences, and there are several reasons for this importance. First and foremost, as Scott (2006: 1119) asserts, there are 'different time-space horizons guiding the lives of migrants and non-migrants' that are not often addressed in sociological analyses of migration that focus primarily on culture, identity and social inclusion. Second, a temporal lens is a means to comprehensively destabilize traditional political understandings of migration that, particularly in settler societies like Australia, remain often predicated on a linear temporal journey from alien to citizen and from arrival to settlement and integration. Finally, I argue that migration, and middling migration in particular, can be an empirical entry point to understanding the multifaceted consequences of global temporal transformation in everyday lives. Fragmentation of the life-course and a loss of security, for example, are global temporal conditions that prompt migration, but migration can simultaneously and paradoxically both mitigate and exacerbate such forms of risk and uncertainty. The temporalities of global capitalism's 'just-in-time' economy compel individuals' mobility (Shields, 2003), yet they are also implicated in bordering processes (Mezzadra, 2011) that contain, suspend and decelerate particular types of migrant bodies while accelerating others. Despite increasing global interconnectedness and 'time-space compression' (Harvey, 1999), migration still involves fundamental temporal ruptures in biographies and daily lives – starting again, reconstituting lives elsewhere, the stretching of pasts and presents and the dispersal of risks and possible futures across multiple places. Mobile lives of 'the middle', which can oscillate between precarity and fluidity, autonomy and heteronomy, desire and anxiety, linearity and fragmentation, are a particularly fertile empirical space to understand the nuanced effects of these temporal conditions on 'ordinary' lives.

I thus seek throughout this book to highlight the multifarious ways that temporality operates within the lives of young and middle-class migrants from Asia to Australia whose open-ended mobilities crisscross multiple spaces, statuses and identities. In order to uncover the complexities and multiplicities of temporality on the move, I draw on the concept of chronomobilities, which I use to describe the temporalities that structure mobile lives as well as emerge from them. I position chronomobilities – which encompass the disjunctures, velocities, synchronizations and rhythms of everyday mobile lives and the meanings they entail – as fundamentally shaped by specific global and national 'time-regimes' of the early 21st century. These are a global socio-temporal regime of 'hegemonic flexibility' in economic and social life, and a subsequent national time-regime of migration governance that I refer to as the 'transification of migration' – a process by which migration has become increasingly and simultaneously transient, transitionary and transitory. I also argue that three 'time-logics' emerge as the primary ways in which time is 'lived' and understood within migrants' own meaning making and narrations of their lives under these broader temporal conditions. These are: logics of sequence, that is, orientations towards past, present, future or before, now, and after; logics of tempo, that is, orientations and experiences of pace, metre and rhythm; and logics of synchronicity, that is, relational experiences of time in terms of synchronicities and asynchronicities with other individuals or collectives. These three time-logics represent distinct but often interlinked modes through which migrants understand and make sense of time-in-mobility. The focus on the three logics – sequence, tempo and synchronicity – allows time to be understood as multiply and simultaneously sequential, rhythmic and relational. I use this conceptual approach throughout the subsequent chapters of this book to find a way through the multiscalar and mutually constitutive relationships between time and migrant mobility – the ways time structures migrants' mobilities as well as the ways new forms and experiences of time simultaneously emerge from their mobilities.

The extended primary research from which I draw my conceptual thinking for this book has involved over 90 formal interviews with migrant participants, as well as numerous informal conversations and observations conducted between 2005 and 2016. However, the empirical chapters of this book draw specifically from fieldwork conducted in the cities and surrounding suburbs of Melbourne, Sydney, Brisbane and Perth, as well as online, between 2015 and 2016. This research involved a series of in-depth narrative interviews and a process of 'focused ethnography' (Knoblauch, 2005) through participant self-documentation where each migrant provided a collection of visual and textual artefacts relating to their migration experience. The research took the specific kinds of migration trajectories undertaken by middling 21st-century Asian migrants to Australia as its empirical entry point. As such, the research did not lend itself to a conventional ethnography of long-term observation at specific field sites, as migrant participants did not all belong to the same social or cultural group, nor necessarily live or work in the same locations. I therefore employed a focused ethnographic approach in which data intensity (the triangulation of multiple narrative interviews with most participants and textual and visual artefacts), and the breadth and intensity of the analysis of individual experience, compensated for shorter-term engagement with participants. These methods engaged 42 migrants (approximately half male and half female), from the top six Asian source countries for temporary visa entries – China, India, South Korea, Malaysia, the Philippines and Taiwan – who all arrived in Australia between 2000 and 2013 and stayed for two or more years. A selection of images from the visual and textual artefact data is included in Chapters 3 to 5. Due to the focus in this research on individual narratives of migration, throughout the book participants' names, and at times other details about their families, workplaces, homes and specific experiences, have been altered to protect their anonymity.

The group of research participants featured in this book was limited to migrants who were in Australia at the time of recruitment to the project, but due to interviews being conducted over two years, some had moved on or returned to their country of origin, either voluntarily and involuntarily, by the end of the project. The sample also potentially does not capture the most vulnerable segments of this population, such as those have overstayed visas and are living in Australia illegally, or those who are experiencing highly exploitative and illegal work situations, because they are likely to be reluctant to participate in research. However, on the basis of my ongoing work across multiple projects on these forms of migration since 2005, the experiences of this group of young migrants tends to reflect broader patterns in the overall experience of 'transification'.

The remainder of this book is divided into five chapters plus a Conclusion. In the next chapter, Chapter 1, I set up the book's central concepts and arguments, drawing on existing literature on the turn towards temporal analysis in migration studies over the last decade. I sketch out in detail in this chapter how I see chronomobilities as structured through specific time–regimes and time–logics. In Chapter 2, I establish the empirical context of migration from Asia to Australia in the 21st century and make a set of arguments around the empirical value of studying these middling forms of migration. I also think through my conceptualization of these migrants *as* middling, seeking to move this empirical category beyond conventional understandings in migration studies that tend to position the 'middle' as a fixed and primarily socioeconomic classification. My central claim here is that rethinking the middle in more expansive terms can shed light on nuanced and divergent experiences of time, beyond polarized ideas of migration creating either temporal liminality through the mobility of the disenfranchised or temporal fluidity through the mobility of the elite. Chapters 1 and 2, then, create a set of conceptual arguments around the importance of rethinking and recentring both time and the middle in the study of contemporary migrant mobilities.

In Chapters 3 to 5, I use data from narrative interviews and visual artefacts to explore the chronomobilities of migrants' lives via their own narratives and meanings. I focus on how hegemonic flexibility and the transification of migration structure interplays of sequence, tempo and synchronicity in migrants' everyday lives, across the themes of work (Chapter 3), place (Chapter 4), and intimate and familial relationships (Chapter 5). The focus on these themes centres migrants as simultaneously labouring subjects, intimate subjects and emplaced subjects with transnational, translocal and global orientations towards the fundamental social projects of the modern self – education and work, social relations and place attachments. Chapter 3 addresses how, for 'middling migrants' from Asia in Australia, hegemonic flexibility and the transification of migration create new forms of mobile labour and new career pathways; transform lived experiences of work time; and shape understandings of the self in relation to time and work. I argue primarily here that young and middling migrants become 'transified workers' whose careers are made up of contingent rather than teleological processes. Chapter 4 connects migrant experiences of temporality to their dwelling within, mobilities across, and attachments to place including nation states, towns, cities and homes. The ethnographic analysis in this chapter is concerned with how time is lived within and across different places, and how rhythms of local, lived time are shaped by the time-regimes that structure migrants' lives. I show how, for middling migrants, different local places across mobility trajectories have different temporal rhythms and paces of life and influence differently ordered biographies. Chapter 5 explores how, for middling migrants in the life-stage of 'emerging adulthood', romantic partnerships and transnational family relationships are highly significant to their experiences of mobility and are complicated by a context in which partner and spouse visas can secure migration futures. This chapter utilizes the chronomobilities approach to explore how middling migrants understand and negotiate 'times of the heart' – focusing on families and intimate relationships – under the conditions of their mobility. The analysis focuses on two highly significant aspects of migrants' narratives in which logics of tempo, sequence and synchronicity have bearing on the intertwined negotiations of intimate and family relationships: reconfiguring intimate timelines and timing in relation to mobility, and how partner and spouse visas transform family relations through time.

Finally, the Conclusion returns to and reflects on the fundamental questions posed by the book as a whole. Why does time matter to the study of migration? How are spatio-temporal formations, and subsequently scholarly understandings, of migrant mobilities changing in the contemporary world? What new insights does a temporal perspective add to the sociology of migration? How can we understand the middle as a range of migration experiences that sit in between the liminal mobilities of those disenfranchised by globalization and the fluid mobilities of those privileged by the same forces?

1

Chronomobilities: 21st–Century Migration and Lived Time

Hyon-Woo grew up in a small town in the southern region of Korea. Her parents had always expected their two daughters would go to university. When Hyon-Woo secured a place for an engineering degree in Seoul, they were thrilled. "They were so proud of having a daughter, going to capital city, getting into [a] good university, [a] good major," Hyon-Woo told me. "They thought that my future is guaranteed." Hyon-Woo, however, was miserable after she moved to Seoul. She didn't enjoy her course and she felt out of place, like an "awkward country-girl". The other students were obsessed, she said, with make-up, high heels and dating the "right" boys. Her classmates' desires and imaginations of their future mirrored the expectations of Hyon-Woo's family: "Follow the mainstream … you have to go to university and then you have to get a job, married before 30, kids before 30 and all that." Hyon-Woo ached for something different, but she wasn't yet sure what that was. She left her engineering course without graduating. Her mother and father were shocked and angry. Hyon-Woo thought to herself, "In that case, I'm going to go as far as possible so you can't say anything to me." Australia as a destination was simply a pragmatic decision. A working holiday visa was relatively easy to get. The Korean *won* was, at the time, quite strong against the Australian dollar, so Hyon-Woo thought she could survive in Australia for some time on her savings, and more importantly, "It was really far away from Korea and totally different." Hyon-Woo arrived in Melbourne with only basic competency in English in 2006. She checked into a backpacker hostel and started to explore the city. She thought she would give it at least six months and try to think about what she wanted to do next.

When I met Hyon-Woo, now in her early thirties, for coffee in Melbourne in 2015, it was nine years since her arrival. She was casually dressed in jeans and trainers, carrying a backpack, her hair cropped short. Chatty and relaxed, her Korean accent was inflected with the slightest Australian twang on certain words. Hyon-Woo had ended up staying on in Melbourne by transitioning from the working holiday visa to a student visa to do a course in social welfare in the vocational education system, known in Australia as 'TAFE' – Technical and Further Education. Her parents, who had been hoping the trip to Australia would be brief and she would return to Korea and to university, were appalled by this decision. Hyon-Woo explained that working in social services doesn't have much legitimacy in Korea, especially in the kind of family she was from. Her parents told her she was "wasting her brain" and sending herself "down to the bottom of the list". After some persuasion, however, they agreed to pay the course fees for TAFE, and Hyon-Woo found casual work as a waitress to support her living costs. Hyon-Woo finished her training and moved on to a temporary graduate visa. These visas allow international students to work in Australia for between 18 months and four years (depending on the level of qualification attained) after graduation. She transitioned through various volunteer roles, to part-time and eventually full-time work in the social welfare sector, working in diverse contexts including refugee settlement, disability services and youth homelessness. She knew if she wanted to progress in this career she would need PR, and she also thought she might want to return to study – something she could not do on the graduate visa without enrolling as an international student and paying costly fees. PR would give her more options, and so she decided, "I'm just going to do it."

In 2011, when Hyon-Woo was still waiting to see whether she would be able to stay in Australia, she was feeling bored during the Easter holidays. She signed up on a whim for a scuba course at a local diving centre. Over the next few years, the Melbourne dive scene came to form much of her social world. She met her partner, Peter, whom she described as "a typical white Australian", through the diving community. Yet, despite a new hobby and a relationship, the three years spent waiting for PR "really dragged". Although confident her application would be successful, Hyon-Woo was frustrated during this time that, as a temporary migrant on a bridging visa, she was refused services like a home loan or even a mobile phone contract. As a result of this ongoing sense of insecurity, she had some last-minute doubts, wondering if she should return to Korea:

'I was pretty annoyed, I was very annoyed. I wanted to settle in, I wanted to get my own place and I didn't want any hassles getting my phone and everything. Just annoying. You can't get a loan from the bank. And being a typical Korean, you want to have the security of your own place. It's very important. Even everyone say I don't act like Korean, but at the same time I've got it with me that I do need to have my own place just to feel that this is my place. And that's a lot of pressure on me that I'm here by myself, yes I have freedom, but at the same time I do want to make my life now. Because I made a decision [to] apply for permanent residency, so I['ve] kind of semi-made a commitment that I'm going to stay here but [the situation] wouldn't let me have the full security that I need. ... It was very frustrating in a way. So because of that, I was thinking at the very last minute, "Should I just go back?"'

But, she continued to wait, more or less committed to a future in Australia but with a sense of her present suspended. In 2013, three years after submitting her PR application, and seven years after she had first arrived in Australia, Hyon-Woo received her PR. It is likely that Hyon-Woo's application took such a long time because, as a welfare worker, her occupation was classified as in demand but also low priority, meaning her application could be indefinitely shunted to the back of the processing queue. Soon after, she left the social services sector, where she had become "a bit itchy to move on" for some time, for an administration job at a dive company. Once she had PR, she no longer had to remain working in the field that had qualified her to stay.

Hyon-Woo had spent many of her early years in Australia avoiding return visits to Korea, to her parents' chagrin. At the dive company, however, Hyon-Woo found her bilingual and bicultural skills put to good use in managing the business's push into the Korean market. She made several business trips to Korea. She decided to study interpreting to formalize the skills she was using at work. In a second interview in 2016, Hyon-Woo had finished her interpreting course and had pulled back from full-time work, although she was still freelancing with the dive company occasionally. Overall, she was ambivalent about whether she wanted to keep working there, or seriously pursue interpreting as a career, or do something else entirely. She described herself as less worried about career these days. Hyon-Woo had recently become an Australian citizen. She had applied at her boyfriend's encouragement, as he felt citizenship was "more secure" than PR. Her boyfriend Peter earned a decent salary and Hyon-Woo was happy working a bit, taking long walks with her dog and diving whenever she could. They planned to move to the countryside in the next few years – perhaps rural Victoria or Tasmania, somewhere with lots of trees, and close to good dive sites. Hyon-Woo said she could never return permanently to Korea. She hates even visiting, because all her old feelings of not fitting in return. Not only is she unable to pursue diving there because it's far more expensive than in Australia, she also said, simply, "I can't be me in Korea." She laughingly noted that she is a "bad daughter" – not only is she unmarried, living with a non-Korean partner and not planning on having children, but she is not following a full-time and financially lucrative career. Some kernel of the filial daughter remains, however. Even though she says that visiting Korea "completely stresses me out", Hyon-Woo has returned at key moments in her family members' lives – when her father retired, when her sister married and again when her sister gave birth to twins. She also returned to Korea to nurse her mother through cancer in 2011, even though it was at a point in time when her pending PR application could have been jeopardized by leaving Australia.

Hyon-Woo felt, by the time we met, that she was "settled" into a life she enjoys, a life radically different from the one that seemed ahead of her when she first left home to go to university. Australia had brought her a new career, a partner, a new passion. Throughout the interviews, however, Hyon-Woo moved back and forth between describing her experiences as marked by significant freedom to plot her own course into adult life and by significant constraints. She said the best thing about living in Australia was that "you don't have to have a set plan for life". But when she thought back to her past self, the girl who arrived in Melbourne with one backpack, who wasn't thinking more than six months ahead, she was pensive:

> 'To be honest with you, if I knew what was going to happen, I'm not sure whether I would have made the same decision of coming into Australia. Because it's been tough in a way. ... I shouldn't care too much because I never thought I would make my life in Australia. Again, I'm not sure whether I would do it if I knew. ... Now yes, I can say it was worth it, I'm happy with what I have, I love my dog, I love my boyfriend, I love my life, I love our plans of our future and everything. But you need to put energy into it, you need to go through tough surroundings to get you there. But if you know in advance, not sure!'

Hyon-Woo's story shows some of the complexities of temporality 'on the move' for young and middling migrants: how migration and career timelines and timings become intermeshed and interdependent; how the temporalities of governance (such as application processing queues) radically alter lived presents; how mobility can function as an escape from normative biographic timelines of 'becoming adult'; how the journey to 'settled-ness' can be non-linear and unplannable; and how tensions emerge in synchronizing one's own desires and mobilities with the timings of others: parents, siblings and partners. Empirically, this book centres on an in-depth understanding of such experience of chronomobilities or 'times on the move'. It focuses specifically on the temporalities of middling mobility through the lives of young adults who have migrated from Asia to Australia in the first decades of the 21st century, a period in which specific regimes of social time and policy time have shaped both imaginaries and experiences of being on the move. By 'imaginaries' I refer to the processes of 'imagining migration', both individual and social, that recognize possibilities and construct future lives, and thereby simultaneously both produce and are produced by migration realities (Salazar, 2011). The way time is lived for these young migrants is multifaceted, involving trajectories through time, differing rhythms and tempos of time, and the syncing and desyncing of divergent times between individuals, places and cultures. Further, I see the lived experience of time at the level of the everyday as fundamentally shaped by the broader-scale temporalities of both contemporary economic and social life and national immigration regimes.

In this chapter, I thus sketch out my approach to rethinking migration and time in a way that foregrounds the multiplicities of lived time, as well as how these multiplicities are structured through national and global temporalities that both explicitly govern and implicitly shape the everyday. In doing so, I develop the thinking I employ in the remainder of the book to understand the interplays between everyday social time, transnational mobility and the temporalities of migration governance in migrants' own narrations of their lives. First, I engage with key thinking on the sociology of time in general, and critical work within the emergent 'temporal turn' in migration studies, in order to argue for the need for new frameworks to understand the multiplicities of migrants' sense of lived time in this context, and to position the specific contribution that this book seeks to make.

Next, I describe the specific time-regimes that form the backdrop to the mobilities of the migrants whose lives are the focus of this book, as a means to establish how thinking through chronomobilities is a way to understand how multiple temporal orders (or time-regimes) and temporal meanings (time-logics) shape and emerge from mobile lives. In this section, I first sketch out how the time-regime of hegemonic flexibility (an amalgam of the temporal social consequences that coalesce around time-space compression, social acceleration and risk) enables migrant mobilities to be faster, more fluid and multidirectional but simultaneously restructures the life-course as de-sequentialized, non-linear and unpredictable. I then outline how, in the Australian context, as in many other former 'settlement' nations of the West, hegemonic flexibility has shaped a new regime of migration policy and migration patterns. I refer to this time-regime as transification, meaning that migration to Australia in the 21st century has become increasingly and simultaneously transient (of limited and contingent durations), transitionary (a stage in an ongoing pathway, rather than an endpoint or arrival) and transitory (a process of multiple, overlapping and non-sequential changes of status, identity and belonging). Finally, I flesh out, in the final sections of this chapter, how I understand the logics of everyday lived time – synchronicity, sequencing and tempo – that constitute migrants' lived experience in this context, and which I draw on throughout the analysis in Chapters 3 to 5.

Migration studies and the temporal turn

While social analysis of time has a long history (see, for example, Durkheim, 1915, 1964; Mead, 1932), contemporary sociologists of time are often interested in how current and emerging forms of social and economic organization inform the social constructions of time and the complexity of modern temporal experience. Adam's (1995) work on the social analysis of time, for example, foregrounds the homogenizing influence of clock time and calendar time in contemporary schooling and work relations. She focuses on how this homogenization can obscure less visible or more ambiguous relations to time. In addition, Adam (1995) highlights how the 'natural' times of the procreative body and the environment remain deeply entangled with complex and evolving social constructions of health and nature–culture relations, whether within 'cancer time' or the times of global pollution. Flaherty (2011), in turn, focuses on the social construction of time and the agencies it produces, analyzing how various social actors strategize and manipulate the resource of time, or what he refers to as 'time work'. Anthropologists and cultural studies scholars have also offered critical insights into the 'times of modernity' in relation to everyday life, such as Sharma's (2014) vivid ethnography of how different time sensibilities of labouring subjects are produced in global capitalism, illustrating the 'chronography of power' that shapes the 'differential and inequitable ways in which time is both made to matter and experienced' (15) by business travellers, city taxi drivers and yoga teachers within a modern economy of time. Jeffrey's (2010) anthropology of young men studying in a provincial city in India similarly develops a case for how rapid social and economic transformation has affected the temporalities of local lives. Despite the promise of education and upward mobility that emerges through India's rapid economic expansion, many of these young men are left 'waiting', unemployed and immobile, in a liminal temporal zone that engenders new yet unstable forms of local practice and politics.

While approaches to the study of time vary considerably, in a very general sense, modern social analysis of time positions the temporal perspectives or time horizons of individuals and collectives as closely linked to their social contexts and social conditions (Bergmann, 1992: 85). This means, of course, that people on the move who undergo the specific social process of international mobility will have 'time horizons' that are shaped by this experience.

Yet, migration research has only recently begun to comprehensively grapple with questions of temporality in migrants' lives. During the 'transnational turn' in migration studies that dominated research in the 1990s and early 2000s, spatial perspectives tended to shape understandings of migrants' mobilities, practices and identities. With the exception of Cwerner's (2001) seminal paper on the 'times of migration', prior to 2010, time was rarely made central in conceptual discussions of the heterogeneity of contemporary migration (Griffiths et al, 2013), emerging theoretically only as implicit or subordinate in discussions of space and spatiality (May and Thrift, 2004). The past decade, however, has seen an emerging focus on the temporal in studies of migration, prompting some scholarship to consider the advent of a 'temporal turn' within the field (Carling and Collins, 2018; Baas and Yeoh, 2019; Wang, 2020). This turn towards the temporal clearly has its antecedents in the transnational turn's now well-established destabilization of linear understandings of migration as journeys between fixed points of departure and settlement (Baas and Yeoh, 2019).

Critical overall to the temporal turn is the work of both Saulo Cwerner (2001) and Melanie Griffiths (2014), who have unveiled the specific qualities of time produced by migrant mobility through the development of varied categories and typologies of 'migrant time'. Griffiths (2014), for example, writes of 'sticky', 'suspended', 'frenzied' or 'ruptured' times in the lives of refused asylum seekers and immigration detainees, while Cwerner (2001) identifies eight typical dimensions of the times of migration, which relate in three 'sets' to different stages of the migration process. These are strange, heteronomous and asynchronous times, which relate to immigrant adjustment; remembered, collage and liminal times, which are more expressive as the immigrant experience develops; and nomadic and diasporic times as part of long-term outlooks across the life-course.

Across a series of publications on international student and migrant mobilities, Frances L. Collins and Sergei Shubin have also individually and collectively elucidated a number of conceptual interventions into understanding migrant times. They draw most often on a Heideggerian approach to critique linear and compartmentalized understandings of migrant life-courses and daily temporal experiences, arguing for attentiveness to the more-than-subjective nature of temporalities, questions of affect, and notions of migration as an ongoing process of 'always becoming' (Collins and Shubin, 2015, 2017; Shubin, 2015) through which spatio-temporal differentiation is implicated within transformations in subjectivity (Collins, 2018). Recent special issues and collections featuring migration scholars working across diverse global contexts further point to the fact that temporality is emerging as a key theme in current thinking about migration globally (see, for example, Mavroudi et al, 2017; Barber and Lem, 2018; Baas and Yeoh, 2019).

Yet, while work focusing on the temporal as both a conceptual framework and a research object in migration studies has increased significantly in the past decade, this focus is yet to coalesce into any unified or dominant approach. And perhaps this is rightly so, because time emerges as a slippery concept across this literature – both measurable and immeasurable, subjective and more-than-subjective, structural and agentic, and, as Cwerner (2001) and Griffiths's (2013) work suggests, taking on different qualities for migrants under different condition, stages and contexts. In the following sections of this chapter, I identify four key themes in the current thinking on migration and time that are most relevant to the project I undertake in this book to understand the temporalities-in-mobility in the lives of young Asian migrants in Australia: time as discipline, biographical time, shared/care time and future times of aspiration and desire. This is not an exhaustive review of studies of migration and the temporal, but rather a critical synopsis of key strands of thinking that inform the framings I develop across this book, and through which I situate my own contribution to the emergent 'temporal turn' in migration studies. In Chapters 3, 4 and 5, I delve in more detail into specific literatures on migration and time that are relevant to the themes of each chapter: work, place and intimate life. Despite a growing body of work on migration and temporality today, as Erdal and Ezzati (2015: 1203) note, the temporal dimensions of migration remain often 'integrated as part of analysis foregrounding other themes, such as identity formation, access to the labour market in countries of settlement, and sustained transnational ties' rather than as objects of analysis in their own right. In the sections that follow, therefore, I focus on contemporary work in which time is made wholly central, conceptually or empirically, to the study of migrant lives.

Time as discipline: temporalities of governance and bordering

Crossing over in some respects with critical border studies approaches, one key strand of literature on migration and temporality focuses on time as a form of discipline in migration regimes and its subsequent effects on migrants' experiences of time. Specifically, much of the empirical work here has centred on 'liminal' or 'suspended' time in the lives of asylum seekers and displaced people (Conlon, 2011; Griffiths, 2014; Brun, 2016); the uncertainties created by the labour mobilities of undocumented workers (Ahmad, 2008; Villegas, 2014); or the restrictive temporalities of border control (Andersson, 2014; Krivenko, 2016). The politics of waiting and of immobility has received significant attention, especially in work on forced migration (Hyndman and Giles, 2011; Mountz, 2011; Elliot, 2016; Stock, 2019). In these analyses, time is often a constraint that works against vulnerable migrants or a resource that they have limited agency over, as processes of temporal bordering curtail not only people's movement across borders but also their movements, capacities and inclusion within receiving states. Stock (2019), for example, analyses sub-Saharan migrants 'stuck' in transit limbo in Morocco, their routes to Europe blocked by 'forced immobility', and the ways this hinders their individual futures. Liminal, suspended or 'frozen' times, and times without futures, are also a particularly salient theme in studies of undocumented or precarious status workers and temporality. Ahmad's (2008) smuggled Pakistani workers in London, for example are 'dead men working', 'prisoners of monetarized time, locked into an endless cycle of work that confines them to a tiny physical space at work and home. … Stuck in a vacuous present fraught with anxiety and question marks about tomorrow, they suffer from a perverse imbalance by which their sacrifices, in terms of the "short-term", are far greater than those endured by the rest of society' (315). Griffiths's (2014) refused asylum seekers and immigration detainees are similarly migrants 'out of time', living with the simultaneous threats of imminent and absent change. In the Australian context, Stevens (2017, 2019) has highlighted the thwarted trajectories of working-class Chinese temporary migrants, for whom 'prolonged and indeterminate temporariness' produces precarity of both labour and belonging, and constrains possibilities of both staying and returning.

Even in studies of documented and more privileged labour migrants, such as Axelsson's (2017) work on how border temporalities affect skilled migrant IT workers in Sweden, or Seo's (2019) study of middle-class Nepali youth who are temporary labour migrants in South Korea, the focus tends to remain on the disciplining temporal effects of specific visa regimes. Seo (2019) shows how the institutionalized timeline of a short-term, rotation-orientated migration system in South Korea, the Employment Permit System, creates restrictive temporal sojourns that mediate Nepali migrants' downward class mobility, although they do retain the capacity to 'resynchronize' their life-paths with middle-class aspirations when they return home. Axelsson (2017) in turn argues that just like lower-skilled migrants, skilled migrants experience significant insecurities through the temporalities of the border, including extended periods of waiting, insecurity of presence, loss of rights and feelings of living in limbo. These experiences reflect Cwerner's (2001) notions of 'heteronomous time', when the control of time is out of reach of the migrant.

Although the disciplinary effects of time are a crucial dimension of the relationship between migrant temporalities and migrant mobilities, a singular focus on the disciplining functions of time as a mode of bordering potentially sidelines other significant dimensions of time in migrant lives. In particular, the focus on migrants as workers in much of the literature discussed here has meant that transformations to leisure, familial or intimate temporalities wrought by migration remain somewhat in the background. For example, the way everyday temporalities are implicated in translocal constructions of place and lifestyle, or the salience of time to the structuring of intimate relationships across space, remain relatively underexplored sociologically compared with the temporal consequences of the border. Arnado (2010) in fact argues that the intensities of labour temporalities for migrant domestic workers often distance them from family time or leisure time. Migration becomes nearly wholly colonized by work time, or operates, particularly for circular or cyclical migrants, as a 'time out' from normal social life (Parreñas, 2008). Yet, for more privileged migrants, like my interlocutors, labour temporalities may constitute only one strand of a bricolage of the lived effects of chronomobilities, and social and lifestyle temporalities may be as significant to mobility as those of work.

In this book, I am centrally interested in the temporalities of migration governance and their effects, specifically on an overall paradigm shift in Australian immigration from 'settler' dynamics towards what I call transification (which I will discuss in further detail in subsequent sections of this chapter). The disciplinary effects of a particular regime of governance, a regime in which bordering is an inherently temporal process, are central to the stories in the following chapters. Hyon-Woo, like many other migrants globally who enter a country with a temporary status, experienced downward labour market mobility, insecure patterns of work, and uncertainty about her career and migration future. Yet, this was far from the totality of her temporal experience. She also consciously drew on the opportunities of the transified migration regime in Australia for a temporary sojourn to rethink her life-course, then as a way to reframe her career ambitions and to reconfigure the sequencing of her life-plan and the tempo of her lifestyle. Despite often lacking control over what Cwerner (2001) terms 'heteronomous time', the temporal constraints of governance were layered over and negotiated alongside the unfolding temporalities of Hyon-Woo's intimate life, familial obligations, and agentic career and lifestyle desires. Like the 'waiting times' Ibañez Tirado (2019) describes for left-behind family members in a migrant-sending village in Tajikistan, there is agency and creativity within the liminal temporal zones that Hyon-Woo has at different times occupied.

As such, I seek to extend thinking on 'time as discipline' in a number of ways throughout this book. First, the stories that make up this book do not, as in many existing studies, focus on migrants from a single ethnic group, single visa status or single occupation. Not only do visas statuses and employment conditions vary across the sample of individuals, but they also vary over time within individual journeys. This frames the disciplinary temporalities of the border not as the casual effects of a specific policy (such as the Employment Permit System in South Korea or deportation policy in the UK) but rather as diverse and divergent impacts that emerge under a broad national immigration paradigm that is made up of a constellation of evolving policies and concurrent migration flows. I seek to show the broad patterns of this paradigm shift across the lives of migrants who belong to a 'cohort' of young Asian migrants who arrived in the early 21st century, but who come from different places and cultures, and who move through different formal statuses and work conditions over time.

Second, I consider not only the temporal discipline of the immigration regime, but also broader socio-temporal forces (particularly the hegemonic flexibility that increasingly shapes young people's lives, whether mobile or immobile) and how they intersect with border temporalities. In relation to these two points, I have also sought not to silo migrant experience by focusing on their labour alone. This book engages with migrant temporalities that are about lifestyle, family, intimacy, place and adulthood. Although temporalities of work and career are critical (and are addressed in detail in Chapter 3), they are one facet of the complex chronomobilities that make up young migrants' lives.

Finally, with a few exceptions (for example, Axelsson, 2017; Seo, 2019), most of the literature on time as discipline in migrants' lives centres on the vulnerable and disenfranchised. Empirical work heavily skews towards low-skilled workers and undocumented or forced migrants. Migrants with more social and economic resources, in contrast, potentially illustrate more ambiguous relationships to the governance of time. They have more capacity, at different points in time, to benefit from or strategize within the immigration regime, as illustrated by Baas's (2017) work on 'middling mobiles' in Singapore. I seek to show in this book's exploration of 'middling mobility' (defined in detail in Chapter 2) that the disciplinary effects of time are not limited to politically and economically disenfranchised migrant groups. Rather, temporalities of friction and fluidity exist in a complex set of relations in the lives of migrants who enjoy relative privilege, but not necessarily elite status. I argue in the next chapter that an analysis of more 'middling' forms of migrant mobility can be useful in drawing out some of the paradoxes and tensions of mobile lives in which friction/fluidity, hypermobility/immobility and precarity/flexibility often coexist and intertwine at different stages and in different ways.

Biographical time: life-course and life-stage temporalities

Life-course theory and other biographical approaches in migration studies (for example, Kobayashi and Preston, 2007; Ní Laoire, 2008; Bailey, 2009) that have emphasized life-stages, events and transitions continue to heavily inform discussions of migration and time (Robertson, 2015b). As Bailey (2009: 1) notes, life-course scholarship 'seeks to describe the structures and sequences of events and transitions through an individual's life' through an interest in 'patterns of order and orders of patterns in the often banal practices of everyday life'.

Thinking about migration trajectories, decisions and experiences in relation to the life-course can highlight how biographical and biological timings intersect with institutional or governance temporalities, and how these intersections in turn inflect migrant mobilities. Biographical perspectives also attune us to the changing of social roles across the lifetime (Elder, 1994), which become complicated when migrants move between cultures with varied expectations of social roles, and when social obligations, particularly with regard to familial roles, become dispersed across transnational space and subject to the temporalities of virtual communication (Baldassar, 2008) as well as of visits, sojourns and departures (Kôu and Bailey, 2014; Zhou, 2015). The normative force of specific constructions of life-stages and life events is also highly significant here. Specific temporal norms set down the 'right' or 'appropriate' timings for life-course progression and concurrently for migration (Wang, 2020; Harris et al, 2020). These two intertwined timelines (of migration trajectory and of life-course progression) can be mutually disruptive (Kang, 2018; Wang, 2020), with migration often interrupting normative passaging through socially designated biographical time (Robertson, 2019). Migration thus creates space for migrants of different ages to actively redefine social roles across the life-course as well as to restructure the timings and conventions of life transitions, from achieving adulthood to managing retirement (Oliver, 2010; Martin, 2018; Varriale, 2019). This is perhaps particularly salient for young adult migrants, who move under the shadow of normative framings of youth mobility that focus on 'sequential timing of life course and the accumulation of experience' (Collins and Shubin, 2017: 21).

The most common focus of life-course and biographical approaches to migration, however, is to consider the way decisions about migration shape migrants' individual life trajectories and to interrogate how place preferences can change over time (Kelly, 2015). As such, temporality remains implicit in the analysis and is commonly assumed to be linear, with time positioned in relation to life-stages, generations and sequential planning, and thus largely as chronological. There are only a few studies that centre temporality and the life-course beyond linear time. Collins and Shubin (2015) argue for looking 'beyond the life-course' to investigate the complex directionalities and rhythms of migrant time, in particular arguing for more relational perspectives, and Wang (2020) brings together two perspectives, of everyday times and of individual lifetimes, to show how mobile Chinese academics exercise agency to mitigate the temporal dissonance that mobility produces in their lives and careers. Kang (2018), in turn, writing about young international students from South Korea and their mothers living in Singapore, argues for understanding the performative functions of time-space as a series of 'ongoing and emergent processes, by which people evoke and perform specific types of personhood and identities associated with particular spatio-temporal settings' (799). What this literature collectively suggests is that biographical time is not a 'universal grid' (Kang, 2018: 799) of chronological movement through life. Rather, life-courses and life-stages are multiple, contested and always being reproduced. Different versions of past, present and future can coexist and interact within individuals' own meaning making, between social actors and across space. Yet, at the same time, normative and fixed ideals of life progression remain powerful in structuring institutional, familial and individual understandings of the temporalities of people's lives.

Attuning to biographical time is particularly important in the empirical context I explore in this book. After all, I position the life-stage of my migrant interlocutors (their transition to adulthood) as central to my analysis of their migration experiences, which I explore further in my framing of middling mobility in Chapter 2. Yet, following on from the aforementioned literature that seeks to situate migrant time 'beyond the life-course', I consider movement through life as having multiple trajectories – through biological ageing; through socially determined life-stages (that can be negotiated and resisted through transnationalism, as was the case with Hyon-Woo); through long, protracted and uneven courses of settlement (what Noble and Tabar [2017] understand as the migrant 'career'); and through unfinished and cyclical mobilities rather than linear movement from one place to another. I also seek to hold 'everyday lived time' (the rhythms, paces and patterns of everyday life) in relation to biographical time, seeing the life-course as implicated in the production of forms of everyday imagined and embodied temporalities. While life-stage is critical to this study, I do not take a conventional life-course approach, rather, as discussed in Chapter 2, holding the life-stage of transition to adulthood as a construct that is flexible in its meanings, fuzzy in its boundaries and only loosely held within structures of a specific biological age. Varied modes of planning and sequencing of life are critical to the ways my interlocutors relayed their stories, but as the case of Hyon-Woo already suggests, unknowability, 'unplannability' and resistance to norms of life sequencing are central to interpreting the biographical temporalities at play in these young migrants' lives.

Shared time and care time: temporalities and transnational families

As well as being understood as a mode of bordering and a constitutive part of the sequencing of the migrant life-course, time has frequently been understood in the migration literature as a social commodity and a social experience that is shared, distributed and negotiated within transnational social fields. As migrants move, they retain their transnational networks not only through back-and-forth mobility between places, but also through specific practices of the synchronization of time transnationally. Despite an explosion of literature since the 1990s on how migrants maintain transnational networks and relationships across space, there is little on how time is reshaped, reordered and negotiated in the processes of making transnational lives and retaining transnational relationships. Most of the work that does emerge here falls within studies of the transnational family, and uses the temporal as a framework to understand the caregiving and communication practices of families who are split across borders due to the migration of family members – that is, how migrants 'share' time and organize 'care time' across transnational space.

In one of the most comprehensive studies of temporality and the transnational family, Acedera and Yeoh (2019) argue not only that the dispersal of family members across different nations alters the spatial dimensions of family life, but that 'the temporal dynamics of the family are also reconstituted, as members rework and reimagine their familial relationships across different temporalities, negotiating the rhythms and tempo of everyday family life from afar' (252). As in much of the transnational families literature, Acedera and Yeoh's (2019) focus is established nuclear families or couples, split by the migration of one adult family member (in this case migrant wives working in Singapore with left-behind husbands in the Philippines). These families 'create rhythms and manage ruptures' (Acedera and Yeoh, 2019: 267) as they seek to synchronize their intimate and familial lives across national borders. Polymedia and its possibilities and limits in the maintenance of transnational family life have been a significant theme in the transnational families literature for some time (Madianou and Miller, 2013; Baldassar, 2016). Acedera and Yeoh (2019) bring an explicitly temporal perspective to this field, interrogating communications technologies as a means to mediate liminality and attain simultaneity of family life in a context in which the border splits families seeking the economic advantages of labour mobility.

Cati Coe's (2015) anthropology of Ghanaian migrants and their families across the US and Ghana also considers the temporalities of care within transnational families. Drawing on the metaphor of entrainment – a biological concept that describes how the pace of biological rhythms can be shaped by exogenous stimuli – Coe (2015) makes a number of critical arguments to demonstrate how 'time and timing are as significant as space and location in migration' (182). Crucially, she adds to the life-course approaches to migration discussed earlier in this chapter by showing how care requires the life-courses of different family members to be carefully coordinated and orchestrated in relation to each other – that is, 'entrained'. Coe (2015) thus highlights that the temporalities of the migrant life-course are not individuated, but understood by migrants as relational and negotiated, with reciprocities and dependencies as significant to the staging of progress through the life-course as individual mobility decisions or aspirations. Coe (2015) also notes, however, that US immigration policy imposes its own temporal order on migrants' lives, often limiting their capacities to orchestrate temporalities of care.

Like Coe, Carling (2017) highlights 'shared time' via the relational dimensions of the migrant life-course over time. Drawing on a study of childhood and motherhood in Cape Verdean transnational families, Carling uses migration history charts to reveal the significance of the trajectories (pathways over time) and conjunctures (critical moment of relative mobility that are defining moments in people's lives, such as departures or arrivals) that mark out the relations and transitions within the transnational family, particularly between mothers and children. By examining the spatio-temporal constitution of Cape Verdean transnational families, Carling (2017) argues that despite the focus on experiential and conceptual qualities of time in much of the literature within the 'temporal turn' in migration studies, linear and measurable forms of time remain highly significant to understanding transnational family life – for example, specific events in time and measurable durations of time. Carling (2017) thus reconsiders mobility as a set of ongoing separations and unifications with people and places, rather than movement across space. Carling's (2017) claim that an emphasis on subjective, experiential and non-linear forms of time should not preclude ongoing engagement with the time's 'banal measureable coordinates' (33) is a critical reminder that despite the diversity of conceptual approaches to time in the literature, and an emphasis, such as in Cwerner's (2001) and Griffiths's (2014) work, on the specific experiential qualities of 'migrant time', quantified time – years, dates, ages and calculable durations – still matter to the analysis of migrants' lives and to the way that time functions to mediate social relations and to connect people across space.

Temporalities of care and communication are reframed not only by the mobility of family members in terms of everyday practice, but also in terms of the meanings and values ascribed to these temporalities within families. In one of the few studies that looks explicitly at the temporalities of the transnational family in the context of more privileged Asian migration, Zhou (2015) emphasizes how Chinese skilled migrant families in Canada redistribute, reorder and revalue the temporalities of care intergenerationally, with grandparental commitments to childcare becoming a resource to accelerate the nuclear family's settlement and ensure their economic success. Zhou (2015) reads these temporalities of care as shaped by the neoliberal contexts of skilled immigration, within which traditional cyclical Chinese time, which centres generational reciprocity and specific socio-cultural meanings of ageing, becomes devalued. Zhou (2015) sees the ageing process of Chinese grandparents becoming subordinated to the priorities of their immigrant children and the neoliberal logic to 'accelerate' the accumulated economic benefits of migration. Reciprocal care for the ageing generation becomes less possible through distance and less valued through the migration process.

What these varied approaches to shared or care times reveal is that migration clearly transforms temporalities of care across generations, and this reshapes traditional cultural constructs of the pace, directionality and meaning of care flows at different points in the life-course. Temporal structures discipline the unit of the family (Acedera and Yeoh, 2019), including immobile family members, rather than just migrants themselves. This literature also reveals that while 'intergenerational and transnational notions of time ... are not simply chronological or predictable' (Collins and Shubin, 2017: 24), measurable and objective timelines and timings are still significant for the analysis of these temporalities (Carling, 2017). There are two experiences of 'shared time' and 'care time' that tend to dominate in this literature: how migrants and their families synchronize communication and care across distance (with communications technology playing a key role); and the synching of family members' life-courses, migration trajectories and decisions with care obligations – the idea of 'linked lives' (Kõu et al, 2017), or what Coe (2015) refers to as 'entrainment'.

However, the situating of much of this discussion within a transnational families or care framing leaves some gaps. The focus in the literature remains often on the 'split' nuclear transnational family, and on explicit and traditional caregiving roles between generations, such as parents or grandparents caring for dependent children, or adult children caring for ageing parents. The role of young people as 'emerging adults' who exist in a middle space, normatively bracketed by dependence on the natal family and the formation of their own nuclear families, seldom comes to the forefront of these studies. Relations of dependence and reciprocity, as well as the temporal stagings of their lives, are potentially more ambiguous for young, middle-class migrants and their families than within labour migrants' 'split' households.

As discussed further in Chapter 2, transnationally mobile young people, especially those from the middle class and the Global North, are still often understood as engaged in mobility as a process of independence and autonomy, a 'breaking free' from the natal family. While they in fact remain very much embedded in reciprocal and intergenerational relations of care (Harris et al, 2020), these might be quite different from the global 'care chain' models that inform much of the literature and remain based on the migration of members of a nuclear family (usually parents who leave behind dependent children) to provide economic support for the global household. Hyon-Woo's experiences exemplify this complexity. Her mobility was a conscious way to escape familial control over her life-path and to achieve a sense of independence over her future. Yet, economic support still flowed to Hyon-Woo from her parents when she was establishing herself in Australia, and later on, there were particular crisis times (particularly her mother's illness) when she had to craft her own migration timings and aspirations around the provision of proximate care in Korea. Unlike migrants in studies such as those of Acedera and Yeoh (2019) and Carling (2017), where the family is split by economic and policy constraints, a focus on young and middling transnational migrants in Australia occurs in a context in which different configurations of family both locally and transnationally are possible, and the relationships migrants form as young adults are subject to potentially more change over time than within an established 'global household'. The temporal disjunctures and synchronicities between proximate and distant relations, such as Hyon-Woo's relationship with her Australian partner and her family in Korea, play out as young people move into new and transnationally dispersed social roles over time as their 'settlings' into adulthood and into place unfold at sometimes uneven tempos.

The other assumption that the following chapters challenge in relation to 'shared times' is that the object of transnational 'shared' temporality is necessarily always towards simultaneity. Liminal times, or temporal ruptures within relationships, are often positioned in the aforementioned literature as constructed by the temporal orderings of restrictive migration policies or economic models that constrain capacities for simultaneity of communication or continuity of care relations. For middling young migrants, however, desynchronization from transnational relationships, whether through seeking out alternative life-paths or reframing the pace or sequence of communication with families, can be part of the aspiration of leaving and of staying away, as moves towards more autonomy or at least reconfigured patterns of reciprocity. Further, 'shared time' is, for my aims, about far more than synchronization of communication for the maintenance of family life across distance – it can also be about consciously synchronizing with local social rhythms (see Chapter 4), desynchronizing career and life-paths from families or peers (see Chapter 3), or reorganizing the pace and sequencing of the formation of non-familial intimate relationships in relation to family expectations (see Chapter 5).

Future time: temporalities of aspiration and desire

While migration aspirations and desires – understood in the most general sense as people's plans, feelings and objectives around potential mobility – are frequently invoked in migration ethnographies, it has only been very recently that migration researchers have begun to explicitly theorize these terms, and, in a few cases, theorize them explicitly in relation to temporality (see, for example, Collins, 2018; Wang and Collins, 2020). In my analysis, I employ these terms in a mostly matter-of-fact and very much overlapping sense – aspiration signals future-orientated plans, thoughts, imaginings and goals; and desire, following Collins (2018), signals the more affective dimension, the longing, yearning and striving, of this cognitive engagement with imagined futures. Yet, it is worth unpacking some of the surrounding significance of these ideas to my subsequent analysis of migrant lives, as well as the role that these terms have come to play in emerging migration literature.

Aspiration is particularly significant to this book for two reasons. First, it links together the two intersecting subjectivities of my interlocutors – both young people and migrants are frequently positioned as 'aspiring subjects' (Baey and Yeoh, 2018; Robertson et al, 2018b), in that they are 'wishful', 'seeking' and 'becoming' as they imagine and move through geographic and life-course mobility respectively. As I have considered elsewhere (Robertson et al, 2018b), the life-stage of youth is particularly constructed as 'a period of "futurity" – in which "becoming" and the making of adult lives are paramount' and is characterized by 'capacity and desire for mobility before the assumed "settled-ness" of adulthood' (615). Second, although as Wang and Collins (2020) note, the debates about migration and time and migration and aspiration have been largely separate, aspiration is implicitly bound up with temporality, specifically with how individuals mobilize present knowledge and resources to make decisions towards future possibilities. Following Crivello (2015), I do not position my interlocutors' aspirations as only pertaining to abstract futures – rather, aspirations actively influence present actions and realities and are constituted through particular spaces.

Further, individual migrants often cannot predict, calculate and foresee their future trajectories in assembling their present strategies (Carling and Collins, 2018). Thus, as much of the literature of migrant temporalities insists, migrant aspirations and decisions unfold in relation to pasts, presents *and* futures (Griffiths, 2014; Shubin, 2015; Collins, 2018). Aspiration, then, situates the temporality of migration as future-oriented, but also as an ongoing process. This is particularly important to consider in a study of migration under transification, because of how the uncertainty of visa trajectories and rapid policy changes destabilize any orientations towards linear settlement. Migrant decision making in general, but in particular in the context of an 'unsettling' of a settler paradigm, seldom occurs at a single moment in time, nor it is necessarily siloed within the time period prior to departure (Carling and Collins, 2018; Wang and Collins, 2020). The stories of David, Carolyn and Hyon-Woo have already illustrated, how, in this way, plans and strategies around mobility exist in flux and endure far beyond single instances of departure and arrival.

Collins's (2018) exploration of desire as a theory for migration studies through the lives of three Southeast Asian guest workers in South Korea further critiques notions of migration decisions as linear and calculative, highlighting how expressions of desire are not reducible to rationales for action. Conceiving of migrant aspirations and desires as purely projective and future-oriented is problematic because migrants' actual stories tend to reveal the extent to which migration hinges on 'opportunism and the time of grasping the moment' (Collins 2018: 977). Collins's (2018) interlocutors describe taking risks, speculating and experiencing unforeseen blockages and disruptions as they seek to achieve their evolving desires for themselves and their families through a series of migration decisions over time. My research participants, although more privileged than those of Collins (2018), share the experience of not necessarily knowing their trajectories in advance; they are similarly 'driven by desires for becoming otherwise' that can channel them 'along unexpected pathways' (977). At first, for example, Hyon-Woo's desire to migrate was simply a desire to be 'far away', a yearning for 'something different' that was not connected to any specific plan for the future or a particular vision of what life in Australia would be like. The decision to stay was also made moment by moment as she waited for PR and was not necessarily rational or strategic – her emotional connections to her life in Australia and sense of 'waiting and seeing' overrode the pragmatic social and economic benefits of returning to Korea.

In highlighting aspirations in my analysis, I seek to emphasize not only how migrants plan for the future, but also how aspiration constitutes these sometimes ambiguous 'states of feeling and circulation of affect' (Carling and Collins, 2018: 913). However, like Wang and Collins (2020), I also seek to retain a sense of how migration aspirations articulate with various other temporalities, including the pace and rhythms of everyday life, progression through the life-course and wider scales of institutional and social temporal ordering. Aspiration is also importantly related to imaginaries of place, examined in detail in Chapter 4, and to questions of social mobility and capital accumulation (Erel and Ryan, 2019) that are particularly significant to the middling cultures of mobility described in Chapter 2.

Aspiration also articulates with my prior discussions of biographical time, in that 'migration aspirations intersect with how individuals plan and utilise their lifetime ... and how to actualise migration aspirations at different life-stages' (Wang and Collins, 2020: 578). In this understanding, aspirations *to* migrate and aspiration for what will emerge *from* migration are both equally significant. As such, I also follow Carling and Collins (2018) in their argument, that, although they are distinct processes, it makes sense to integrate analysis of 'aspiration and desire for migration' and 'aspiration and desire through migration', given how inseparably intertwined they often are empirically. When I evoke the idea of aspiration, therefore, I am interested in 'the link between processes of "desiring mobility" and "making futures through mobility"' (Robertson et al, 2018b: 615) and how these processes emerge in migrants' lives.

Chronomobilities: framing the multiplicity of lived times

Like Kang (2018: 809–10), I see value in using 'a temporal framework [that] allows us to understand the situated and shifting nature of the migrants' placements in time, which appear not in a unitary sequence of time, but at multiple scales, for example, both experiential and discourse levels and the local and global contexts'. As Cwerner (2001) articulates, however, and as I have argued elsewhere (Robertson, 2015b), the multiplicity and ubiquity of time in social life 'precludes the success of a unifying or totalising theoretical project' (Cwerner, 2001: 14) in understanding the temporalities of migration. A totalizing framing is thus not my aim. Rather, I seek to demonstrate systematically throughout this book some of the specific intersections of lived temporal orientations and temporal scales that emerge from a particular group of migrants' own narratives of their mobility experiences. In doing so, I build primarily from four key premises that emerge across the literature discussed previously.

First, again drawing from Cwerner (2001), any discussion of migrant times needs to hold in place that time belongs to multiple scales of social life, from individual experiences to social systems. Migrant experiences of time are shaped by the experience of transnational mobility and its governance and simultaneously by socio-temporal orders that inflect social life beyond the migration context. While my understanding of 'temporalities-in-mobility' is very much centred on 'how (im)mobilities are not only shaped by spatial boundaries, but also produced by temporal boundaries and structures' (Acedera and Yeoh, 2019: 268), I am also interested in how these chronomobilities both produce and are produced by various temporal cultures, imaginaries and identities. As such, while what Acedera and Yeoh (2019) call the 'micro-temporalities' of everyday life cannot be understood without attention to the meso-temporalities of immigration policies, other scales and modes of temporality – global and local cultural understandings of time; the localized rhythms of life in a town or a city; the tempos of a specific workplace; imaginaries of national temporal 'lifestyles' – all matter to daily temporality and are all in different ways inflected by the experience of mobility.

Second, migrants are not merely acted upon by time but create and negotiate new forms and meanings of time. While Griffiths (2014) and many other scholars of migration and time write primarily about precarious lives on the edge of mainstream society, my interlocutors are both 'in' and 'out', secure and precarious, at different moments and in different places. In this context of middling mobility (interrogated further in Chapter 2), it is particularly important to see time not only as a constraint that migrants must strategize through and mitigate against, but simultaneously as a resource, a lifestyle and a desire.

Third, time's abstract and experiential qualities do not swallow its measurable ones, and in fact any binary analysis of 'time as objective' versus 'temporality as subjective' (Hoy, 2012) perhaps unhelpfully excises the extent to which the qualities and quantities of time, its subjective and measurable dimensions, interweave and inter-bleed in migrants' own sense-making of the role of time in their daily lives.

Finally, temporality, like mobility, must be understood as relational (Sharma, 2014) – that is, it connects, separates and mediates between people, places and things, and creates relations between them. In this way, time is charged with changing meanings that are consistently negotiated between people (Cheng, 2014), and further transformed by mobilities between places. It is normative and institutional, yet also, as explained in my third point, experiential, imaginative and transformative. In the remainder of this chapter, I work from these premises to sketch out my framework for understanding the chronomobilities of migrant lives, which I then deploy throughout the empirical discussion in Chapters 3 to 5.

Global time-regimes: hegemonic flexibility

In order to understand the way experiences of time both structure and are structured by contemporary migrants' mobilities, there is a need to first examine how time functions in relation to the macro-global social transformations that shape many aspects of social and economic life today, including but not limited to migration. Specific transformations of both space and time are central to theoretical understandings of social life under the conditions of globalized modernity. In this book, I understand social life in the 21st century as dominated by a time-regime of flexibility. 'Hegemonic flexibility' brings together several key concepts around spatio-temporal transformation in modernity that have become, since the late 1990s, foundational to the contemporary sociological canon. The first concept is 'time-space compression' (Harvey, 1999) or 'time-space distanciation' (Giddens, 1991). Time-space compression describes how technological advancements, particularly in transport and communication, as well as accelerations in capitalist processes of commodity production and consumption, have diminished distance through the intensified speed at which objects, information and people move. The second concept is social acceleration (Rosa, 2013; Virilio, 2006) which posits that contemporary social and political life is marked by a 'speeding up' of tempo and velocity in relation to advancements of technology, as well as in relation to the pace of broader social change and the pace of everyday life. The third is sociological orientations towards risk (Giddens, 1991; Beck, 2009) that position social life as increasingly shaped by anticipatory orientations towards future uncertainties.

Hegemonic flexibility refers to the way that these constellations of macro-temporal conditions (risk, acceleration and time-space compression) have come together to shape modern social life. It has material effects on the temporalities of individual lives as well as of communities. For example, the life-course – that is, the sequencing of age-related social roles across various domains of social life, including family, work, education, health and leisure (O'Rand, 2003) – has undergone significant change. Capitalist orientations towards 'short-termism' (Sennett, 2006) and the 'flexibilization' of labour have done away with the 'job for life', as well as linear and immediate transitions from education to work for young people. The life-course, explored in more detail in relation to my interlocutors specifically in Chapter 2, has broadly become increasingly deinstitutionalized, and no longer entails a sense of linear or predictable progress over time and orderly transitions across sequential life-stages. Diversifying social norms, 'sped up' by social acceleration and intensified global cultural flows, have also contributed to the transformation of many life transitions that were in the past more or less fixed and sequential, such as education, employment, marriage, family formation and retirement. Particularly for the middle class, this has created increasing 'options', but also increasing anxieties, around the organization of life. A time-regime of flexibility is also manifest in daily routines and in the construction of the self. Daily rhythms of work and leisure have become desynchronized, and technologies of connectivity have disembedded much of our social lives from 'real', or rather, 'embodied' time (Urry, 2000). The erosion of continuous and locally embedded communities, combined with the risks and uncertainties created by globalizing forces, have led to a distinctly modern refashioning of the self as a reflexive project made up of multiple and often fragmented social identities (Giddens, 1991).

Overall, hegemonic flexibility has embedded uncertainty, transience and desequentialization into social organization, which in turn has left individuals, families and communities needing to adapt and recraft projects of social life. These conditions form the global socio-temporal backdrop to the migrant lives described in this book. Contemporary ethnographies of migration processes and imaginaries have only just begun to suggest how temporalities of migration are reshaped by global time-regimes, with Zhou (2015), for example, noting how 'neoliberal accelerative logics' (177) come to colonize and dominate the organization of transnational family life, and Coe (2015) noting how 'to the extent that migration is conceived as a mode of "getting ahead" (a spatial metaphor), it is also a metaphor of time: getting ahead earlier or faster' (183). While my exploration of chronomobilities in this book is centred on everyday life, my analysis seeks to hold the backdrop of hegemonic flexibility as a time-regime consciously present in my analysis of migrant experience.

National time-regimes: the transification of migration

In the following section, I outline current temporal changes to migration policies and patterns with a focus on the Australian context. I describe these changes as a process of the 'transification of migration', which I see as a time-regime that shapes national policy making and subsequently migrant lives. This section provides the national context for the empirical analysis of the chronomobilities of everyday lives that makes up the subsequent chapters of this book, and also develops the aspect of the chronomobilities approach that seeks to understand everyday temporalities in relation to the temporalities of border paradigms. The transification of migration is a set of interlinked social and political processes that lead to key changes to how migration is both governed and lived. Transification suggests that migration is simultaneously constructed as transient (that is, of limited and contingent duration); transitory (a stage in an ongoing pathway of mobility, rather than a destination or endpoint of 'arrival'); and transitionary (a process that involves multiple, overlapping and non-sequential changes of status, identity and belonging). It is a process constituted by both changing forms of migrant agency and changing local, national and transnational structural conditions. Policy processes that are themselves transient and transitory – wherein policy changes occur frequently and rapidly – are important aspects of these structural conditions, which render migrant lives continuously uncertain and inchoate. The transification of migration is occurring in differing forms and with differing intensities globally, but I concentrate here on outlining its effects in the Australian case, which has resonance with other former settler contexts, such as Canada, New Zealand, the UK and the US.

Australia provides a case study par excellence of a former 'settler' nation that has undergone a transification of migration in the 21st century. From the Federation of the continent's British colonies in 1901 until the late 1990s, mass migration to Australia was fundamentally linked, politically, economically and culturally, to nation building and the long-term growth of the citizen population. Over the past 20 years, however, as in many other receiving contexts globally, migration in Australia has become a 'just-in-time' process to import flexible, transient and expendable labour to meet the needs of rapidly changing economies (Aneesh, 2001; Neilson, 2009). Three key changes are significant here. First, temporary visas have become more accessible and increasingly prevalent in comparison to permanent visas. Second, migrants increasingly experience transition across legal categories and other typologies of migrant mobility (such as skilled or unskilled, student or worker, labour migrant or lifestyle migrant). Third, migration has become a desequentialized, non-linear and often unfinished life project, involving varied stages and durations, and multidirectional trajectories. These changes position migrant mobilities beyond movement between only 'home' and 'host' contexts, highlighting the parallel significance of intra-national mobility and serial transnational mobilities across third or fourth countries and beyond.

Overall, under this time-regime, the paradigm of permanent settlement in Australia has been replaced. But it has not been replaced with a conventional 'temporary worker' model in which migration is relatively uniform, circumscribed to specific short-term durations. Although temporary migration has increased rapidly, transitions between temporary categories and between temporariness and permanence have become the norm. For example, the primary temporary skilled work visa scheme in Australia between 1996 and 2017 was the 457 programme, which allowed migrants with specified skills four years of work and residency rights. By 2012, around half of all 457s were granted to migrants already onshore, that is, holders of other temporary visas or 457 visa renewals. Mares (2016) estimates this represented around 60,000 people moving from one temporary visa to another between 2012 and 2014 alone. Furthermore, since 2011, international graduates of Australian degrees have had access to post-study work visas of durations between 18 months and four years under the 485 graduate visa scheme. In the same two-year period between 2012 and 2014, approximately 93,000 international student graduates extended their stay in Australia by switching to temporary graduate visas, 457 temporary work visas, or working holiday visas (Mares, 2016).

As Wright and colleagues (2016: 4) note, the growth in these forms of multistage migration through the creation and consolidation of pathways between student, working holiday maker, temporary skilled, and permanent visas is one of the most significant paradigm shifts in Australian migration policies and processes in the 21st century.

The full expanse of the constellations of policies that have brought transification into effect in Australia are, however, complex, contested and ever-changing. Indeed, Australian policy relating to these visa pathways continues to evolve as I write this book. A more thorough analysis of the policies and politics around Australia's transition from settler multiculturalism to what Walsh (2014) has termed 'a state of transience' can be found elsewhere (see, for example, Mares, 2016 and Koleth, 2012). Specific policies and their consequences are further explained in relation to the narratives of individual migrants in the subsequent chapters of this book. It is the sociological consequences of this time-regime that form the foundational concerns of this book, rather than specific policy developments. Of central interest are the lived temporalities that emerge through migration becoming increasingly transient, transitory and transitionary, and how migrants make meaning from them. Indeed, transification as a process is more than just a consequence of policies. It is also a consequence of dynamic social and cultural processes driven by migrant desires to craft global careers and seek economic and lifestyle opportunities in multiple places at different stages of their lives.

Although all the migrants I interviewed during the research that underpins this book initially arrived in Australia on temporary visas, I engage the lens of 'transification' (a process) rather than the descriptor 'temporary migrant' (a status) in understanding their experiences. This is because although they all arrived with temporary legal statuses of limited duration, many understood their own journeys as far from fleeting sojourns, and most eventually (although not always initially) sought out PR as a goal. However, permanent status did not necessarily denote permanent settlement in terms of their life projects. Rather, migration was often described as potentially ongoing – many of my interlocutors said they would, in the future, probably or possibly move on, either back 'home' or elsewhere. These mobilities were more than just imaginaries, with some moves taking place over the course of the research. One participant relocated from Perth to Beijing for a year for her husband to take up a job, and two others left Australia for indefinite periods, one for Oman and one for Brunei. Others had plans to move on to the US or Europe, mobilities sometimes made more possible by the acquisition of Australian citizenship. Some had specific plans to return to their countries of origin if or when their visas ran out, once they had saved specific amounts of money or achieved particular career goals, or when they were ready to start families. Some had already returned home for a few years and then come back to Australia. Participants' moves to Australia were also often preceded by other mobilities, either transnational, such as overseas work and study, or intra-national, such as from hometowns to major cities.

Migration for these individuals is thus an ongoing life project consisting of multiple arrivals and departures, and becomes simultaneously transient, transitory and transitionary. The idea of transification as a new migration paradigm is not exclusive to Australia, but in fact reflects a broader picture of how migration is changing in the Asian region. As Yeoh (2017: 144) notes, 'Today, migrations in and out of Asia ... by and large do not take the form of permanent ruptures, uprooting and settlement, but are more likely to be transient and complex, ridden with disruptions, detours, multi-destinations, and are founded on interconnections and multiple chains of movement.' Some of the consequences of transification on everyday lives and choices are already apparent in the migrant narratives I have explored so far. As Hyon-Woo's story attests, the new pathways are attractive to young middle-class people from Asia on the very basis of their flexibility and possibilities – to work, to study, to experience different lifestyles, to maintain connections to multiple places. Yet, over time these forms of migration also have the potential to fundamentally transform the experience of time. Experiencing transified migration can suspend, speed up or slow down the flow of time. It can move one forward in a particular trajectory or hold one back. New synchronicities and asynchronicities are created, and pasts, presents and futures reordered. Such emergent chronomobilities have significant effects on people's relationships to work, to place and to each other. It is the intricacies of these transformations that I explore in subsequent chapters, utilizing the idea of multiple logics of lived time, outlined in the following section.

The logics of 'lived' time: sequence, tempo and synchronicity

Understanding how time emerges within migrants' own meaning making and narrations of their lives requires an engagement with the multifaceted nature of lived time. As I have already argued, my analysis of temporality-in-mobility throughout this book is shaped by key thinking within the temporal turn in migration studies, in which, despite a variety of concepts and approaches, migrant times are understood as simultaneously relational, structural, embodied and imagined, and as equally produced by migration regimes, social relations across space, cultural norms and individual desires. Following Carling (2017), I see measurable, linear time as entangled with more experiential dimensions of time in everyday life, and thus seek to avoid conventional and limited distinctions between 'objective' and 'subjective' times. My analytical entry point into this temporal complexity is to structure my analysis of migrant chronomobilities around three logics of lived time: sequencing, tempo and synchronicity. The migrants interviewed for this book talk about and perceive time in relation to their mobility (that is, their experience of chronomobilities) largely via these three temporal logics, which represent subjective experiences of time, but are at the same time constructed through and embedded within, rather than separate from, clock and calendar times. These logics are not discrete, but rather intersect at different points and in multiple ways as migrants make sense of their varied experiences of mobility.

What I term logics of sequence involve a sense of progression of time and ordering of time characterized by the meanings and understanding of pasts, presents and futures and before, now and after. This does not imply, however, a necessarily linear, unitary or ordered sense of chronology in the lived experience of the unfolding of time. Mobility or immobility, for example, may involve experiences of remaining 'trapped' in the past, living in multiple simultaneous presents, or imagining multiple futures that may or may not be reached after unknown durations. Aspirations are a critical aspect of the logic of sequence in that they encompass, as discussed earlier in this chapter, particular affective and imaginative orientations towards possible futures. Logics of sequence are often, in migrants' narratives, concerned with the sequencing of the life-course, and in particular in this empirical case, with the progressive building, through significant events and milestones, of adult lives while on the move. Yet, I use the concept of sequencing rather than biography or life-course because the concerns here surround 'more than' the ordering of the individual life-course. Sequence can attend to the ordering of migration processes, of daily, weekly or monthly schedules and routines, of the progress of a new relationship into different stages of intimacy, of affective progression of 'belonging' over time – in short, any social process that requires a reflexive orientation to the ordering of events in time or a sense of progression through time.

Logics of tempo concern pace and rhythm, such as acceleration, deceleration, repetition, disruption and so on. A sense of how mobility may speed up or slow down time either in relation to daily routines or life trajectories is an example of logics of tempo in practice. For example, as explained in Chapter 4, daily life in Australian cities and towns may represent a slower tempo than life in Mumbai, Seoul or Taipei, which might be seen positively or negatively by individual migrants in relation to their lifestyle desires. In contrast, living in

Australia with a temporary status might encompass a frenetic sense of months quickly passing as visa expiry dates loom, as illustrated by David and Carolyn's narrative in the previous chapter, or the temporal 'dragging' and suspension of the present that Hyon-Woo felt in waiting for her visa to be processed. This logic encompasses some of the senses of stuckness, waiting, deceleration and suspension that dominate in existing studies of temporal bordering, but also, conversely, the logics of speed that inflect much of contemporary life. It also links, like sequencing, to the idea of aspiration – as demonstrated in Chapter 4, desires for particular tempos of lifestyle critically shape desires to move towards particular places in ongoing migration trajectories.

Logics of synchronicity represent relational or collective forms of temporality, specifically how migrants try to 'sync' or 'desync' the timings of their lives with others across and within space. This syncing involves family members and friends, as well as the alignment of one's own sense of time with those of larger collectives, such as transnationally dispersed diasporic communities, or local communities. As explored in detail in Chapter 5, much of the 'doing' of love and family across transnational space involves logics of synchronicity, whether negotiating with partners or parents the right time and place to get married, or aligning daily schedules so communication with loved ones in distant time zones can occur. As in Hyon-Woo's case, migrants' own decisions about their presents and futures might clash with familial or cultural expectations about 'when' they should be doing certain things or for how long. While I draw here on existing understandings of temporality from the transnational families literature, I understand synchronicity beyond the coordination of care and communication across borders and generations, seeing it additionally as a means to understand how migrants seek synchronicity within place, with local temporal norms, and with varied social actors beyond and within their family and kin networks. Synchronization and desynchronization occur between local and transnational times, between migration aspirations and career aspirations, between different actors and between different cultural modes of time. Synchronicity can be a driven and agentic process of migrants actively seeking to link the rhythms of their lives with others, or a process that emerges in a less conscious way within their transnational and local practices of making lives on the move.

Logics of sequence, tempo and synchronicity represent distinct modes through which migrants understand and make sense of time in their lives, yet also work together to constitute the overall experience of chronomobilities – the temporalities of being on the move. In Chapters 3 to 5, I draw on these three logics of time throughout my analysis to foreground 'lived' time as more than just how time is structured or how it is used, but also how it is social and relational, embodied and everyday, and significant to the self-fashioning of individual as well as collective identities. Via these logics, my analysis of lived time includes cultural and social understandings of the life-course or the individual biography as well as the immediate, embodied and affective experience of time, day to day, in migrants' work, leisure and social experiences. This includes everyday tasks and daily rhythms and their physical and emotional consequences on migrants' minds and bodies; the feeling of time passing; the meanings migrants make of their pasts, presents and futures in relation to each other; and how individuals orient the self in relation to their experiences of time-in-mobility.

Conclusion

In this chapter, I have sought to work through the complexities of the relationship between migrant temporalities and migrant mobilities, and to build the framework that guides my understandings of this relationship and the experiences it produces in migrants' lives. The concept of chronomobilities underpins my analysis in the remainder of this book. This portmanteau achieves two fairly prosaic aims. It simply and concisely suggests and reiterates the indivisible and mutually constitutive nature of temporality and mobility, and it names a framework made up of time-regimes and time-logics that provides the scaffolding for making our way through the complexity and multiplicity of migrant experiences of time.

In building this framework, I have drawn considerably on existing research that centres time in the study of migration. This research sits within the broad field of migration studies, but cuts across the disciplines of geography, cultural studies and sociology as well as across the interdisciplinary spaces of ethnic and racial studies and critical border studies. While space–centric analysis dominated migration studies' transnational turn of the 1990s and early 2000s, the past decade has seen the emergence of a 'temporal turn', which, although still very much in an emergent phase, has provided significant and important ways to rethink migration experiences in the 21st century. I have given critical attention in this chapter to strands of literature within the temporal turn that focus on the disciplinary temporalities of the border; the relational dimensions of shared and care times across transnational space; the role of future imaginaries via aspiration and desire; and the interlinking of life-course mobility with transnational mobility. Much of this literature signals towards the multiscalar and multidimensional qualities of time, and uncertainty, waiting, precarity and non-linearity are prevalent themes in relation to contemporary migrant experience.

My approach to time, however, differs from and builds on this existing body of work in that it takes an explicitly sociological approach to unpack how multiple logics of migrant temporal experience are constructed and reconstructed via the overlapping and intersection of specific layers of social and political temporal ordering. I have outlined in this chapter a global socio-temporal order, or time-regime, of hegemonic flexibility that draws together broad understandings of transformations to time in social life, foregrounding accelerations, desequentialization, uncertainty and risk. Underneath this, I position the specific temporal paradigm of 21st-century migration governance in Australia as one of the transification of migration. These two regimes work together to structure the systems and cultures within which the migrants in this study move and experience time. I have also laid out the intersecting logics of lived time that critically enfold migrants' everyday experiences – logics of sequence, synchronicity and tempo. This approach to migration and time aims to continue the temporal turn's challenge to temporal fixedness and linearity in the study of migration, but without resorting to frictionless metaphors of fluidity and flow, and without limiting analysis to a dialectical understanding of structural forces of the border existing in contestation with migrants' aspirations and desires. Rather, I centre the interplay of multiple temporal regimes and logics in understanding the structuring and the meaning of migrant temporalities.

I use the idea of chronomobilities throughout the remainder of this book as a means to find a way through the multifarious and mutually constitutive relationships between migrant time and migrant mobility that thread through the life stories of the young migrants interviewed during this research. The themes I address in the following chapters cannot touch on all the aspects of chronomobilities that matter in the lives of my migration interlocuters. Time has infinite depth and breadth as a research object and as a research lens, and as such remains 'knotty and slippery' (Robertson, 2013), both empirically and theoretically. The framework have I outlined here is by necessity incomplete, and, although as I discuss in the book's final chapter, it may have applicability to other contexts, in the following four chapters, it remains understood via the empirical context of middling mobility in contemporary Asia–Australia migration processes. What I hope the chronomobilities approach broadly achieves, however, is an unveiling of the relationship between migration and time that foregrounds temporality and mobility as interrelated, multiple, multidirectional, mutually constitutive, and operating simultaneously and vertically across multiple scales, as well as an attentiveness to a mutual permeation of tangible and subjective notions of time in practice. Moreover, my orientation towards the temporal by no means obscures or denies the role of the spatial in understanding contemporary migration processes. The centring of the temporal throughout the book occurs very much through an understanding of time as inseparable from space and movement.

In Chapter 2, I explore the wider contexts of 21st-century, middle-class Asian migration, as well as establish my use of the term 'middling mobility' to describe the experiences of my research participants. I argue that an analysis of more 'middling' forms of mobility can be useful in drawing out some of the paradoxes and tensions of mobile lives in which friction and fluidity, hypermobility and immobility, and precarity and security, often coexist and intertwine at different stages and in different ways. I seek to show that researching migrant lives 'in the middle' can usefully highlight often hidden nuances around the interrelationships of temporality and mobility, and of spatial mobility and social mobility, by opening up analysis of the uneven experiences that exist in between the liminality of the migrant precariat and the fluidity of the mobile elite.

2

Asian Migrants of the Middle in Local and Global Context

Woojin and I first chatted late one evening via Skype. I was in my home office in Sydney, he was in his bedroom in a shared house in a town of about 15,000 people, about a five-hour drive from the city. Woojin was in his early twenties, with the clean-cut features of a K-pop singer,[1] and slightly hesitant, although comfortably conversational in English. He was excited about participating in the research, seeing it as a good chance, he said, to practise his English but also to reflect on his journey in Australia. Like Hyon-Woo, Woojin is from a small town in Korea; his family lived comfortably, but his parents were not university educated. After completing his compulsory military service after high school, he trained and began work as a welder, which was a secure job. Like Hyon-Woo, Woojin's future seemed mapped out according to a standard life-path – work hard, save money, marry and start a family, and support his parents into their old age. But also like Hyon-Woo, he felt vaguely bored and dissatisfied. He thought learning English might improve his chances of more diverse career options, and he wanted to see more of the world. As for Hyon-Woo, a working holiday visa to Australia was quick and cheap to obtain, and Woojin had a few friends, also welders, who had already followed this path. He arrived in Western Australia in 2012. He initially struggled to find work, but a friend from Korea recommended him for a welding job in a regional town of New South Wales where he eventually settled. He recalled the long drive across the continent from the west coast to the east as one of his most memorable experiences in Australia – the wide-open, dramatically empty landscape, the wildlife, the endless sky. These were images of Australia he was familiar with from television and online but he had never thought, growing up, that he would ever see them with his own eyes.

As a welder, Woojin's skills were in demand in the regional town where he settled. Despite some initial problems with his English at work, he earned a good salary and the cost of living was relatively cheap, especially when compared with that of his Korean friends who were struggling to make ends meet in Sydney or Melbourne. He saved money, travelled around the country during his time off, made a few friends. He felt that in many ways his profession as a tradesperson was more respected in Australia than in Korea. The 'tradies' (as they are colloquially known in Australia) he worked with earned good money and ranked highly in the social hierarchy of the town – they had large houses and expensive cars and took their families on holidays overseas every year. Woojin was eventually offered sponsorship for a four-year skilled visa by his employer, which could lead to PR. Although it took him several attempts to pass the required IELTS test to meet the visa requirements, he was happy about this opportunity, not necessarily because he was sure he wanted to live in Australia permanently, but because PR would offer him the flexibility to leave and return. It would also, as it did for Hyon-Woo, allow him to change jobs more easily or return to study. Woojin's parents were able to visit him in Australia and he took a holiday with friends to Taiwan, all opportunities and experiences he said he would never have imagined possible before he left Korea.

In a second interview with Woojin a year later, however, he was planning to return to Korea. He had experienced ongoing problems with his employer, describing bullying and discrimination, a situation exacerbated by his dependence on the employer for visa sponsorship. Ultimately, the offer for permanent sponsorship had been rescinded. Woojin had also decided to leave his welding career behind and apply to university in Korea. He had become interested in the union culture and workplace relations of the construction industry in Australia – radically different from his experience of trade work in Korea. He was determined to study industrial relations or human rights law and become a lawyer. Like Hyon-Woo, he had used his distance from his family to delay questions of marriage and children. He knew a return to Korea would mean some pressure from his parents to settle down and have a family, but he said he could largely ignore this pressure: "I don't care," he said, "it's my life, not their life." Leaving Australia was not necessarily a permanent decision in Woojin's mind. If he didn't pass the law school entrance exam, he said he might return and try again for a permanent visa in Australia. He was particularly careful to explain that his career change was not about the money or prestige a law career would bring. It was about his own identity and passion for justice, shaped by his experiences as a worker: "I want to do the right thing … I don't care about the money, I just want to get the truth … my ultimate goal is to be this man. It's kind of very … complicated. But I want to make [a] … better society, a better world, you know."

Experiences like Woojin's, as well as Hyon-Woo's, described Chapter 1, and David and Carolyn's described in the Introduction, are not easily placed within the conventional typologies of migration studies, and within conventional understandings of the relationship between transnational mobility and social mobility. Both migration and transnational mobilities research has tended to divide those who move voluntarily across borders into binary categories: 'expatriates', 'cosmopolitans' or 'globals' – the elites who mobilize their significant economic and cultural resources to circulate fluidly across national borders (see, for example, Bauman, 1998; Sklair, 2001; Elliott and Urry, 2010) – and 'immigrants' or 'migrant workers', the disenfranchised and often undocumented workers from the Global South who move out of economic necessity and form a migrant underclass in host countries (see, for example, Constable, 2007; Giles et al, 2014; Kathiravelu, 2016). Further, the literature on 'middling transnationals' that first emerged in the mid-2000s positioned the concerns of this middle category as primarily around White and Western young people moving between sites in the Global North, such as between the Antipodes and global cities such as London (Clarke, 2005; Conradson and Latham, 2005a).

How then, do we understand the experiences of migrants like Woojin and Hyon-Woo in relation to existing concepts in migration studies, and within the context of the specific socioeconomic locations, life trajectories and cultures of mobility that surround Asian migration today? In order to understand these kinds of experiences, one of the key things I seek to do in this book is to rethink ideas of 'the middle' in migration studies, particularly migration sociology. In this chapter, I both lay out the foundations for this rethinking, and further establish the empirical context that underpins this book.

First, I give a brief description of the regional social and economic dynamics that shape 21st-century flows of young Asian migrants to Australia, including an outline of some of the general drivers of middle-class transnationalism in the six sending countries of concern, revealing how local social, economic and cultural conditions inflect the outward mobility of young people in these different contexts. My central argument here is that, despite the varied national backgrounds and migration trajectories of my research participants, the concept of middling mobility is a productive way to understand the cultures of mobility that shapes their lives. I then build an argument for how I understand middling mobility throughout this book as a specific form of migration that is marked by various states of ambiguity, 'in-betweenness' and transition. I address how the migrants whose lives I analyze inhabit multiple spaces of the in-between in terms of their socioeconomic locations in different places, their life-stage, and the scholarly and policy categories of migration that they occupy. Throughout the chapter, I engage in a critical discussion of how migration scholars understand middling or middle-class migrant mobility in the 21st century, drawing on previous work on transnational, Asian middle-class families; the pioneering work on 'middling transnationalism' of the mid-2000s; and more recent studies of Asian middle-class young people and the role of transnational mobility in life-courses, particularly in the transition to adulthood. I finish the chapter by arguing that analysis of chronomobilities 'of the middle' presents new ways of thinking through both contemporary migrant experiences and the spatio-temporal transformation of contemporary social life more broadly.

Twenty-first-century middling migrant mobilities in the Asian context

It is timely to rethink ideas of middling migrants and middling transnationalism as we enter the third decade of the 21st century, especially from the vantage point of Asia-Pacific circuits of migrant mobility. The rapid growth of a 'global middle class' is a 21st-century phenomenon. Figures from the Organisation for Economic Co-operation and Development (OECD) show an increase from 1.8 billion in 2009 to 3.2 billion in 2020 and a projected 4.9 billion by 2030, with the bulk of the growth from the Asian region, which by 2030 will represent 66% of the global middle-class population (Pezzini, 2012). Financial analysts and media commentators tend to view Asia's consumption-hungry and upwardly mobile middle class as key to the region's rising economic power and the new world order of the 21st century as the 'Asian century'. Yet who precisely falls within the middle of Asia's class hierarchies, positioned between the working and upper classes, is highly context-dependent and usually measured on national variables around consumption power, relative income, education levels and local perceptions of wealth and status (Roy, 2018). This means establishing quantitative and measurable boundaries of 'middle-classness' for a group of migrants from different sending countries in Asia in contexts of ongoing transnational mobility is far from straightforward. As this chapter explains, the conceptualization of 'the middle' that is deployed in this book is not intended to be a fixed class signifier. In terms of the socioeconomic position of my interlocutors, I understand being 'of the middle' in a deliberately loose way that can account for variations in sending-country economic dynamics and demography; the socioeconomic landscapes migrants encounter in Australia; and cultural understandings of what it means to be middle-class and on the move.

The specific cultural and social contexts of my interlocutors' sending countries are highly significant to shaping their mobility trajectories, and the reasons each of these individuals found themselves in Australia were always at least in some ways reflective of specific policies of their home-country governments and specific social influences within their home cultures. These conditions are worth briefly exploring in each case. Five of the migrants were from the People's Republic of China (PRC), where the 1978 'open-door' policies that relaxed restrictions on emigration, the one-child policy and the rapid economic development of the past quarter century have given the youth of the 21st-century PRC far greater capacities and aspirations to be mobile than previous generations. The creation of a new entrepreneurial elite and a burgeoning middle class comes with transforming lifestyle expectations for many in China (Tomba, 2004). These include aspirations for international travel, with China now the world's largest international tourism market, with more than 127 million outbound trips in 2015 (UNWTO, 2016). Further, Pieke (2007) sees the interlinked and rising trends of student and professional migration from the PRC as critical to a 'new Chinese migration order' globally. Increasing wealth has brought foreign study within the reach of a salaried middle class, making the Chinese by far the largest group of international students in most Western countries, including in Australia. Emigration of skilled and professional labour is closely connected to educational migration via the education–migration nexus (Robertson, 2013). Various authors have noted the increasing importance of post-study work experience abroad for Chinese graduates of international universities, given the increasing underemployment of returnees and devaluing of Western degrees in the local Chinese job market (Waters, 2006; Hao and Welch, 2012; Yu, 2016; Tu, 2018). Like the middle-class Hong Kong and Taiwanese transnational families that received considerable attention in the migration literature in the 1990s and early 2000s, mobile Chinese young people today are often supported by family strategies for education, investment and 'flexible citizenship' (Fong,

2011). My PRC-born interlocutors were all only children, and all had initially entered Australia on student visas for undergraduate or graduate study. They were also uniformly financially supported, as least initially, by their parents, and most agreed that the obtaining the 'package' of the Western degree and overseas work experience was important to their futures. As demonstrated by the story of Percy in Chapter 3, my Chinese interlocutors tended to plan, at least initially, to compete degrees in Australia, work in their chosen field for a few years, and then return to China to 'settle down' and support their parents as they aged.

Twelve of the migrants interviewed were Indian. The emergence of a 'new' middle class after the country's economic liberalization in the 1990s is well established in sociological analyses of contemporary India (see, for example, Fernandes, 2000; Brosius, 2012). The younger generation of this middle class in particular is recognized as aspiring towards Western consumptions patterns and 'cosmopolitan' lifestyles (Forsberg, 2017). However, as in many of the other sending-country contexts, in India the aspiration towards a global lifestyle is often produced within the realities of constricted opportunities for young people domestically. As Jeffrey (2008) attests, the benefits of neoliberal globalization have only been truly accessible to a very 'thin' stratum of highly privileged urban youth in India. High educational attainment has not led to secure pathways to professional employment for many young people (Jeffrey, 2009), and for the bulk of lower middle-class families, liberalization has made life more difficult due to 'inflation, increasing financial stress and debt, increasing competition for jobs and housing and a marked decline in living standards' (Brown et al, 2017: 533). International mobility, in the form of study, work or both, is thus often positioned in analyses of the Indian middle class as a way for families to gain some advantage within a competitive labour market (Forsberg, 2017). But the role of youth transnational mobility and its relation to class in India is symbolic as well as economic. Tuxen (2018) notes that the procurement of the 'foreign stamp' of living overseas is often critical to the reproduction of middle-class status for young urban Indians, regardless of a tangible economic return, and Radhakrishnan (2008) further highlights the cultural aspirations towards 'global Indianness' that increasingly shape the professional classes in the growing Indian diaspora. Young Indians who enter Australia on temporary visas are very much embedded within these cultural and economic imperatives towards mobility. While earlier work often positions young Indians in Australia as highly motivated to achieve the 'holy grail' of permanent residency (Baas, 2012), my Indian interlocutors were on the whole ambivalent about fully settling in Australia, often remaining open to return or on-migration elsewhere as opportunities arose. For this group perhaps more than any other, an overseas experience was seen as a 'normal' stage in a life-path, with their peers, siblings and cousins commonly also undertaking these experiences.

Six Malaysian migrants participated in the study. As a former colonial state, Malaysia's post-independence journey has been marked by the creation of a burgeoning middle class with significant transnational links globally, including in Australia. Malaysian students were a key demographic within the soft diplomacy of the Colombo Plan of the 1960s and 1970s, where students from Asia studied in Australia then returned to leading roles in business and government in their countries of origin. Significant networks of alumni of Australian education are still present in Malaysian industry and government today, and several major Australian universities have branch campuses in Malaysia. One of my participants studied at one of these campuses before coming to Australia for graduate study; another was drawn to Australia because her brother had studied at an Australian branch campus locally. Also significant to young middle-class Malaysian migrants is the legacy of the controversial 1971 New Economic Policy that sought to address social and economic disparities between racial groups in Malaysia through various preferential programmes favouring the Bumiputera (ethnic Malay and indigenous) population over Chinese-Malaysians and Indian-Malaysians (Lee, 2012). With 90% of public university places reserved for Bumiputera students, international education has become an increasingly popular choice for middle-class Chinese-Malaysians in particular. The young Malaysians I interviewed for this study reflected these previous patterns of migration from Asia to Australia – all were Chinese-Malaysians, except for one, who identified as Eurasian. They were mostly from relatively affluent families, and at something of an advantage compared with some of the other groups due to their existing English fluency. Most had visited Australia as tourists, often more than once, prior to coming for more extended stays on student and then work visas.

Four participants were from Taiwan, where a 'new middle class' of professionals and small- to medium-sized business owners emerged in the 1980s and 1990s, building their wealth on Taiwan's integration into the global market as an export economy (Lan, 2006). Lan (2006) sees a metropolitan and transnational lifestyle, including overseas travel, as an important cultural marker of middle-class status in Taiwan, and Pieke (2007) argues that education, skilled migration and business migration, particularly to the US, Canada and Australia, has been a normal part of Taiwanese middle-class life since the late 1980s and 1990s. Taiwanese transmigrants in the West, including to Australia, have often been highlighted as entrepreneurial, highly educated and investment and lifestyle motivated (Tseng, 2000; Chiang, 2008), with the Taiwanese featuring prominently in Australia's business migration stream in the late 20th century (Ip, 2001). For Taiwanese transnationals, residence rights in the West have been an important form of capital accumulation for a number of decades, not only for investment and work opportunities, but as a form of 'political insurance' against the threat of reunification with the PRC (Pieke, 2007; Chiang, 2008). Further, ongoing circulation between Taiwan and settlement contexts is common (Ip, 2001). My Taiwanese participants, who were all female, all had some extended family connections in Australia as a result of previous waves of skilled and business migration. They noted that their parents retained concerns about Australian citizenship as a good safety net, although they were themselves generally more interested in travel and lifestyle experiences than the 'insurance' of the passport.

Korea is an interesting case in this research because, compared with China, India, Taiwan and Malaysia, there was only a relatively small 'settler' Korean community in Australia prior to the 2000s. Ten interviewees were from Korea. Much of the rapid growth in Korean migration in Australia this century has been driven by temporary working holiday and international student visa streams. For example, in 2003–04, only 9,522 working holiday visas were granted to Korean nationals (DIMIA, 2005); by 2012–13, this had jumped to 35,220 (Phillips, 2016). This bump in incoming youth mobility is driven by cultural shifts in Korea, where a growing number of young Koreans are either taking overseas breaks during their undergraduate study, or postponing the transition to employment and family formation after graduation via short-term transnational mobility, primarily through English language or working holiday programmes (Yoon, 2014a). Yoon (2015) sees this youth mobility phenomenon as a product of Korea's state-driven globalization push since the 1990s, with today's young Koreans growing up in a political discourse that heavily promoted 'global talent' and a 'global generation' as critical to both national and individual success. The transnational mobility of Korean youth, has, more so than any of the other source countries in this book, been driven explicitly and directly by government policies, particularly President Lee Myung-bak's 2008–13 administration, which introduced and heavily promoted mobility opportunities for young adults, particularly outbound overseas internship and training opportunities. Despite the rhetoric of both self-development and national 'global talent' that these policies employed, as Yoon (2015) critically notes, a weak domestic labour market for youth was a key driver and 'one of the policy's effects was to discard the surplus labour force mostly at its own expense' (84). Among my interlocutors, as well as the many other young people I spoke to informally while writing this book, Koreans were far more likely than other nationalities to initially enter Australia for English language study or on working holiday visas, and many described having very easy access to information about these programmes through promotions at their high schools and universities. Many, like Carolyn and David, however, were eventually sceptical about their opportunities if they returned to Korea, realizing that the push for English fluency and 'global' experience in practice had limited value in the domestic labour market.

The case of the Philippines differs somewhat from other sending-country contexts in this study, although it is also positioned, as an 'emerging' economy, within narratives of a rising Asian middle class. Labour export was first introduced by the Philippines government in the early 1970s as an economic development strategy. Today, the country is well known as a top source country of workers for the global labour market, particularly in terms of the 'feminized' migration flows of women into expanding markets for domestic and healthcare workers. This emigration is heavily state-driven, with remittances from the ten million Overseas Filipino Workers (OFWs) (who tend overall to be a younger demographic) bringing in 10% of the Philippines' gross domestic product (Flores, 2019). As the fifth largest supplier of temporary migrants to Australia at the time this study was conducted, there were five Filipino participants in the sample. Three of these requested to participate together in a group interview, and only one responded to requests for follow-up interviews. As such, the data I have on the Filipino experience is narrower than for the other nationalities. Based on these few cases and on secondary data, however, Filipino young people are more likely to enter Australia under sponsored skilled temporary work visas, and the top three occupations for Filipino nationals on temporary skilled visas are nurses, motor mechanics and cooks (DHA, 2018). Reflecting the overall pattern of labour-focused migration (in comparison to other groups who tended to move more in and out of work and study) the Filipino participants all entered on 457 skilled work visas, rather than student or working holiday visas, although one had since transitioned to a student visa. Although all except one had some level of post-secondary education in the Philippines, the four male participants were working in landscaping and construction, and the female participant as a care aide. This group were older on arrival than most of the other participants and their experiences reflected in some ways a traditional model of Filipino outmigration. They were all regularly remitting money back to families in the Philippines, and two of the men had spouses and children that they were supporting at home. While able to bring their families on dependent visas, both said it was too expensive, and that they would reunite the family if and when they achieved PR. Yet, like the other participants, all spoke about their own self-development and the lifestyle benefits of coming to Australia, as well as the economic benefits. These experiences reflect Limpangog's (2013) findings on Filipino women in Melbourne, for whom migration enabled a recovery of a declining middle-class status in the Philippines as well as the exploration of a different lifestyle.

Despite variations in political, social and economic conditions in specific national contexts, across the Asian region, rapid modernization, urbanization and rising levels of education have seen significant expansions of the middle class over the past half century. Eased bureaucratic restrictions on travel and the decreasing costs of air travel and transnational communication have led to increased transnational mobility, especially of this expanding 'middle strata' of Asian societies (Lee and Piper, 2003). Significant previous work on Asian middle-class families and transnational social capital has established that aspirational norms assume transnational mobility will confer particular kinds of cultural capital, and consequently upward social mobility (Ong, 1999; Waters, 2009; Thomas and Ong, 2015). Pertinently, Gomes (2016) notes that it is increasingly transient mobilities, like international education or short-term overseas work – rather than classical settler migration – that shape middle-class identities across Asia. Migration in general – and transified forms of migration in particular – although still practised by a relatively small number of people overall, has become in Asia, as Scott (2006: 1105) has argued in the European context, 'a normal middle-class activity rather than something exclusively confined to an economic elite'. As Mapril (2014) has argued, migration – as a resource and as discursive formation – can in fact be understood as constitutive of the new Asian middle class.

My interlocutors mostly clearly sat within this cultural and social milieu of a mobile 21st-century Asian middle class. But there were also some, like Woojin, who moved across its edges, both economically and culturally. All had the economic resources to pay the costs of airfares, visas and living in Australia, which are high relative to many other migrant-receiving contexts globally. And, while some had more affluent backgrounds than others, they were uniformly, in relation to other flows of migrants from their sending countries, positioned in between highly skilled or elite mobilities and low-skilled labour mobilities. Like Fathi (2017), I must bracket my analysis of the class positioning of my interlocutors with the caveat that this analysis is subjective, relational and limited to the narratives and experiences of this fairly diverse group of migrants within a particular context of 21st-century Australian migration from Asia. Yet, while the variations in their specific backgrounds and circumstances reveal the broadness of the 'middle space', all these migrants experienced the oscillations between flexibility and precarity and opportunity and risk that their mobility engendered in remarkably similar ways. They also all shared middle-class imaginaries and aspirations around their mobility, namely, that moving to Australia, whether for the short or long term, would enable the accumulation of combinations of 'global' (that is, English) language fluency, 'global' work experience, and experientially significant cultural and leisure experiences.

What I have suggested in this section is that there is a normalization of transnational mobility for the Asian middle class; yet, the relationship between social mobility and spatial mobility remains complex in practice. As Naafs and Skelton (2018: 1) note, 'while many Asian youth have the possibility of aspiring towards very different futures than their parents could have imagined at the same age, the routes into such futures can be more risky, demanding and insecure'. My conceptualization of middling mobility seeks to understand the lived experiences of mobility within this context. It is a context in which the relationship between social mobility and spatial mobility for migrants of the middle is rarely smoothly correlative, either upwards or downwards. My approach thus critiques the widely accepted view of 'aspirational' transnational mobility in both Asian and Australian contexts – that international experiences provide young people with enhanced life chances and competitive job skills, as well as benefit national and local communities more broadly through remittances, skills transfer, cultural diplomacy networks and an increasingly cosmopolitan and agile workforce (Robertson et al, 2018). In the following sections, I look in more detail at how to productively rethink this middle space of migration.

Middling mobility: rethinking the 'in-between' space

As argued in this chapter's introduction, for a significant period, migration research tended to divide those who move voluntarily across borders into two binary categories. The first is the elite professionals, capitalists, and other 'highly skilled' migrants who mobilize their significant economic and cultural resources to circulate fluidly across national borders and most often between global cities – encapsulated in the images of 'expatriates', 'cosmopolitans' and 'globals' (Bauman, 1998; Sklair, 2001; Elliott and Urry, 2010). The second category comprises the disenfranchised workers from the Global South who move out of economic necessity and form an exploited migrant underclass in host countries – often labelled 'immigrants', 'guestworkers' or 'migrant workers' and including irregular or undocumented migrants. Empirically, this binary has served to importantly illuminate how transnational mobility is implicated in the production and reproduction of global inequalities of metropole/periphery; White/non-White, Global South/Global North; and how the imperatives, capacities and outcomes of individual mobility are crucially yoked to sets of multiscalar power relations, described by Massey (1993) as globalization's 'asymmetrical power-geometries'.

In recent decades, however, there has been increasing recognition of the proliferation of migrant mobilities that exist on a spectrum in between these two poles of the mobile global elite and the disenfranchised immigrant. Conradson and Latham's (2005b) seminal exploration of middling transnationals importantly established that a focus on 'middling' experiences draws attention to the more mundane, everyday and 'ordinary' practices of transnational lives. Subsequent empirical scholarship on middling transnationalism or middling migration has highlighted the everyday lives of varied kinds of migrants who occupy a middling socioeconomic stratum and who move for a combination of cultural, lifestyle, social, professional and personal reasons. These types of migrant mobilities are increasingly significant globally. Due to unprecedented growth of knowledge economies, burgeoning middle-class populations in sending regions and increasing focus on 'skilled' intake in receiving countries, a significant proportion of migration today into post-industrial contexts is of the relatively skilled and educated (Scott, 2019). Middle-class 'cultures of mobility' are concurrently growing and spreading, with transnational mobility, as previously argued in the Asian context, becoming an increasingly normative part of the imaginary of middle-class life trajectories globally (Robertson et al, 2018).

Existing scholarship on this significant 'middle space' of migration includes the movement of professionals and expatriates from the West (Scott, 2006; Walsh, 2006; Lehmann, 2014); the temporary movements of young middle-class people as 'rites of passage' to adulthood such as 'working holidays' and 'overseas experiences'

(Wilson et al, 2009; Matthews, 2014; Kawashima, 2010); and the movements of 'lifestyle migrants' seeking individualized, anti-modern and escapist life projects through migration (Benson and O'Reilly, 2009). New scholarly categories of migration have arisen here from the analysis of 'the middle', and these often shift the focus of analysis in particular directions. Benson and O'Reilly's (2009) category of lifestyle migrants, for example, moves questions of migration away from the global circulation of labour or skills, focusing instead on mostly Western subjects who present their migrations primarily as journeys of self-realization. Transnational mobility can be read in analyses of lifestyle migration as less about traditional notions of upward mobility or economic security through crossing borders, and more about forms of countercultural practices and networks, such as in D'Andrea's (2006) work on 'neo-nomadism'. Lundström (2014) uses multi-sited ethnography of privileged Swedish migrant women in the US, Singapore and Spain to bring to the fore the significance of race and class and the complex hierarchies of privilege that operate across different receiving contexts. Critically, she uses the category of 'white migrations' to describe these women as a move to critique the implicit racialized boundaries between 'expatriates' and 'migrants'.

There remain, however, some gaps in this body of work. Scholarship of middling migration has perhaps not yet fully accounted for new global conditions and for the differential experiences of the middle along the lines of location, directionality, nationality and race. Studies of expatriates, working holiday migrants and lifestyle migrants most often focus on the experiences of White and Western subjects – albeit with some recent exceptions, such as Yoon's (2014a, b, 2015) work on Korean working holiday makers and Kato (2013) and Kawashima's (2010) on Japanese, or Ho's (2011a; 2011b) on young skilled Singaporeans in London. Middling migrants from Asia living in the West, although an increasingly significant and rapidly growing migrant group, remain relatively under-researched within this strand of migration research. There has also been an overall critique of the concept of middling migrants that argues that the concept is too inclusive and broad, and therefore fails to account for nuances and diversity within the 'middle', particularly in relation to the significance of life-stage (Ryan et al, 2015).

Further, in spite of an expanding body of work, the concepts of middling migration or middling transnationalism too frequently remain narrowly located within static notions of the middle as a socioeconomic status, where they are usually tied to studies of migrants who remain fixedly middle-class at home and away. Smith, for example, (2005: 235) defines middling transnationalism simply as 'the transnational practices of middle-class social actors'. In addition, Collins (2014) argues that middling migrants are usually defined in the literature as those 'whose education and occupation reflect a middle-class status in their home countries but also as they migrate to new destinations' (43). These definitions tend to fix migrants as 'middleclass at home' and 'middleclass abroad', as well as fixing 'the middle' itself as a static social category. There is a sense in recent examinations of new forms of migration, however, that 'the middle' can be more variegated and contradictory than these definitions suggest. To be 'middling' is not a fixed status, but rather a spectrum of social locations and experiences that migrants may slide across and between depending on the contexts and circumstances of their mobility. Furthermore, mobility can paradoxically be a way for migrants to procure or reproduce middle-class careers and lifestyles, but also to destabilize and reframe them (Scott, 2006). The 'unevenness' of the middle seems especially apparent in relation to 'middling' young people who move from relatively 'peripheral' places to global cities of the West. Rutten and Verstappen (2014) for example, show such unevenness clearly in their analysis of young Indian men in London, who end up in low-status and low-skilled work, despite their comfortable middle-class backgrounds at home. A similar process occurs for the highly educated Poles and Lithuanians in the UK studied by Parutis (2011). Both Rutten and Verstappen (2014) and Parutis's (2011) interlocutors use downward social and economic mobility in the UK somewhat strategically to build economic and social capital that will reinforce their middle-class positioning at home, or as a means to 'escape' parental control and build 'life experience' for a brief period.

Following from Baas (2017), I use the term middling mobility to describe my interlocutors' experiences, seeking a definition of the middle that is both more specific and more expansive than the approach taken in earlier work in the migration field on middling transnationals and middling migrants. This framing sees 'the middle' as the broad space in between migrant marginality and elite mobility, as well as a way to understand the experiences of migrants who occupy multiple and intersecting spaces of 'the in-between' in relation to social mobility, spatial mobility, temporality and mobility 'type'. It is a socioeconomic category in which migrants have access to resources, and are relatively educated, but are not socially located in a fixed or uniform middle, but rather a middle that changes over space and across time. In what follows in this chapter, I further sketch out my conceptualization of middling mobility as multiply constructed, and not just as a signifier of socioeconomic status or class positioning. I argue that this concept of middling mobility renews and expands some of this previous thinking in a way that can highlight hidden nuances around the interrelationships of temporality and mobility, and of spatial mobility and social mobility.

In relation to terminological distinctions around migration versus mobility, the journeys I describe in this book are migration journeys, in both subjective and political senses, and I thus refer to my interlocutors as middling migrants throughout the book. The use of the term 'mobility' to conceptualize their experiences, however, importantly acknowledges that these migration stories are constituted by multiple and intersecting mobilities, beyond a single spatial border crossing from home to host country. As Brickell and Datta (2011: 9) note, studies of transnational migrants have tended to under-theorize the significance of movement across localities within national boundaries. The spatial mobilities that are significant to the journeys of the migrants in this book are not just forms of two-way transnationalism, but include intra-national mobility between towns, regions and cities, and onward mobilities to third or fourth countries. Furthermore, the term mobility also encompasses the non-spatial mobilities of status and social location that are also crucial to the dynamics of these migrant experiences. Middling mobility thus presents a sense of in-betweenness and transition across different legal categories, social categories and conventional scholarly categorizations of migration as well as mobility across national borders. Also significant is life-course mobility – the often-uneven movement through emerging adulthood that interlaces with geographic mobility in these young migrants' lives. This more expansive understanding of 'the middle' is crucial to understanding the chronomobilities of migrant experience that I explore in this book, but is also potentially crucial to migration studies more broadly as migrant mobilities become increasingly spatio-temporally and socially complex.

Between social locations and between migration 'types'

If we return to thinking about Hyon-Woo and Woojin's experiences, it is clear that, in many ways, they fit into a migratory middle as a space somewhere in between the mobilities of the elite and the mobilities of the disenfranchised. Yet, in other ways, they complicate and slip between some of the existing scholarly conceptualizations of the middle described in the previous section. Both Hyon-Woo and Woojin entered Australia on working holiday visas. These are one-year temporary visas that allow young people aged under 31 years to live and work in Australia via reciprocal bilateral arrangements intended for cultural exchange and extended tourist experiences. These visas have limited work rights, and, at the time of the fieldwork, the option to extend for a second year if visa holders undertake three months of specified work in regional areas.[2] Both Hyon-Woo and Woojin ended up being able to stay on in Australia via skilled migration pathways – at the time they applied, both welding and welfare work were determined by Australian migration policy as skilled occupations in high demand. Both Hyon-Woo and Woojin thus utilized their skills and education in their migration projects, and both experienced middle-class lifestyles in Australia in terms of economic capacities to travel, consider higher education and pursue leisure activities. Neither was driven to migrate purely by economic necessity. To some extent, their desires to stay and to move were intrinsically linked to desires for different life experiences and lifestyles. As such, they reflect existing models of middling mobility as a privileged form of movement that centres on self-actualization and lifestyle choice (King and Ruiz-Gelices, 2003; Conradson and Latham, 2005a, 2005b).

To see their mobility as entirely autonomous and privileged, however, does not account for the full scope of their experiences. Hyon-Woo experienced periods of economic insecurity and at least initially, downward social mobility – from a promising engineering student at a top university to a waitress and then a social welfare worker – much to her parents' dismay. Her subsequent career trajectory was fragmented, as she moved through unpaid, casual and eventually full-time welfare work, and then freelance work and part-time study. Her parents remained perplexed about her patched together and temporally contingent employment across social welfare, small business administration and interpreting. But despite sometimes struggling financially, Hyon-Woo didn't see her zigzagging trajectory as much of a problem in the long term. She had enjoyed the welfare work and it had ultimately been a means to an end in terms of securing a permanent visa. Her desire to stay in Australia was grounded in things outside of work and economic gain – her relationship, her appreciation of the lifestyle, her passion for diving and nature, and her rejection of perceived values of ambition and consumption in Korea.

Woojin remained in the same type of work he had done in Korea, but experienced a form of social mobility related to the different cultural status afforded to trade occupations in Australia, particularly in a regional context where skilled trade work is often more highly paid than most available white-collar work. His work was more stable, better paid and in some ways had a higher status than Hyon-Woo's. Ultimately, however, he experienced severe workplace harassment and bullying that was exacerbated by his dependency on his employer for a visa. This is a common condition for contemporary migrants in Australia, where the transification of migration often 'traps' migrants within certain industries or with certain employers (Robertson, 2017) if they wish to secure another visa.

For both Hyon-Woo and Woojin, leaving Korea was also something of an escape from a predetermined pathway to adulthood – a rerouting of their lives away from the normative biographic temporalities shaped by cultural, and particularly parental, expectations. They sought through their mobility not to reproduce but to break away from normative Korean middle-class life scripts. Both were driven by their somewhat amorphous desire for 'something different', rather than fixed aspirations for the future. While Woojin's return to Korea could on the surface be read as a project of upward social mobility – completing law school and fluency in English would firmly place him in the elite professional sphere – he was adamant that this transition should not be understood in terms of conventional Korean middle-class desires for the accumulation of economic and cultural capital. This new pathway had come about due to a passion for worker protection, drawn from his experiences of exploitation as a tradesperson.

I use the complex and sometimes contradictory experiences of Hyon-Woo and Woojin to suggest that the middle, as a social location, is itself mobile. As discussed earlier, occupying the middle as a mobile subject can be a decidedly uneven experience, particularly for non-Western young people travelling to the West. While they may end up in low-status and low-skilled work despite their comfortable middle-class backgrounds at home, this downward social and economic mobility while living overseas can be strategically used to build economic and social capital that will procure, reproduce or reinforce normative middle-class careers and lifestyles in the long term (Rutten and Verstappen, 2014). Yet, mobility can also be a strategy to destabilize, reframe or defy these same norms (Scott, 2006). As Hyon-Woo and Woojin's stories attest, despite the uneven economic and social outcomes of mobility, the process can have value for young people as a means to 'escape' parental control and culturally normative life scripts – to experience 'something else' and to craft alternative futures.

Such experiences of the middle were not exclusive to Hyon-Woo or Woojin, but were reflected in the mobilities of all the migrants I met in the course of my research, regardless of their country of origin, education or occupation. Transified migration further intensifies this sense of in-betweenness of social locations and class identities, as temporary visa statuses and uncertain futures often result in deskilling at work and downsizing of lifestyles. I met migrants who were working on prestigious PhDs at top universities in Australia, and who had several years of high-level professional experience in their fields at home. They were hoping to qualify as skilled migrants after graduation, but while they studied were cleaning offices or waiting tables for less than the minimum wage. I met young women and men who lived in cramped, shared flats in the outer suburbs of Australian cities, who juggled punishing schedules of shift work at restaurants or in factories. Their homes were sparsely furnished and barely decorated. They bought basic homewares second or third hand and shopped at discount grocery stores. Yet, on annual holidays they would return to privileged, middle-class lifestyles at their parents' homes in Kuala Lumpar or Mumbai, with domestic staff catering to their needs and nights out at clubs and restaurants. Others, predominantly the Filipino participants, were professionally qualified in their home countries but were unable to maintain a middle-class lifestyle there due to scarce employment opportunities. Abandoning their professional careers and working in landscaping or construction (on skilled 457 visas) in Australia, and sending money home, allowed their families to access more middle-class consumption patterns and, if they had children, better education.

Middling mobility is thus not just about mobile people who occupy a social location within the middle class. Rather, it is constituted by moves across the overlapping but often incongruent social hierarchies of different places and cultures, in unexpected and sometimes 'zigzagging' patterns of social location, dislocation and relocation. It involves uneven outcomes and fragmented and unfinished mobility trajectories, within which individuals may move up, down and even sideways across transnational and translocal social and economic landscapes.

In addition to their dynamic sense of social location, the migrants featured in this book also often fall between or move across legal and scholarly categories of migrant type. Globally, many migrants move between statuses – sometimes strategically and sometimes because they are forced to do so – such as moves from documented to undocumented or from asylum seeker to labour migrant (Schuster, 2005). As Baas (2017) notes, however, it is the 'mobile middle' who can most 'actively negotiate and test the flexibilities of a migration program in order to be able to work and potentially stay on' (Baas, 2017: 47). As such, the spaces that middling migrants occupy between established and recognizable categories can be 'principally dynamic and fluid' (Baas, 2017: 50), in relation to both legal categories and scholarly typologies. For example, young and middling migrants often strategically use changing visa categories to extend stays (Baas,

2017; Ho, 2011a; Robertson, 2018; Roberts, 2019). Visa transition is one of the most prevalent features of transified migration, and all the migrants involved in this research transitioned across different visas at least once, and many did so multiple times. Hyon-Woo moved from a working holiday visa to a student visa, then to a temporary skilled graduate work visa. She then spent nearly three years on bridging visas while her PR application as a skilled permanent migrant was processed, and finally she became a citizen. Woojin also entered Australia on a working holiday visa and then transitioned on to a temporary skilled work visa. His attempts to be sponsored for a permanent visa were ultimately unsuccessful, but even if he had to return to Korea, he could potentially seek a new visa to again return to Australia. Furthermore, within the context of middling and transified migration to Australia, specific visa categories are, as scholars have noted in other contexts (Baas, 2017; Yeoh and Eng, 2008), far from homogenous in relation to income levels, skill levels and experiences. A migrant on a working holiday visa could spend six months working in a well-paid professional job in an urban centre, and then three months doing unskilled farm labour in a remote location. Workers on 457 skilled visas include chefs working late-night shifts and earning the minimum wage as well as highly paid corporate consultants.

Along with significant status mobility, the migrant narratives in this book also demonstrate how conventional typologies of migrant 'type' exist in complex, and not always clearly aligned, relationships with migrants' actual motivations, practices and decisions. For example, is Hyon-Woo, who was motivated to stay in Australia by her leisure activities and her search for a different way of living what Benson and O'Reilly (2009) refer to as a 'lifestyle migrant'? Having studied on a student visa and then transitioned to work is she also a 'student-migrant' (Robertson, 2013)? Do her recent business trips to Korea place her at the fringes of what Sklair (2012) terms the 'transnational capitalist class', or does her freelance work status make her part of Standing's (2011) 'global precariat'? How can Woojin's varied positioning as a trade worker, both economically and culturally, be understood as mobile across both space and time? When he goes back to Korea, with his law school ambitions, travel experiences, significant savings, and newly minted bilingual capital, does he become an elite, cosmopolitan returnee? Or, is he a 'failed migrant', returning after poor treatment in the host country and a lack of options to stay on? Are Hyon-Woo and Woojin, and other migrants like them, settlers, sojourners, circulators or something in between?

These questions are challenging to answer because migration studies largely continues to rely on bounded typologies of migrants, based either on a fixed sense of their spatio-temporality (for example, 'second generation', 'temporary', 'return', 'permanent', 'circular') or a fixed sense of their motivations and agency (for example, 'labour migration', 'lifestyle migration', 'student migration'). This has resulted in limited conceptual capacity to capture the complexity and connections within often overlapping forms of transnational mobility, or to adequately account for those who do not fit or stay in these categories (Robertson et al, 2018a). An exploration of middling mobility can thus, I argue, push against the tendency to typologize in migration studies that sometimes limits analysis of the spaces migrants occupy across and between categories.

Between youth and adulthood

Australian migration policy strategically seeks to draw on middle-class youth populations in Asia as a new consumer, labour and reproductive force to shore up the nation's future. As a result, Asian migrants experiencing transified migration in Australia are by and large young when they arrive. The majority of the migrants whose lives I explore in this book were in their late teens or in their twenties when they initially arrived in Australia, although some were in their thirties and beyond at the time of the interviews. This reflects the age distribution of migrants globally, which generally peaks in the mid- to late twenties (OECD, 2013), as well as the overall focus of Australia's current immigration selection policy in prioritizing migrants at earlier stages of working life (Wright et al, 2016). In Australia, these policies are influencing national demographic trends. The median age of Australian residents born in Asian countries is decreasing. For example, the median age for Chinese-born residents decreased from 39.8 to 35.5 years between 1996 and 2014, and for Indian-born residents it decreased from 40.6 to 33.2 years. Median ages of the Australian-born, and of more established migrant cohorts such as the UK-born and Italian-born are, in contrast, contributing to an overall ageing population (DHA, 2015).

While direct permanent settlement pathways also favour younger applicants, transified migration processes in Australia particularly favour young migrants in their twenties and early thirties. Visas of initial entry for transified pathways are often youth-focused. This is either explicit, as in the case of working holiday visas where migrants have to be under 31 years of age for eligibility, or implicit, as in the case of student visas where the connection with tertiary education means the most common age range (representing 43% of all international student entrants) is between 20 and 24 years (AEI, 2016). Further, there is an age criterion in the points testing of applications for permanent skilled migration – migrants aged between 25 and 32 receive 30 points; this reduces to 25 points for those aged between 33 and 39, and 15 points for those aged 40 to 44. No age criterion points are given for applicants older than 44 or younger than 25. Migrants under 25 thus often have to enter on temporary visas with the hope of applying for permanency once they cross the age threshold for points. Migrants already living onshore on temporary visas must also often 'race the clock' to meet other eligibility criteria to qualify for permanent visas before they 'age out' of the maximum points age group (Robertson, 2014).

The transient, transitionary and transitory temporalities of transified migration are thus inextricably intertwined with a life-stage in between youth and adulthood. Sociologically, this life-stage has conventionally been understood as 'transition to adulthood' – a concept governed by particular normative ideas of transitions through education to employment, away from dependence on the natal family, and towards the formation of adult partnerships and nuclear family (Thomson and Taylor, 2005; Cuervo and Wyn, 2011; Skrbis et al, 2014). More recently, developmental psychologists have identified that in industrialized societies since the late 20th century, there has been a lengthening and unsettling of this transition, captured in the concept of 'emergent adulthood'. Emergent adulthood is characterized not by linear and normative transitions, but 'relative independence from social roles and from normative expectations' (Arnett, 2000: 469) – a period in which people in their twenties and early thirties are afforded self-focused and explorative freedom before settling into stable adult life.

The experiences of my migrant interlocutors were heavily influenced by the complexity of navigating the process of 'becoming adult' – both in the normative sense and in the sense of emergent and explorative adulthood – alongside their mobility. I therefore use the idea of middling mobility to also understand the cultural and social structures that inform the experience of mobility during the in-between life-stage of young adulthood. Such an exploration is particularly significant in the context of young, middle-class migrants from Asia, where constructions of youth and adulthood are in the process of transforming. While the idea of an extended stage of freedom and exploration in the time between childhood and adulthood is relatively established in the cultural imaginaries of the West, it is still an emergent (and often an exclusively middle- and upper-class) phenomena in many parts of Asia. However, as Martin (2018) notes, economic and social change in Asia, most notably the rising ages of marriage and increasing participation in tertiary education, are contributing to a 'stretching' of youth, often understood as the period in between adolescence and marriage. In alignment with Sala and Baldassar (2017), I seek to theorize life-stages in a flexible way that can allow for the variance of cross-cultural, and indeed cross-generational, diversity in what constitutes 'youth' and 'adulthood'. In general, however, for the migrants in this book, cultural understandings of their life-stage encompass *both* 'transition to adulthood' (as a process through the normative markers of marriage, stable employment, family formation and independent living) *and* 'emergent adulthood' (as a period of 'unsettling' and individual identity exploration). In fact, for middling migrants, mobility choices and capacities often intersect with contestations between these two models of 'moving towards' adulthood. As we have seen in the narratives of Woojin and Hyon-Woo, migration can be central to the creation of an explorative space of emerging adulthood that temporarily suspends or permanently rejects the normative transition-to-adulthood life-scripts of the Asian family. Yet, in the case of David and Carolyn, mobility can also inhibit and constrain desires for transition to adulthood in terms of delaying career transitions and having children.

Such navigations of becoming adult are, of course, shaped by the global time-regime outlined in Chapter 1, within which desequentialization of the life-course and increased social and economic insecurity are, particularly for the middle classes, continually producing more options alongside less certainty and more risk. For youth studies scholar Carmen Leccardi (2012), the complexities of transition to adulthood for 21st-century youth are inherently tied to the global socio-temporal transformations that I characterize as 'hegemonic flexibility'. Leccardi (2012) sees the twin forces of social acceleration and the 'crisis of the future' (a sense of uncontrollable risks and corresponding great uncertainties) as leading to a contemporary form of time that 'seems to erase not only temporal continuity but also the notion of the life-plan as developed in the modern era' (226), thus radically changing the transition to adulthood for today's youth. Not only has the transition to adulthood become extended, it has also become more fragmented and less institutionally supported, leaving young people to '"navigate by sight" rather than following pre-established routes' (229), and producing biographical patterns that are 'increasingly distant from linear life trajectories' (230). Leccardi (2012) also reminds us, however, that despite diversification and less cogency across 21st-century biographies, temporal norms remain powerful in regulating their construction.

In the migration literature, ideas such as transition to adulthood or emergent adulthood and their intersections with migration experiences are seldom made explicit. This is despite the fact that transient forms of transnational mobility (from the European 'grand tours' of the 17th and 18th centuries to the 'gap years' of the contemporary context) have for a long time been a part of cultural imaginaries of becoming adult for young people in the West. The transnational mobilities of middling Western young people have frequently been framed around these notions of cultural experience, self-actualization and self-development, as a period of freedom and experimentation before settling down into adult careers, marriages and families (Robertson et al, 2018a; Tsai and Collins, 2017). Literature on the circulation of middle-class migrants from Asia to the West, however, seldom foregrounds the experiences of young people nor considers the significance of transition to adulthood to these mobilities. This reflects the more general trend towards 'adultism' in migration studies (White et al, 2011). The literature on educational mobilities is one exception here. In these studies, young people, as students, play a key role in leading family mobility strategies for capital accumulation and class reproduction (Waters, 2006, 2015), or seek out an instrumental form of cosmopolitan identity in order to further global careers (Matthews and Sidhu, 2005). An emerging literature has also begun to highlight the intertwined motivations of Asian youth in undertaking transnational sojourns. Working holiday makers from Taiwan, Japan and Korea see global experiences simultaneously as forms of leisure and self-development, opportunities to postpone transitions into employment, and strategic opportunities to enhance employability and English language skills for their futures (Tsai and Collins, 2017; Kawashima, 2010; Kato, 2013; Yoon, 2014a, b). And as Lan (2019) significantly highlights in her discussion of Chinese *youxue* (travel and study) mobilities, from the late 2000s, the 'experimental and experiential' dimensions of overseas experiences have become significant to a new generation of youth, further destabilizing the assumption of the earlier literature that East Asian young people are primarily motivated to 'become mobile' by instrumental concerns. Yet, for the contemporary generation from Asia, as described at the beginning of this chapter, transnational mobility is increasingly about dealing with rising economic and social uncertainty, as well as about personal growth or social mobility (Lan, 2011; Collins, 2014; Marcu, 2012; Yoon, 2014a, b).

The experiences of Hyon-Woo and Woojin reflect such decidedly uneven and often contradictory experiences of middling mobility that occur within a global context of temporal fragmentation and temporal uncertainty. This has been demonstrated in other empirical contexts, particularly in Europe. Marcu (2017: 7), writing of young Eastern European migrants in Spain who circulate throughout the year across Europe in fragmented and temporally contingent patterns of study and work, notes that her interlocutors 'live somewhere in between precarity and flexibility'. The openness of EU mobility politics combined with the post-recession uncertainty of the region create this temporal ambiguity at the micro-scale of young people's decisions about work, study and location at different times of the year. Scott's (2006) work on British skilled migrants in Paris similarly describes a generation who have come of age in an economy where the 'logic of flexibility' (1122) is hegemonic. In contrast to the older 'colonial' generation of expatriate Britons in Paris, the young set of professional or 'lifestyle' expatriates that Scott (2006) studies 'appear to have more accepting attitudes towards career-path change and future mobility' (1122), and see moving internationally in one's twenties and thirties as a normalized stage 'in an increasingly fragmented career life path' (1114). Mar (2005) presents one of the few Australian studies that engages critically with ideas of the middle as a contradictory space of aspiration and fragmentation. In his analysis of the lives of skilled migrants from Hong Kong, he positions middling migrants 'as the most anxious of subjects'. Mar (2005) locates this anxiety in the uncertainties of the social mobility–transnational mobility nexus, as his interlocutors remain 'insecurely poised between demands of material necessity and aspirations for upward social movement' (367).

We see in these existing studies different glimpses of what a chronomobilities approach can draw more cohesively together in exploring the ambiguities, contradictions and tensions of mobile lives 'in the middle': how the biographical temporal scale of the life-stage intersects with broader economic conditions of insecurity; how aspirations for social mobility are increasingly tied to uncertainty of outcomes; and how, in terms of lived experience, hegemonic flexibility can, for a mobile middle, engender divergent experiences of opportunity and escape as well as anxiety and precarity. Two forces converge on the current generation of young and middling migrants: the globalization of both economic and social insecurity and the globalization of cultural imaginaries of the individualized life project. The middling mobiles from Asia whose lives I explore in this book thus negotiate their mobility within this convergence across a number of tensions. These include most significantly, tensions between normative and linear life scripts that still hold significant cultural weight in home families and communities and more individualized and flexibilized senses of the 'modern' biography; and tensions between cultures of mobility that correlate transnational mobility with upward social mobility and cultures of mobility that correlate transnational mobility with alternative pathways. As Marcu (2017: 2) notes, it is important to 'analyse how transnational youth mobility can be understood as a means of managing precarity and uncertainty'. But it is equally important, I argue, to simultaneously understand how transnational mobility can manifest through a desire *for* temporal uncertainty – for the opportunity to deviate from normative and linear life-scripts, and as, Hyon-Woo and Woojin experienced, to 'go far away' and 'see what will happen'.

Conclusion

The migrants' whose lives I explore in this book are multiply situated in between: in between social locations; in between conventional categories of migrant type; in between youth and adulthood; and in between transforming cultural and social understandings of transnational mobility for the young and middle-class. Their lives both reflect and challenge established understandings of middling migration as an identity and a practice. In this book, I use the concept of middling mobility to describe the lived experiences of my migrant interlocutors within this context. I understand the middle as multiply constructed, not just as a signifier of socioeconomic status or class positioning. Rather, I argue that the experiences of my migrant participants occupy multiple and intersecting spaces of the in-between. They move between different social and economic locations across a spectrum that sits in between the elite and the disenfranchised. They also often fall between or move across conventional understandings of mobility 'type', crossing between skilled and unskilled work, economic desires and lifestyle desires, sojourn and settlement. Furthermore, they exist in the middle space of the life-course, experiencing the transitions from youth to adulthood while on the move. I have argued, therefore, in this chapter for conceptualizing the middle space of migrant mobility beyond the socioeconomic, as a way to understand the spatio-temporal complexity that shapes the lives of young migrants from Asia who occupy a dynamic middle space in terms of their socioeconomic locations in different places; their life-stage; and the complex nexus between social mobility and spatial mobility in a global era in which hegemonic flexibility is fundamentally reshaping career, migration and life trajectories.

Thus, although the middle remains important in my analysis as a relational socioeconomic positioning, this positionality is neither fixed nor homogeneous, but rather mobile, contingent and differentiated. There is a complex and not always linearly correlative relationship between social mobility and spatial mobility within the broad socioeconomic spectrum of the middle. Further, the middle, as a socioeconomic stratum, needs to be understood not just in terms of the material resources and constraints of migrants, but also in terms of the evolving cultures of mobility that go hand in hand with middle-class identities globally, and particularly in Asia.

This approach allows more nuanced attention to the potential unevenness of middling experiences, and the fact that the middle can be a spatio-temporal, as well as a socioeconomic, zone of mobility. Young Asian migrants' transnational mobilities under regimes of transification and hegemonic flexibility are marked by ambiguity, in-betweenness and transition. These transnationally mobile subjects are middling in terms of their material resources and social locations in between places and within transnational fields. Yet, they are also often middling in terms of the intentions and desires around their mobility, which, as we have seen in the cases of Woojin and Hyon-Woo, encompass entanglements of leisure, labour and tourism within migration projects that have indeterminate outcomes. I also seek to capture in my analysis the fact that it is not just the mobility of these migrants across national borders that matters, but also their upward and downward social mobility, their mobility across visa statuses, their labour market mobility, and their mobility within nation states.

Through the concept of middling mobility, I further locate the everyday experiences of my research participants as embedded within specific time-regimes that crucially inflect middle-class experiences globally in the current iteration of globalized modernity – what I refer to and unpack in Chapter 1 as the hegemonic flexibility of economic and social life and the transification of migration paradigms in a formerly 'settler' context. The middle can thus encompass a 'complex and messy middle-ground' (Scott, 2006: 1107) where 'citizenship vulnerabilities and class fluidities' (Ho and Ley, 2014: 38) structured through migration governance rub up against migrants' own desires to use mobility strategically to create new pathways and identities. The middle is an in-between space, but it is also a space of transition or becoming. It can signify constraints (being 'stuck' in between) or progression, renewal and acceleration. Middling mobility is a set of processes of moving through life and through migration that exists beyond the straightforward accumulation of capital and thus beyond linear senses of upward social mobility and transitions to a fixed adulthood.

This new approach to middling mobility and my particular attention to the multiple scales and logics of its temporalities matters to the sociology of contemporary migration beyond my specific empirical case of young Asian migrants in Australia. The ambiguities and nuances of the temporal condition of hegemonic flexibility, as described in Chapter 1, and its varied impacts on the migration experience, can perhaps best be seen through the lived experiences of middling migrants. For these migrants, hegemonic flexibility and the transification of migration can simultaneously and paradoxically become embodied experiences of freedom and constraint, closure and openness, anxiety and opportunity. The literature that has focused on the temporal governance of the displaced, undocumented and disenfranchised, in contrast, can limit temporal analysis of migration. As Brun (2015) argues, representations of such migrants as 'living in limbo' position them as passive in their longing for the past and consequently devoid of agency, or, they are represented as 'dead men walking' (Ahmad, 2008) – interstitial and instantaneously deportable subjects. As privileged but non-elite, however, experiences of middling migrants' mobilities can unveil uneven and divergent outcomes of mobility in a context of hegemonic flexibility, and this has broad implications for understanding migration's consequences in an increasingly complex and differentiated global environment.

Throughout this book, I tease out how the structural import of conditions like hegemonic flexibility and the transification of migration, as well as the cultural expectations around the promise of mobility, affect the everyday mobility decisions and experiences of young people as they move across geographic and cultural boundaries. I do so by considering middling mobility in relation to life-stage as well as in relation to economic resources, migration categories and social locations. The following chapters move through three of the most significant aspects of my interlocutors' lives – the work migrants did, the places they lived, and the relationships they formed along the way. These themes structure the book primarily because they were what stood out, again and again, in the stories young migrants told about their lives as well as in the images and documents they shared with me. The times that mattered, the memories they highlighted, the aspirations that shaped their anxieties and dreams for the future all circulated around work (what they did, and what they wanted to do), place (where they were and where they wanted to be) and love (who they were with and who they wanted to be with). But these chapters also remind us about some significant constitutive elements of temporality in everyday life – experiences of time are very much produced through engagements with capitalism, through embeddings and disembeddings in place, and relationally through intimate and emotional attachments. I begin, in the next chapter, with work and careers, as it is career ambitions that drive many normative understandings of why middle-class young people (and particularly young people moving from Asia to the West) move across borders. However, the detailed picture in Chapter 3 of the complex relationships between the 'times of work' and transnational mobility's affordances and limitations, presaged somewhat in Hyon-Woo and Woojin's stories, challenges these ideas of linear relationships between geographic mobility and career mobility.

3

Times of Work: Transified Workers and Contingent Careers

I met Percy, from Shandong province in China, at a café outside his local public library in Perth, Western Australia's capital. Impeccably dressed in business-casual attire, 25-year-old Percy was initially courteously formal, as if he were attending a job interview. But he soon relaxed as we chatted about life in Perth, which happens to be my own hometown. Percy arrived in Perth to study gas engineering when he was 19. Western Australia appealed to Percy because the state's north was in the middle of an extraction boom, including in natural gas, so there would, he thought, be good job opportunities with multinational firms. He arrived with the "rough idea" that after graduation he would work in Australia in gas engineering "for a couple of years, if I still like it", before deciding whether or not he wanted to return to China. As an only child, Percy told me that maintaining close contact with his parents was a top priority. Perth was also appealing, he said, because unlike the more populous east coast Australian cities it is on the same time zone as his hometown, "so it would be much easier to communicate with my family. There's no time difference."

Percy supported himself by working as a waiter and a kitchenhand during his study, as well as volunteering with mentoring programmes and other student activities at his university. He was unsuccessful, however, in his applications for summer vacation internships with mining firms, a crucial first step in becoming competitive for graduate positions in the industry. By the time he graduated, the extraction boom was also winding down, and a job did not materialize. Percy saw the combination of his market disadvantage as a migrant and the unfortunate economic timing as the key contributions to his lack of transition to work in his field:

'I didn't have my permanent residency back to the time I applied for my vacation work so regretfully without the real industry vacation work experience it would be very difficult to go to the industry directly. ... We compete with local students, so they grew up here, they know everything here so they have the advantages to compete with us. ... Always I ask myself, what if it was 2010 or 2011 when I looked for the vacation work? Things could be totally different because I have several seniors in mining engineering, they [are] all native Chinese person from China, they just came here a couple of years earlier than me to study engineering disciplines and even before their graduations they have secured their graduate positions with the giant companies within the industry. So, well, definitely it's a factor that the industry has been down. So the prosperity has been at least halved. So opportunities has been reduced.'

Like Hyon-Woo, as described in the previous chapter, Percy was able to procure an 18-month temporary graduate work visa after he finished university. During this transition period post-graduation, Percy was focused on making sure he could meet immigration requirements and, in his words, 'accelerate' his PR application. At this stage, he saw PR not necessarily as a path to permanent settlement, but rather as an important gateway to being able to obtain professional work in his field. Percy described to me how, although he met most of the criteria for PR, he was at the time under 25 so would not receive additional points for his age in the points-based assessment. To make up for this gap in points, Percy took a test to become an accredited Mandarin–English translator – the National Accreditation Authority for Translators and Interpreters (NAATI) accreditation. He was able to successfully apply for residency based on this qualification, as translators and interpreters in certain community languages are in-demand occupations that garner additional migration points. NAATI accreditation was, in fact, a common fall-back plan for many bilingual migrants I met whose professional skills and other criteria were not quite enough to gain sufficient points for residency. As he prepared for his PR application, Percy found work as a service attendant at a hospital through a university friend. Despite its distance, both geographically and professionally, from the gas rigs, Percy spoke positively about working in the hospital as a potential transition point between his restaurant work and more professional roles, and as a chance to meet new people and learn new things:

> 'I tried to get myself still in the workplace and refresh my mind. And then probably when the right time comes I could still jump into the boat [for engineering]. So I just had to be optimistic and keep myself occupied. ... It was a big team and all the colleagues come from different culture and social backgrounds. So they were pretty nice. And I did learn a lot from most of the colleagues I work with.'

Despite not having full-time work, Percy described an intense schedule of balancing IELTS study, NAATI training, shifts at the hospital and professional networking with an active social life, as he was keen to maintain connections with his "Aussie" friends from university and perhaps meet a girlfriend. Percy saw great value at this stage of his life in 'investing time' into activities that would enable him to progress to the professional future he envisioned:

> 'After my graduation, I participated into some like the professional networking events either in terms of my major, like relevant to engineering, chemical engineering and petroleum industry, or in terms of the Australia–China relationship. Because I could meet some like-minded young alliances and hear from their professional perspectives and to motivate me to grow to a higher level. And also learn how to behave professionally. So definitely I believe I will be the beneficiary for that. So it's worth to invest more time interacting with those professionals.'

Percy received his PR in 2015, less than 18 months after his graduation. It was only a few months after this milestone that we first met in Perth. In this interview, Percy was optimistic now that he had PR that his career would soon take off. But he was also open to imagining alternatives to engineering as he continued to work at the hospital and undertake freelance translation work. With the milestone of PR achieved, he had realized he was only now at the 'real' beginning of his professional life in Australia:

> 'I've spent five years to pursue for a degree in engineering. And ... I also have a passion for engineering and to be

a professional engineer. ... I think I have done some achievement in terms of personal development like communication skills, interpersonal skills, teamwork after so much experience in the working, study and the extracurricular activities. ... I still haven't got a job relevant to my major, but by now I understand actually even [if] eventually I couldn't come back to the engineering profession it will still be alright as long as I discover my passion, my interest and even though in other area, sectors I will still go for it because there is more to it actually. ... Be stubborn to your goals but flexible about the methodologies. So my goal would be to live my life and to do something I'm passionate about and to fulfil my values. ... That would mean the degree will be one thing, but it's not everything. I could always try to diversify my portfolios through different professional jobs, activities and events. ... At least [now] I'm a permanent resident ... so you don't need to worry about like one day I might go back to China or just leave without saying anything. ... I realized that the real journey, the real tough journey was just to start it, which is the job seeking and there is the real life. PR is not the end it's just the beginning for a new stage.'

In a second interview a year later, Percy was happy to have progressed to an office job, as a consultant at an education and migration agency. Owned and staffed by Chinese migrants, the small business facilitated and offered advice on visas and educational options for Chinese international students. Many of Percy's clients were in situations that reflected his own life-path. Finding this job had been a relief for Percy. His patched together working weeks of shift work at the hospital and long hours alone in his room working on translation projects had begun to feel "so boring". His new schedule was also a busy one, however. He was putting in extra hours to learn the ropes in a new industry, and felt he had to be "always on" for clients. And he continued to balance work with his ongoing volunteer commitments in the Chinese-Australian community:

'I think at this stage I have to catch up with everything as fast as possible, because I'm still in the like learning process, and as you know, like the tertiary education system or the secondary education system in Australia actually are quite complicated. ... I think it's the nature of the job I'm doing right now, because as agents definitely we had to provide the premium service to make sure every single client will be satisfied with our service. ... So, I check my mobile you know always open, turned on, and also as you know, those extracurricular activities do occupy some of my spare time. Plus, I also have some other activities I would like to do, catch up with friends, blah-blah-blah, so sometimes ... I'm pretty busy. ... I still devoted myself into several organizations, like I have been a translations officer for an organization called Australia–China Youth Association.'

In this second interview, Percy said he was no longer holding on to the aspiration to one day have a career in engineering. In that sense, he felt he was starting again in the education field. But he did not see this necessarily as a long-term career, but rather, a foot in the door to professional employment that he had positive hopes could lead to something else further down the track. Percy's optimism had perhaps dimmed a little by the second interview. He noted that it was "very hard" to find another professional direction after dedicating so much time to engineering. But he remained positive that this new role would allow him to "go somewhere", even if he was no longer certain where this might be:

'I must grab this opportunity, otherwise it's very hard for me to do something else, because my background is in engineering, and I really don't have other like professional professions or some other specialities in other areas. So, probably education is like a stepping stone for me, go into the sector first and then from here as a platform I could go somewhere else, but without this starting point it's rather hard for me to start something officially professionally.'

As Percy's story attests, work is a highly significant part of middling migrants' experiences in Australia. Coming to Australia is almost always motivated, at least in part, by career-related goals, as professional experience is deeply embedded into the aspirational narratives of transnational mobility for the Asian middle class (Doherty and Singh, 2005). Work is also intrinsically tied to migration goals and outcomes due to the focus in the Australian migration regime on formal qualifications and specific work experience as criteria for many visas. Work means multiple things to migrants in the middle – it is income generation for basic needs, it is both a reason to move and a

Figure 3.1: Percy

A decorative Christmas display on the hospital ward where Percy worked, featuring effigies of Princes Harry and William. Many of the medical staff at the hospital were British migrants.

Figure 3.2: Percy

The kitchen of the Italian restaurant where Percy worked as a kitchen hand while he was at university. Percy valued his diverse work experiences as opportunities to learn about 'Aussie' culture and to make friends from around the world.

gateway to stay, and it is part of the meaning making that surrounds their transition to adulthood. However, as Percy's experiences show, the temporalities of working lives for young and middling migrants are shaped in complex ways by their mobilities, whether in terms of how the rhythms of working days and weeks become structured, or in terms of how migrants understand the development of their careers and professional lives across their pasts, presents and imagined futures.

In this chapter, I seek to understand experiences of work and career for migrants like Percy in terms of their chronomobilities – the temporalities that simultaneously emerge from and structure mobile lives. The migrant narratives outlined in the previous three chapters have already revealed something about the complex temporalities inherent in the working lives of middling migrants under time-regimes of hegemonic flexibility and transification. The experiences of David, Carolyn, Hyon-Woo and Woojin, described in the Introduction and in Chapters 1 and 2, hint at how the transient, transitory and transitionary nature of migration journeys affect transition into the labour market, transitions in and out of skilled and unskilled work, and the suspension, disruption and rerouting of career paths. It is apparent from these stories that there are complex relationships between the 'times of work' and transnational mobility's affordances and limitations. This chapter therefore seeks to show in more detail how hegemonic flexibility and the transification of migration create new forms of mobile labour and new career pathways, transform lived experiences of work time, and shape understandings of the self in relation to time and work. The experiences of work and career that I engage with throughout this chapter sit within the middle space outlined in Chapter 2. Working lives and career aspirations for the middling migrants I spoke with often come to float, as they did for Percy, in between the precarities and risks and the flexibilities and possibilities of mobility.

As noted in Chapter 2, the majority of the young Asian migrants I met in the course of my research for this book had similar middle-class and university educated backgrounds, with a few exceptions, such as Woojin, who were skilled trade workers. They generally assumed that they would find themselves in professional or skilled careers in Australia, an assumption that was buoyed by consistent messaging from migration agents and the Australian government that Australia suffers from a skills shortage. Yet, after arrival, most engaged in a wide variety of different types of work, skilled and unskilled, paid and unpaid. Across the interviews, I heard about migrants' experiences as gardeners, factory managers, manicurists, babysitters, fruit pickers, baristas, pizza delivery drivers and sushi chefs, as well as office administrators, events coordinators, software engineers, nurses, teachers, consultants and accountants. Some individual migrants had experienced an almost dizzying diversity of jobs over time. Saji was a trained pilot and had a bachelor's degree in commerce. He had, over a period of less than two years, worked in a fish and chip shop and in a Chinese restaurant, was as an art gallery attendant, a volunteer at a school with underprivileged children, and drove trucks for a grocery chain, before finding an administration job with a large security company that led to a junior business development role. Jody, from Malaysia, had a bachelor's degree in architecture and a graduate degree in communications. Over the course of several years, she had acted in independent films, sold vegetables at a market stall, coordinated community events and edited a community magazine, worked in community outreach in local government and managed a wedding venue. Other migrants experienced more consistency with the roles they worked in, but physically moved multiple times to access work and migration opportunities. Jacob, for example, a software engineer from India, had planned to settle in Melbourne, but when his visa became stuck in indefinite processing he found work in New Zealand for a period and later relocated to Perth for another job. Anastasia, a naturopath from Taiwan, left a settled life in Brisbane for a regionally sponsored visa in a town 600 kilometres north of the city. She moved back to Brisbane and a less secure job when her boyfriend was unhappy with small-town life. Despite the wide range of occupations and workplaces that my interlocutors moved through, what their working lives had in common were their experiences of time-in-mobility in relation to work and career. I explore these chronomobilities in the following sections of this chapter.

I first outline some of the relevant current thinking on the interrelationships between migration, work and time. This brief discussion establishes the importance of middling mobilities to more nuanced understandings of these interrelationships. I then outline how hegemonic flexibility and the transification of migration work in concert to structure middling migrants' chronomobilities around work and career in particular ways. I argue first that hegemonic flexibility and the transification of migration construct young and middling migrants as transified workers and shape their careers as contingent rather than teleological processes. I show how middling migrants in this context must reconfigure the self in relation to work and in broader chronologic relation to their pasts and futures. I then describe the specific impacts of the overlapping logics of sequence, synchronicity and tempo that shape time at work, namely, what I refer to as 'the indenture of the present' and 'the intensities of the everyday'. My overall argument in this chapter is that hegemonic flexibility and the transification of migration produce particular kinds of worker subjectivities and career trajectories that lead to specific lived experiences of tempo, synchronicity and sequence in migrants' working lives.

Migration, work and the temporal

The specific temporal experiences of my interlocutors as workers must be read within a broader global context of the changing nature of employment in Western societies under the conditions of contemporary capitalism. As noted in Chapter 1, globalized modernity's orientation towards hegemonic flexibility has transformed traditional and teleological understandings of labour and of career structures for many workers globally, migrant and non-migrant alike. The compression of space-time (Giddens, 1991; Harvey, 1990) through technology has disembedded labour from specific sites and hours of work; short-termism has increasingly casualized and contractualized labour (Sennett, 2006); and the economic risk of uncertain futures is increasingly borne by the livelihoods and bodies of individual workers (Beck, 2009). Demands for flexible labour make modes of employment increasingly temporally marked by insecurity and uncertainty (see, for example, Amin, 1994; Sassen, 1999). Non-permanent and part-time work is a significant part of these temporal transformations in working lives, with young people and migrants often disproportionately represented in these types of work in Western labour markets[1] (Winson and Leach, 2002; Peck and Theodore, 2010). Furthermore, careers are increasingly marked by a sense of 'turbulent unpredictability' in which 'labor force participants must take it upon themselves to learn how opportunity structures operate, strategise how to access them, and invest time, psychic energy, and financial resources to take advantage of them' (Smith, 2010: 279–80).

While these conditions affect many workers, both mobile and immobile, for migrant subjects, transnational mobility adds layers of complexity to the temporal restructuring of work. As discussed in Chapter 1, studies of time, work and migrant precarity tend to focus on time as a form of discipline and on its material and affective impacts on temporary and undocumented migrant workers, often showing how insecure migration produces insecure working conditions and limited work opportunities (see, for example, Anderson, 2007; Ahmad, 2008; Batnitzky et al, 2012; Villegas, 2014). Despite their more privileged status, middling migrants may often experience an interlinking of insecurity of work and insecurity of migration status, and security of presence can become dependent on work, due to, as is the case for many migrants in Australia, the linking of employment contracts or work experience to visas. Particular temporal work practices can also create illegality and deportability for middling migrants – such as working beyond the hours allowed on a visa or overstaying visas in order to work.

However, there has been little focus in the literature on migration, work and time on the experiences of middling or skilled workers, who are often seen as privileged via fast processing and accelerated pathways to future residency (Yeoh and Lin, 2013). There are a few notable recent exceptions, however, as migration scholars begin to grapple with the complex aspirations and mobilities of educated but not necessarily elite migrants. Emergent work on middling migrant workers and time provides a significant backdrop for the discussions in this chapter, because it suggests that analysis of migrant temporality beyond the wholly liminal times of the marginalized can reveal nuances that destabilize established analytic binaries and temporal frames. Axelsson (2017), for example, highlights how desirable skills do not necessarily dissolve the temporal 'thickness' of borders to allow frictionless entries and transitions. Rather, the IT professionals entering Sweden in her study experience 'limbo' time – waiting and delays to admission, labour market access and ongoing settlement. Rather than providing a space of privilege, these temporal experiences create an 'in-between space' that 'has spatial and temporal consequences in terms of temporary losses of mobility rights, elongated pathways to permanent status, insecurity of presence and lives placed on hold' (Axelsson, 2017: 987).

Collins and Shubin's (2015) study of Western English teachers in South Korea also challenges some conventional assumptions around migration, the life-course and temporality. Notably, Collins and Shubin (2015) refuse static and linear notions of time, instead revealing complex directionalities and temporal 'openness'. This sits in contestation to positionings of migration as 'planful' and life-course approaches that privilege chronological sequencing. Collins and Shubin (2015) also crucially challenge the assumption that transnational mobility for Western youth is tied to lifestyle and self-development narratives. Rather, in their study, young Westerners in Seoul – although middle-class and tertiary-educated – are often seeking escape from the inertia of underemployment and debt at home. In the context of the EU economic crisis, Marcu's (2017: 7) study of young Eastern Europeans who live in a state of 'permanent temporariness' in Spain importantly highlights how it is possible for mobile lives to be lived 'polyrhythmically' – that is, 'somewhere between precarity and flexibility'. Marcu (2017) also notes the crucially 'mooring' effects of stable professional work for the young and mobile, even as people continue to physically move.

I follow these recent interpretations of middling migration, work and time in several ways. First, I understand the work experiences of middling Asian migrants as occupying a spatio-temporal in-between in which precarity and flexibility can exist alongside each other or transform into each other over time. I see the course of the career as entangled with the temporalities of the border and the affordances and limitations of mobility, and also see career trajectories and work experiences as intimately interlinked with other life transitions. My chronomobilities approach, however, seeks to go further in understanding how specific features of migrant temporal experience are constructed. My focus on logics of synchronicity, tempo and sequence in migrant experience brings together and interweaves perspectives on time and work that have hitherto remained somewhat discrete, that is: understandings of trajectories through time; forms of rhythm and pace in relation to work and mobility; and relational or synchronic understandings of time. A central premise of this chapter is that work and migration pathways are inextricably intertwined. Conditions of mobility shape work experiences, and work experiences shape the possibilities of ongoing mobility. The central question for this chapter thus concerns how hegemonic flexibility and the transification of migration shape the temporal experience of work and career for middling migrants across diverse employment circumstances.

Transified workers

This section focuses on how transification positions middling migrants in the labour market, and how this affects their employment prospects and experiences. My central argument here is that transification creates barriers to entering professional employment, and that these barriers lead to migrants' initial engagements with the labour market comprising semi-compliant and deskilled work, often casual and low-wage and sometimes informal. Further, I argue that perceptions about migrants' temporalities and mobilities, specifically their positioning as transient and as hypermobile, stigmatize them as 'undesirable' workers in spite of their skills and qualifications, and also in spite of the fact that many reside in Australia for the long term.

For example, Percy's status as an international student was a barrier to vacation internships, which (alongside an economic downturn in the mining industry) subsequently hampered his graduate transitions when he obtained a work visa. For Percy, his positioning as undesirable for vacation work was not necessarily bound up with his impermanence as a student-migrant – as vacation work by its very nature involves an employment arrangement of very limited duration. Rather, from Percy's perspective, the problem stemmed from his lack of a locally located past, in comparison to local students who "grew up here" and "know everything here".

Alice, similarly, had an established corporate IT career in Taiwan, but after arriving in Australia had worked across various, far more junior roles in administration and marketing for small businesses. She believed her difficulties in job hunting in Australia hinged crucially on her transient visa status, which limited her options even after she had been living in Australia for several years and had accumulated local work experience. Alice explains: "Your visa is not permanent, so most of the people will never hire you. When they call you, they hear, oh you don't have a permanent resident, then they hang up on you straightaway." Alice's experiences looking for work echoed across most of the interviews – online applications often included the question 'Are you a permanent resident or citizen?' and migrants looking for professional roles felt strongly that answering 'No' to this question meant they would be instantly "screened out".[2]

Sometimes migrants are evasive about their visa status on applications until they secure a job offer, but most end up, at least temporarily, in deskilled, casual and informal employment. Initial conditions at work in Australia for my interlocutors were thus often, if not outright exploitative, mired in the bargain of 'semi-compliance' (Ruhs and Anderson, 2010). Ruhs and Anderson (2010: 195) define semi-compliance as 'the employment of migrants who are legally resident but working in violation of the employment restrictions attached to their immigration status'. In the case of my interlocutors, I include under the umbrella of semi-compliance violations of general employment law as well as breaches of immigration conditions. For middling migrants, the most common regulatory breaches in their employment arrangements are underpayment, cash-in-hand informal payment, unpaid hours (of overtime or for 'training') and working different hours or roles than permitted by visa conditions. Both Alice and Percy, for example, found themselves in deskilled or semi-compliant working arrangements at different times. Alice worked in office roles well below her skill level and was illegally underpaid by one of her employers. As a qualified engineer, Percy experienced deskilled shift work at the hospital, and insecure freelance translation work.

Working 'at the edges' of legality, can, however, as Ruhs and Anderson (2010) note, serve the strategic interests of migrants. Non-compliant employers may be more inclined to bypass or inveigle immigration requirements to the benefit of the worker (Robertson, 2015a). Small employers, who manage contracts and human resourcing informally, also have greater capacity for such 'flexibility'. Accepting low-status positions and even exploitative conditions in small businesses can thus, for middling migrants, be in part a strategy to move forward and achieve migration security. This was the case for Alice, who accepted a job at what she described as a "dodgy" education company. Her boss was willing to be flexible with her position description on paper to meet immigration criteria, but only if Alice accepted an illegally low wage.

When talking about the challenges of finding work, migrants were highly conscious of how intangible perceptions of their transience and their mobility worked in concert with explicit visa limitations to construct their labour market disadvantage as transified workers. Vera, for example, from China, had been in Australia for five years on a series of student visas. She described how both the tangible (students can only legally work 40 hours per fortnight when semester is in session, for example) as well as the intangible temporalities attached to her visa status affected her employment opportunities:

> 'By law we are allowed to work 40 hours fortnightly. During the holidays, we can only work intermittently. But because of the restrictions, if they hire us, for example [major department store] David Jones, they have to think how will I be able to make the shift for her to fit in the 40 hours requirement? Which is a pain in the arse. ... So we have to worry about shifts and all that extra trouble. That's how I understand it. And also, I think because of our side, sometimes I could stay in Australia for two years, three years in a row, but most of my friends fly back to China during Christmas, stay in China for four months or two months. Then come back and quit their job and find another one. So the bad reputation. They always think of us as come and go, not trustworthy.'

Vera's experiences highlight how forms of temporal governance that restrict the hours student visa holders can legally work construct them as transified workers who are "extra trouble" when it comes to the scheduling of work shifts. Vera experienced the logics of asynchronicity created by transification, in that the temporal conditions of her visa 'mismatched' with the normal scheduling processes of employers. Vera also, however, noted how the rhythmic mobilities of transnational student-migrants – who often return 'home' to spend the long semester break over the Australian summer with their families – construct a further stigma around their reliability as workers who "come and go" and are therefore untrustworthy. The annual tempos of mobile student-migrants' lives, which seek out synchronicity with educational institutions' schedules, visa restrictions and transnational familial obligations, construct transified workers as not only insecure, but also, crucially, 'suspect'. The department store retail work Vera uses as an example here is casual and often seasonal. Employers offer no ongoing commitment to employees beyond the next shift. Yet, long-term, uninterrupted emplacement and availability is still considered part of the 'desirable' criteria for workers for these roles.

Such perceptions around middling migrants' patterns of mobility as inherently asynchronous with employers' expectations can affect their chances of retaining as well as finding work. This may even be the case for migrants who, unlike Vera, have no explicit temporal restrictions on their work rights. Saji, for example, told me about the job he briefly held as a delivery truck driver for a supermarket chain. Saji had been pleased to find this job, despite it being a casual, shift-based role. He had spent several months in low-paid restaurant work while he waited on a bridging visa for a permanent partner visa to be processed. The truck driving was a step up for Saji in terms of both hours and pay, although he ultimately hoped to find a professional business role. Saji informed his boss several weeks in advance of a trip he had planned with his girlfriend to visit his sister, who was living in the US. Saji's boss responded angrily and stopped granting him shifts in the weeks leading up to his trip:

> 'I had actually booked the trip in August or September-ish and my trip was actually due in, we were leaving here, departing here on the 6 December. So when I went to work, I thought I would give them a month's notice, or a month-and-a-half notice to Coles [supermarket chain] saying that I would be actually away during their peak time which is at Christmas time. It was about a six-week trip it was, so obviously as you can imagine, it didn't go well, in fact, well at all with my boss at that time, and she pretty much stopped giving me shifts for the last four weeks basically. But I was there and available to work 24/7 so I could save more money. But because she knew that

I actually sort of cheated on her, that I would actually be leaving her for the Christmas time, to punish me in return, I think it was like, we're not giving you any hours at all. … We went for the trip so knowing that I wouldn't have any job to come back to.'

Middling migrants like Saji and Vera have the resources (often in the form of savings, access to credit or family support) to travel relatively frequently to maintain transnational connections with family. Transnational obligations, however, affect their desirability and subsequently their treatment as workers. Their mobilities are asynchronous with employers' expectations that workers will be continually available, even in relation to work that is itself casual and short-term.

In this section, I have argued that multiple perceptions circulate around transified workers and limit their access to the labour market. Temporally and spatially, they are constructed as 'deficit' workers because they purportedly lack both locally emplaced past experience and future stability. They have temporal restrictions on their work rights that are perceived as difficult to synchronize with the regular scheduling of labour, and their regular and irregular transnational circulations further their stigmatization as unreliable workers, prone to be periodically unavailable to work. Workers who migrate under regimes of transification are thus constructed as transified workers in the sense that they are considered neither 'completely' temporary nor 'really' permanent. They may come and go according to visa constraints or their own preferences for mobile lives and livelihoods. The migrant worker who is both transified and middling holds an often ambiguous position in the labour market – skilled yet underemployed, fluid yet constrained, exploitable yet strategic.

The impacts of transification on workers in Australia that I have described here reflect earlier work on middling migrants in other contexts, which notes that they are often willing to undertake work below their skill level in anticipation of future opportunities (Conradson and Latham, 2005b; Parutis, 2011). It also shows that, in practice, earlier deskilling and subsequent 'resume gaps' may continue to influence career and migration trajectories in the long term (Ho and Ley, 2014). A specific logic of sequence is at play here. Initially, the present is sacrificed for the future, but later, this very sacrifice of time can limit the actualization of desired futures. Even after legal statuses shift to permanence, opportunities might be already lost and careers difficult to rebuild, as migrants must 'start again'. Transification thus not only creates insecure work in the present, but contributes to what I discuss in detail in the following section – contingent careers over the long term.

Contingent careers

As educated and mostly middle-class subjects, middling migrants tend to see their engagements with the labour market as more than 'jobs', that is, more than simply economic activity that generates income. Rather, these migrants imagine work via linear logics of sequence, that is, as an 'orderly ordering' of formal training and professional roles over time that build a unified professional trajectory and professional identity – in other words, a career. The concept of a career as the normative outcome of engagements with the labour market is, of course, closely tied to middle-class identities and particularly to transitions to middle-class adulthood (Arnett, 2001; Valentine, 2003). In this section, I use the idea of contingent careers to describe how the careers of middling migrants unfold over time, and to describe the daily experience of work and time that such unfoldings engender.

Increases in 'contingent work' – that is workers on short-term and insecure contracts – are a key feature of global fragmentation and labour flexibilization in modernity (Wallace and Brady, 2001). Contingent roles are not considered to be part of a career, but as 'McJobs', or low-paid positions without future prospects. Here, however, I use the metaphor of contingency somewhat differently in my conceptualization of contingent careers. I use the idea of contingency as a chronomobile metaphor that brings together a number of temporal characteristics of middling migrants' working lives under time-regimes of transification and global hegemonic flexibility. In the analysis that follows, describing the careers of middling migrants as contingent encompasses dual meanings. I suggest first, that careers involve unanticipated, unpredictable and unforeseen circumstances, and second, that careers become dependent on particular events or conditions. I also see these two dimensions of contingence as mutually constitutive – the events or conditions that shape careers may be in and of themselves dynamic or unpredictable, and unforeseen circumstances may create new conditions and dependencies. The way that careers of middling migrants unfold becomes contingent on a variety of different factors – on opportunities, on visa constraints, on policy changes, on transforming individual desires, on the needs of partners and families and on economic necessities. Careers are also significantly contingent on macro-temporalities of the economy and of labour markets. For example, Percy's capacity to transition to engineering work after study was dependent on securing vacation work, which was in turn hampered by his positioning (as described in the previous section) as an undesirable transified worker. Percy's transition was further affected by the unanticipated conditions of an economic slow-down in the extractive industries in Western Australia. New dependencies were thus created as Percy sought alternative avenues via the NAATI accreditation to obtain PR, which then led to unanticipated opportunities as a freelance translator, and eventually an unforeseen career path in the education industry.

Contingency is also a useful metaphor as it captures the space in between precarity and flexibility that middling migrants occupy as their careers unfold – a dynamic and unpredictable zone where risks and opportunities are unevenly and unpredictably dispersed over time. Yet, within the turbulence of the contingent career, moments of active choice, negotiation and purposive investment are enacted to exert control over the future. Hyon-Woo's story, as outlined in Chapter 1, illustrates how contingency functions as an ongoing vacillation between precarity and flexibility that may entail both unpredictable forces and active choosing. Temporary insecurity (of both migration and work) was a choice for Hyon-Woo that enabled her to enact forms of autonomy that resisted the secure and ordered transitions of a normative middle-class career. Despite many years in short-term and low-paid work in Australia, mobility also opened up more expansive career options than had seemed possible for her in Korea, in relation to both different types of work and opportunities to balance work with leisure pursuits. Periods of precarious work for middling migrants are thus not wholly liminal time – the 'dead' or 'frozen' times of undocumented migrant work described by Ahmad (2008) or Villegas (2014). Rather, within mobile lives of the middle, precarious work times are often transitory durations that contain the possibility of new and sometimes multiple futures. Contingent careers thus involve the negotiation of ever-evolving and overlapping conditions that affect career choices and chances, as well as the often contradictory experience of forms of work that are simultaneously pregnant with both insecurity and possibility.

For my interlocutors, career trajectories were never straightforward and rarely proceeded as expected. Contingent careers consist largely of detours, fragmentation, reversals and suspensions that are all either directly or indirectly a result of mobility and its affordances and constraints. The majority of migrants I interviewed had, like Percy or Carolyn (the nurse who featured in the Introduction), pictured their career before they arrived in Australia via a teleological sense of sequence – a linear and successive unfolding of smooth transitions and a more-or-less upward professional trajectory over time, which if they arrived as students, would often begin with a frictionless transition from study to work. They also tended to initially envision a synchronicity of migration and work timelines – most expected (or hoped) that qualifications and experience would lead to career progression and its concomitant migration opportunities. Many, like Percy, remained optimistic when they initially found themselves in deskilled and semi-compliant work, seeing these jobs, rather than 'dead ends', as potential stepping stones to desired careers – an imagined trajectory of migrant work that Parutis (2011: 36) describes as 'any job, better job, dream job'. The ultimate destination, however, almost never matched the original aspiration. Many, including Percy, became radically rerouted into different industries, or, like Alice, remained "stuck" in the long term in under-skilled roles. Over time, linear logics of career sequencing had to be abandoned and reconfigured by most participants as contingent realities replaced teleological imaginaries.

How migrants individually made meaning from this reconfiguration of their career times varied considerably. Yet, amid this ambiguity, there were two dominant and apparently polar patterns of meaning making that migrants employed in reflecting on their work histories, presents and futures – an embracing of flexibility and normalizing of contingency versus a deep and ongoing sense of unmooring, anxiety and regret about lost and irretrievable time. Saji, for example, very much embodied the former response. He had arrived in Melbourne at 17 to train as a pilot, intending to return to India afterwards and work for a national airline. He worked at a fast-food franchise to earn money while completing flight school. When he returned to India, the aviation industry was experiencing a downturn, and he had no luck finding a pilot job. Instead he worked in his father's accountancy firm and for a time in a multinational call centre, while completing a bachelor's degree in commerce. Saji then returned to Australia, primarily to pursue a romantic relationship with Victoria, an Australian woman. Victoria had been a co-worker at the fast-food restaurant. She and Saji had kept in touch as friends, deciding to pursue a relationship after she had visited him in India. Arriving back in Australia on a tourist visa, and then moving to a bridging visa while he and Victoria applied for his partner visa, Saji was hoping to be able to find a job related to his commerce qualification in the town a few hours' drive from Melbourne where Victoria was now working professionally as an engineer. The bridging visa and his lack of Australian business qualifications hampered his hunt for professional work, so Saji began the hop-scotching path across hospitality, gallery work, volunteering and truck driving, as described earlier in this chapter. As mentioned, Saji, now in his early twenties, eventually found an administration job at a security firm and worked his way into a junior business development role.

In reflecting on his highly fragmented career path and the way his aspirations and goals had shifted since his dream, at 17, to work as a pilot for a commercial airline, Saji positioned his own contingent career as a migrant within a wider framework of modern career flexibility. He saw himself not in terms of the very material limitations that mobility had placed on his career development, but instead considered himself a flexible 21st-century subject, who, along with his locally born peers, had the empowering capacity to always "start off fresh" with something "new":

> 'I think that's really 21st century at the moment. I think people are really open to that and that's how people are sort of, it's like the new way to do things. I mean everybody is getting bored with what they're doing really earlier than what they used to get before. ... You know, people are changing careers, going back to university, studying different things, doing completely different things. They talk about at an age these days everybody is going to have seven different professions and stuff, so, I mean, you never know. ... Victoria [girlfriend], also, I mean, we have the same thing, if we sort of don't like what we're doing we'll go back to university, study again, start off fresh.'

I describe this sense of embracing and normalizing contingency as the portfolio self. It was a frequent response when the migrants I interviewed reflected on their experiences of transified work and contingent careers. Many discussed the stages in which they had experienced deskilling through precarious, menial and low-paid work as diversifying their portfolios, developing new skills, becoming a better person or becoming open-minded. They had no regrets about time spent in difficult or even exploitative jobs. Such narratives entail understanding fragmented forms of work as ultimately fitting into a teleological understanding of self-development, which can at times, serve as a discursive rationalization of unpredictable experiences. The portfolio self thus involves a distinct kind of sequencing of the self – a self for which all past work experiences, regardless of their fragmentation, add value to the present, and for whom the future is always open. The capacity to start again and find new paths is held up

Figure 3.3: Kun Woo

Kun Woo, a political science scholar who was hoping to build an academic career in Australia, worked for several years at the noodle restaurant chain Wagamama. The shifts were usually fun and often a time out from the stress of trying to further his professional career. A co-worker gave him the nickname 'Champ' and this photo of his name tag was an important memento of his time there.

in this narrative as a vital set of skills for the modern career, and this kind of open trajectory is seen as desirable and modern.

Such responses are not unique to my interlocutors, but very much reflect identified patterns in the sociological literature on 21st-century careers. Within the biographies of global modernity, workers must remain ever flexible, absorb evolving risks, and craft the self as an individuated subject (Bauman, 2013; Beck, 1992). Many interviewees, like Saji, perceived their attitudes here as connected to their youthful identities and synonymous with their generation. They felt 'desynced' from the past temporal norms of their parents' generation, where stable and linear careers were expected and valued. Presenting a portfolio self was an especially prevalent response from the younger participants who were in their early or mid-twenties when they were interviewed.

In comparison to migrants who responded to contingent careers by refashioning themselves into flexible subjects, another group of participants felt the material and subjective marginalization of contingent career pathways sharply. Darya, an Indian in her thirties who was born in the United Arab Emirates, exemplified this response. Darya had a master's degree in social work from a top British university and several years of work experience in non-governmental organizations (NGOs) in India. She was appalled to find that her skills and qualifications mattered little when she came to Melbourne to commence her PhD and began to look for jobs. Darya was forced into what she described as exploitative and 'demeaning' work, including wrapping gifts at a local market and doing photocopying for a professor in her department:

> 'So it took four years before I could get my first university job that complemented my PhD of skills. I was doing some [social work] practice work. I was tutoring refugees, babysitting, working in the pharmacy and also gift wrapping and doing all sorts of really odd jobs to keep myself financially afloat. ... It's very fragmented. "There's a job going wrapping presents for $4.00 an hour, will you do that?" "Yeah, I'll do that. I need the money."'

After many unforeseen delays completing her PhD, some of which were far beyond her control, Darya transitioned through a succession of short-term junior research positions in the university sector. Although she eventually relocated to Sydney and found secure employment in a university teaching role, the setbacks and delays that her mobility had wrought on her career still troubled her immensely, especially when she compared her situation with that of her peers at home:

> 'Absolutely, this has delayed my career trajectory. Probably by ten years. I have friends in India who are directors of NGOs now and I'm a lecturer. Just somebody who has to deal with students who don't care. I have friends who are in decision-making capacity. ... In Australia I don't have the same standing. ... I'm not grounded anywhere but that's because I lost my youth you see, that's where you ground yourself. You build yourself in a company or you build yourself as you start off as an intern and become the vice president or whatever else. People do those sorts of things in India. They stick with one organization for long and grow and those sorts of opportunities in fact no longer exist in Australia. Australia is the strangest country where there's the highest casualization. I don't know why people want to move to Australia but there's the highest casualized workforce in the world right so you never go through the ranks, you never grow and as a result because you don't go through the ranks, you're never grounded.'

Darya's experience of sequence in the contingent career was not one of a portfolio of ultimately valuable experiences, but of ongoing fragmentation and insurmountable delay. The career setbacks accumulated to the point that Darya felt she would never catch up, as her career radically desynced from the linear trajectories of her immobile peers in India. On the surface, Darya had led a highly cosmopolitan and mobile life and had all the trappings of successful transition to both adulthood and migration security. She had not only PR but a tenured university job. She had married and had a child, owned her own home, and travelled often, both to India and elsewhere. But she could not reconcile this present with the years she had 'lost' in terms of her career. The sacrifices and humiliations of the past, in which she felt continually devalued professionally and in Australian society, continued to affect her present and her future. In terms of a logic of the sequencing of her career, the alternative future she could have had haunted and destabilized her 'now', leaving her feeling forever ungrounded. Darya said that she and her husband talk about returning to India "every second day". But having so recently secured her university position as well as her residency, they are worried about starting again, and about uprooting their daughter who was born in Australia. Participants like Darya who felt this sense of indefinite unmooring tended to be older (in their thirties) when interviewed. The unmoored self was particularly acutely felt by those who, like Darya as well as Carolyn and David from the Introduction, had left established careers at home before coming to Australia, or who had children or were planning children. At a later stage in the transition to adulthood, stability and teleology of careers had become more important, and the long-term impacts of their insecure pasts were becoming more apparent. Their anxieties over the time they had 'wasted' as transified workers was often also reflected in their sense of belonging, many feeling disenfranchised with and critical of Australian society. Many, like Darya, were considering returning to their home country. But the many years of investment into Australia led to fears of having to start again if they returned home. These migrants were often conscious that their contingent career pathways in Australia would not provide the career capital for a fluid re-entry into work in hyper-competitive Asian markets. Their sense of unmooring was thus underpinned by a kind of temporal limbo, as they remained unhappy with the outcomes of life and work in Australia but were also reluctant to move on.

In this chapter so far, I have outlined in general terms how transified work and contingent careers come about, and how migrants make sense of them. In the following two sections, I turn my focus to two of the most prominent everyday lived experiences of working times that emerge from transified work and contingent careers: the indenture of the present and the intensity of the everyday.

On pause: the indenture of the present

Experiences of 'indentured temporality' (Robertson, 2019) are a key feature of transified work and contingent careers. What I describe in this section as the indenture of the present refers to any specific durations of time during which migrants remained suspended or contained within a work situation, and unable to move out or forward. Often this suspension is required to obtain a migration outcome or to further a career goal. The term indenture of course evokes the colonial history of Asian migrant worker mobilities throughout the Asia–Pacific, including to Australia. But I do not intend to imply that today's middling migrants experience oppressions commensurate with the indentured servitude of the colonial era (Robertson, 2019). Instead, I use the idea of indenture to evoke how the conditions of transnational mobility structure durations of immobility and containment, and how, in relation to their careers, such containment is often understood by migrants via a particular logic of sequencing involving the temporary sacrificing or 'mortgaging' (Bastia and McGrath, 2011) of the present for the future. The most common experience of indentured temporality for middling migrants is working an unfulfilling, difficult or poorly paid job for a possible migration outcome.

Alice, for example, stayed in a marketing role at an unscrupulous education provider for four years to accumulate the experience she needed to qualify for PR with 'marketing' as her listed occupation. When I first met Alice, she was in her mid-thirties and had recently achieved her PR, and when talking with me about this milestone she became tearful. Having "secured the bottom line" on migration security, she explained that she was finally free to pursue her career "passions". She had left her semi-compliant employer, who had been instrumental in getting her permanent visa, and found a new digital role in the travel industry. She felt, much like Percy, that PR allowed her career in Australia to officially "start". In Alice's case, this beginning occurred ten years after her arrival:

> 'One thing about my permanent resident. I feel like, okay, I can actually doing something I really want. So because before you getting your permanent resident, you feel like, okay you need to continue working in marketing, and

then if you have passion for other areas, you still can't do it because you haven't secured the bottom line, for you to stay in Australia. So I've now get my permanent resident, I started thinking, "What do I really want do?" So now I'm working in [travel franchise], you know those? So I'm going to get my PR, and get a job I like, so life starts.'

For many migrants, like Alice, a suspension of career progression is structured through a direct or indirect dependency on the employer that ties the migrant's future to a specific working arrangement. In what follows, I explore in some detail the story of Abigail, in her mid twenties when interviewed, from Malaysia. Her story highlights not only the career impacts, but also the affective and embodied impacts of periods of indenture as 'the present suspended'.

Abigail had come to Melbourne for two years of boarding school as a teenager and stayed on to study commerce at university. Her dream was to one day run a dance school, an aspiration her parents were willing to support when she was ready to "settle down". Although eligible to apply for an 18-month post-study work visa, she had always planned to return to Malaysia after her university graduation, as her older sisters had done and as her parents expected. But, Abigail explained, she "met a boy", which drew her to use the 18-month visa to stay on and pursue the relationship. When that relationship ended, Abigail described herself as too upset by the break-up to decide to either stay or go back: "I just wanted to just stay at home and just cry." (The impact of intimate relationships on mobility decisions is explored in more detail in Chapter 5). She spent several months "wasting time" and unsure of her plans, vacillating between returning to Malaysia or staying just a bit longer, until she stumbled into a job managing rental properties at a real estate agent and started a new relationship.

Work did not play a significant role in Abigail's decision to stay, and she had little real interest in pursuing real estate for a long-term career. She remained somewhat ambivalent about staying in Australia during much of her first year working at the real estate firm. But her relationship was going well, and a family contact who worked in the immigration industry encouraged her to request a 457 visa sponsorship from the company.[3] Under the 457 programme, she would have to remain with the sponsoring employer for two years to be eligible for residency. Abigail had no strong desire for PR at this stage, nor any wish to make a career out of real estate. But she didn't want to be forced to leave her boyfriend behind when her temporary visa expired. Abigail described in some detail what happened at work when the company directors received a formal request to action her sponsorship:

'At this stage, I had already kind of lined up my situation to my department manager. I was like, "You know, if I ever was in this situation, would you be able to sponsor me?" And he was like, "Of course, we'll do anything to keep you, blah, blah, blah", not knowing again that it will happen. Anyway, next thing you know, he receives this email from this immigration officer and they kind of, I don't know, ignore it. That's the best feeling I got, except for my immediate manager. He pushed them a little bit harder. But then she sent another email, "That needs to be done." And then the directors took me aside for a meeting, and they got really angry. … It's pretty funny, but my direct department manager, actually, he said he knew that they just wanted me to really want the visa. If I was sitting there, all arrogant, "Oh, you don't have to sponsor me", they just wouldn't. So, he leaned over and goes, "Start crying." I swear, that's what happened. He goes, "Start crying." And this was not an act. It was actually really sad. The whole situation was really sad. And I looked [at] him, I'm like, "Shut up." And I turned around and water works, just tears down my face. And I'm just crying and crying. I'm like, "You don't understand. The people I've worked with are like family, and I don't have family here. And, you know, I understand if you don't want to sponsor me but I …" … And I was like, "I'd be happy to stay until you find someone new, or if you sponsor me, you know, I'll work very hard. I'll stay with the company for a long time." And that's really hard to find in real estate. So, yeah, and then they decided to sponsor me.'

Here, we see Abigail's response to the stigma described earlier in this chapter, of the transified worker as unstable and lacking commitment, ready to leave at any moment. Abigail's tears were a performance of stability and long-term investment, a deeply embodied enactment of the faithful and grateful employee. Abigail's emotional response was far from inauthentic, she was stressed and worried about the consequences of the meeting, and she wanted to keep her job. Yet, breaking down emotionally in front or her employers, claiming that they were "like family" to her (despite her actual ambivalence about the work), was directly tied to her transification. Such embodied performances of long-term commitment, although not always as dramatic as Abigail's, are a common and daily strategy for insecure middling migrants to build trust with their employers, and to mitigate the stigma of the transified worker (Robertson, 2016).

After the meeting, the directors agreed to support Abigail's sponsorship, and her 457 visa was granted relatively quickly. On the one hand, she was pleased, yet at the same time the reality of her situation began to sink in. Abigail was by this stage more serious with her boyfriend. They had moved in together, and she had adopted a dog. She was beginning to see a future in Australia, at least a future "for a while". She was now certain she wanted to transition to PR, simply for the sake of not having to take into account another looming visa expiry date as she thought through her future plans. But, obtaining PR meant staying with the real estate company for two years of indentured time. When I met with Abigail in the apartment she shared with her boyfriend in a chic inner-Melbourne suburb, we drank tea as her dog yapped happily in the other room. She still had a year-and-a-half remaining with the company before she would be eligible for PR. While there were aspects of the work she enjoyed, and she was friendly with some of her co-workers, by and large she felt stuck. As she saw non-migrant colleagues coming and going in a high turnover field, the containment of her own situation became harder over time:

> 'You know, with every job there's an up and down. ... Being in real estate, it's very high turnover. And I love my friends that I make, but then they go, and you get other people that you don't want to work with, and that's when the job becomes so heavy. ... There are times where I'm like, "I wish I could just get out of the company and go somewhere else", but you know, I wouldn't. I know I wouldn't. And forcing myself to stay somewhere, that sucks. ... I feel like they own me. You know, I can't do anything. It's not like they treat me badly or anything. They don't. But I just do feel like I owe them or, yeah, they could pretty much tell me to do anything and I'll just jump and I'll jump. How high, you know? And for, yeah, two years and more it's a long time, yeah.'

In terms of the sequencing of her career, the indenture of Abigail's present seemed to suspend her capacity to figure out want she really wanted to do in the future. Still unsure of what she really wanted from her career, or how long she really wanted to stay in Australia, PR represented for Abigail the ability to simply take a break – to have time out from working and to consider her next move with the security of a permanent visa:

> 'My plan, and I don't know if it's possible, but my plan is to finish up the year, get my permanent residency and then I just want to take a break from working. I think having that security of being able to stay here with no job, it's actually just really good. ... I just want to have a break for a while and then I'll find a job again, whether or not they'll take me back or I'll do my own thing. ... You can't take a break with these visas. You always have to be doing something, and that's – yeah. ... The whole time your mind's like, "Okay, I've got 18 months, 17 months, ten months", you know?'

For many migrants like Abigail who are tied to employers for specific periods, careers can remain in these forms of suspension for several years. When the present is indentured, it is not just career progression that must be deferred into the future, but often even any sense of career planning. The relations of dependence created by the indentured present have embodied and affective consequences for workers in their dealings with their employers, even if they are not explicitly mistreated. Often, workers must synchronize their bodily and affective performances at work with what they see as the desires of their employers for long-term commitment. For Abigail, this involved crying on cue in a meeting to performatively prove her commitment to the company, as well as the ongoing sense that she had to be immediately responsive to any demand: "they could pretty much tell me to do anything and I'll just jump".

Dark tunnels: the intensities of the everyday

Abigail described her daily experience at work during her indenture at the real estate firm as "so heavy", as well as having a feeling of being "stuck" and as if the days were overly long. For Abigail, this deceleration of the tempos of the everyday was interwoven with a suspended sense of sequence – that the future was on hold and that she could not take a break until she had PR. Many migrants had similar everyday experiences of feeling that the passing of time, whether it moved quickly or slowly, was experienced more intensely when transified work and contingent careers kept them in jobs for economic or migration necessity rather than intrinsic interest or long-term career goals. In this sense, the actual objective quantities of time spent at work were less significant to logics of tempo than the subjective sense of how the hours seemed to pass. Whether migrants felt the work was 'taking them somewhere', moving them forward in a chronologic sense, was significant here in shaping daily and weekly tempos of pace and rhythm. Percy, for example, was just as busy, if not more so, once he started working at the education consultancy. But he no longer felt that his work hours dragged by as they had done when he was doing freelance translation work and service shifts at the hospital. Instead he felt energized by his schedule. In part this was because the work was more challenging, and in part because he now felt "at the beginning" of a "real" career.

However, future-focused migration anxieties can also create intensified time even when migrants are pursuing their desired career paths. Colleen, for example, from China, was in her late twenties when we met, and was training for her Australian teaching qualification, a career that she was excited about. She was keen to use her qualification to apply for PR, but teaching was intrinsically fulfilling, not simply a means to a migration end. Although she enjoyed her study day to day, Colleen described her final year of study and practice teaching as "extremely long", not only because of the intense schedule of her training but also because of the ever-present possibility that sudden policy changes could affect her migration plans:

> 'The year that I view extremely long was the year I studied the secondary teaching qualification, because it was really full-on, study, assignment after exam after prac, like no break at all that year. And [it] just meant that I couldn't have any social life that year. So that was an extremely long year, because lots of [migration] policies were changing at that time ... and it's like going through a dark tunnel or you don't know what's at the end.'

In Colleen's narrative, the frenzied pace of her weekly schedule was interwoven with the unpredictability of her future. This created a sense of an inability to plan, and a slowness of the passing of time. A paradoxical logic of tempo emerged for Colleen, as time both sped up and slowed down simultaneously. The tempos at a daily level (busy days) effected a sense of slowness in terms of the chronologic or sequential passing of time (a long year), creating the heavy sense of moving through time as though through a "dark tunnel".

Dark tunnels of intensified daily time are also created when transified work and contingent careers place middling migrants' routines outside of the standardized nine-to-five schedules of local professional workers. Like Percy, many middling migrants experience stages in their contingent careers when working times are characterized by intensified hours of work that are also non-standard, such as shift work or weekend work, or the juggling of schedules across multiple workplaces. This usually occurs because, as described in the early sections of this chapter, transified workers are often limited from full-time work and standard hours by explicit constraints on their visa or by their low status in the labour market. Work schedules can tend towards the piecemeal — a cobbling together of multiple casual or informal jobs, often in industries such as hospitality where non-standard hours are common. Many middling migrants also juggle paid work with long hours of study either for formal education or to meet other migration criteria like IELTS scores. Many migrants I spoke with were reluctant to refuse overtime (even if unpaid) or extra shifts, either because they were dependent on their employers for potential future offers of visa sponsorship, or because of concerns that they would lose their job and be unable to find another one. Such experiences reflect previous work on the relationships between immigration precarity and labour precarity in relation to lived time, as 'precarious immigration status funnels migrants into precarious working conditions which in turn affect their ability to control their work and nonwork schedules' (Villegas, 2014: 281). Here, the dark tunnel of intense work time takes the shape of a segregation of the migrant from the 'normal' tempos of daily life, leaving them 'out of sync' with social lives, leisure time and family routines.

Mark, from Malaysia, now in his forties, came to Australia 15 years ago on a tourist visa, initially working illegally to save money. When he obtained a student visa to study graphic design, he was able to bring his wife and two young children to join him. But supporting them financially meant working every night at a restaurant as well as studying full-time, a punishing schedule that he maintained for nearly five years:

> 'You have to study very good and you have to pass all the subjects. And then I tried to do it and studied at daytime and work at night time, seven day, seven night at restaurant, so no stop, four or five years, that's right, working very hard. ... The emotion, it's from my family, if I can't pass all my study, I have to go back to Malaysia.'

For Mark, there was emotional as well as financial pressure to maintain this schedule, coming from dual investments from his wife and children in Australia and his parents in Malaysia. If he failed his course, he would have to uproot his wife and children to "start again" back in Malaysia, but he would also have failed to provide return on investment to his parents, who had helped to finance his study. The intensities of Mark's work temporalities continued after graduation. He was unable to find full-time graphic design work, and freelance jobs could not sustain a family of four in Sydney, driving him to continue with long shifts cooking in the restaurant, seven days a week. For Mark, working long and non-standard hours for such an extended period had radical affective and material impacts on his sense of social belonging, even after many years of living and working in Australia, as his schedule left him "no time" to see friends and take part in significant annual events like Christmas and Chinese New Year:

> 'When I graduate I try and talk to my friend, "I'm very good for graphic design", but they say, "Okay, you can do me just like a freelance job." I can't get a full-time job. Because I still got family, I want to support them, and then back to restaurant working full-time ... that's long hours, I start work at ten and finish at ten at night, that's 12 hours, no stop. ... I think my life is very boring, working six days, when the day off, I just stay at home. No friends. When a big day like Christmas, New Year, I have no times to celebrate for my family. ... And, how can you make a friend? And they say, "Oh, my birthday, Mark, come and join my birthday." "No sorry, birthday always on Friday, I need to work, I can't." When Chinese New Year, Christmas, they organize a dinner, "Mark, come for the Christmas dinner." "No Christmas, I need to work", because Christmas time very busy, I can't take off. So then how can I get a friend? No friend.'

Sima, in her late twenties and from India, had an Australian master's degree in accounting. She became similarly 'desynchronized' from social and family life, operating in a parallel and liminal temporal zone, during a period in which her temporary work visa required her to work a minimum of 30 hours a week for one year to be eligible for PR. Sima had been unable to find professional work as an accountant. As she tried to balance the hours imposed by her visa conditions with the precarious scheduling of casual work in food

Figure 3.4: Ji-Min

Ji-Min, from Korea, had to rebuild an established career in the international development sector when she came to Australia. She described this picture as "heading for the light" – representing her career journey.

service, her weekly routine became an intense juggling of over 70 work hours across two workplaces:

> 'I again started in the food services. But here it was like casual base and I was getting work for only like three shifts in a week and it will be like 12 hours. I had to work full-time [as a condition of my visa]. My visa was telling me to work more and they were like, "Oh I don't have work. I don't have work." Like every time I use to call my supervisor, thrice in a time, will you believe that?... And then she understood, she was trying to giving me work, but as a casual I mean they have to give more priority to the permanent ones. So it wasn't enough. ... So I find work same in the food service in another place too and then after I was meeting my visa conditions. ... I was working two different places, I had non-stop work for one year, I didn't take a single day off, it was like 6.30 to 2.30 at one place, I use to go straight from this place to another place and start work again at four o'clock and I use to finish at 9.30 at night, come back home, have dinner and sleep. ... Seven

days a week. ... More than 70 hours in a week, because being casual what happens is ... if you start refusing the work maybe the next week you will not have anything, so I will not say no, whatever comes in, I'll just grab it.'

Sima's intensified work schedule meant she could not provide care for her young son. She had no choice but to send him back to India to be temporarily cared for by her parents. This decision meant that despite her frantic schedule, she found this period of her life to be marked by an intensely heavy slowness, an almost utterly suspended sense of time passing. Both the tempo of each day and the chronologic sequencing of events in time altered for Sima. Focusing only on work, her days blurred into one another with a frenzied monotony:

'Oh it was so slow, it was very slow. When I arrived after leaving him [my son] there [in India] it was like this time has stopped, and then I kept myself so busy with the work I didn't feel like it is Monday or Tuesday I was just going to the work. As soon as I got up in the morning I wasn't sure like, "Am I going to workplace number one or am I going to workplace number two, what is the date today?" It was like as soon our alarm beeps go brush your teeth, get ready for the work, you know it was just one focus, work and work that's it. ... I forgot that it was my birthday. It was in November and I really forgot and one of my friend she rang me at 12 o'clock midnight, "Happy birthday my dear." And I said, "What?" She rang me from Sydney and I was like, "Is it my birthday? I don't even remember."'

Sima's story shows how the logics of tempo of transified work and contingent careers involve the paradoxical simultaneity of divergent velocities of acceleration and deceleration. Busyness unfolds contemporaneously with monotony – days are full, but weeks are endless. Time becomes a dark tunnel, not only because of such intensified velocities, but also because the present has often been suspended for a possible but uncertain future. It is worth noting that these futures are not just about ever-upward career progression. Many middling migrants, like Carolyn and David, whose experiences were described in the Introduction, come to Australia initially to seek a work–life balance, a more relaxed pace of living that they saw as intrinsic to Australian culture and in contrast to the rhythms of the Asian metropolises they had left behind. Living through the intensities

Figure 3.5: Adra

Adra, from India, provided this image from when she worked as an engineer on an oil rig in remote northern Australia. Although a good experience for her resume, she hated the fly-in, fly-out shifts that meant weeks away from her home and friends in Perth. She was often rostered to work at the last minute, and this affected her ability to make social plans or take holidays. She did not remain long in the job.

of the everyday and the indenture of the present is, however, a stage often required to reach a secure position in Australia that then allows an enjoyment of this desirable lifestyle temporality. These experiences of seeking out slow futures are discussed in more detail in Chapter 4, which focuses on how time is understood in relation to place, and in Chapter 5, which unpacks the synchronization of intimate lives across both space and time.

Conclusion

As Collins and Shubin (2017) note, the transnationalism of young middle-class people seeking work and educational opportunities today is far from a straightforward narrative of capital accumulation – rather, such journeys are in many respects 'unmappable' and 'unknowable' in advance. Moreover, these journeys must be recognized as shaped by the career flexibility and lifestyle fragmentation synonymous with our current era of advanced globalization (Scott, 2006: 1106). The everyday temporal consequences on work and careers for middling migrants are shaped by the global and national time-regimes of hegemonic flexibility and the transification of migration. Young, Asian middling migrants to Australia become positioned as transified workers who experience contingent careers, and complex temporalities of sequence, synchronicity and tempo arise out of these positionings.

Perceptions about young middling migrants' asynchronous temporalities and mobilities characterize them as undesirable transified workers, creating specific worker subjectivities and specific experiences of finding and retaining work. This characterization shapes their opportunities in the short and long term as well as their immediate and ongoing relationships to employers when they do find work. These young migrants become seen as 'risky' because of their perceived asynchronicity with the regular temporal processes of hiring and scheduling, but then are also understood as potentially exploitable because of their uncertain migration futures. Deskilling and semi-compliance thus often characterize migrants' initial engagements with work. Sometimes there is an element of strategic investment here as migrants seek to leverage present working arrangements for future migration outcomes, but such periods of precariousness can also have long-term consequences in delaying or rerouting careers.

In relation to young and middling migrants' long-term careers there is a fundamental tension between imaginaries of careers as teleological progressions and the realities of careers as temporally contingent under the conditions of hegemonic flexibility and the transification of migration. Contingency consists of unexpected detours, new dependencies and circumstances, and reimagined aspirations and desires, all framed within a sense of mobility as always unfinished and the future as ever uncertain (Robertson, 2019).

Contingent careers are thus unpredictable zones in which precarity and flexibility become unevenly dispersed across a migrant's career in ways they often cannot foresee. Yet, migrants still seek to purposefully sacrifice and invest their time in anticipation of shaping their career futures, even as these futures are continually made fuzzy by contingency. Most middling migrants oscillate between seemingly contradictory ways of understanding their careers and selves, often toggling back and forth between narratives of openness and flexibility and of insecurity and anxiety when reflecting on how their mobilities have shaped their careers.

The logics of everyday lived time that arise from transified work and contingent careers involve the indenture of the present in which work satisfaction in the present is sacrificed for the future. This leads to chronologic suspensions, delays and reversals of the sequencing of career paths as well as the impetus for embodied performances of stability and 'long-termness' in the workplace to synchronize with employers' desires and expectations. Transified work and contingent careers may intensify embodied time, daily schedules and the sense of the passage of time, creating dissonant, uncomfortable velocities that my interlocutors felt they had little control over.

Despite the significance of work to middling migrants' aspirations, it is important to understand their lives beyond their engagements with the labour market, as lifestyle, love and attachments to place coloured their decisions and experiences just as much as their careers. The chapters that follow move on to understanding the 'times of place' and the 'times of the heart': how hegemonic flexibility and transification transform middling migrants' relationships to place and to others in their transnationally dispersed intimate and family lives.

4

Times in Place: Moving, Dwelling, Belonging

Anastasia came to Brisbane in 2011 from Taipei, Taiwan, to do a master's degree in food science. Already familiar with the Australian lifestyle after visiting her aunt, who had migrated some years before and lived on the Gold Coast in Queensland, Anastasia had always thought she would stay on perhaps a bit longer after her study, but she didn't have a clear plan. Four years later, she found herself packing her belongings into her car, preparing to drive 600 kilometres of coastal highway from Brisbane to the small regional city of Rockhampton, a journey of seven hours. Living in regional Australia in a place built on the agricultural and mining industries with a population of around 80,000 had never been part of Anastasia's aspirations. But, she had gradually realized over the course of her degree that she was more interested in the interpersonal and holistic elements of nutrition than the laboratory work and so decided to continue her study with a diploma in naturopathy. Having worked part-time at a health-food store during her study, Anastasia saw a robust market in Australia for natural therapies and nutrition. But she also knew that her naturopathy aspirations limited her visa options – if she remained in food science she would be better placed on the list of 'in-demand' occupations for immigration purposes. But, as she told me, she wasn't willing to commit to a future career path only for the migration opportunity, so she decided to gamble a less certain migration future against her real career ambitions: "I just don't want to [go] kind of like against my dream and I just decided to still do the naturopathy and see how it goes."

However, as her diploma year drew to a close and she studied for her final exams, Anastasia began to worry more about her visa – she just wasn't ready to go back to Taipei. She interviewed by phone for a naturopath job at a health food business in Rockhampton. Once she had been offered the job, she asked if the employer would sponsor her for a visa under the regional skilled migration scheme. Under this policy scheme, designed to redistribute skilled migrants into locations with labour shortages, migrants who are willing to work in regional areas have better chances of sponsorship than in major metropolitan areas. The business agreed to sponsor Anastasia. Much like Abigail in Chapter 3, this offer would tie Anastasia to the job, and subsequently to living in Rockhampton, for two years if she wanted to stay in Australia.

The move from Brisbane to Rockhampton was a radical rupture for Anastasia. Her four years of student life in urban, multicultural Brisbane had drifted by with relative ease. She had a close group of friends and her aunt lived not too far away. She said of Brisbane: "I fit in well. Like I mean fitting into that city life well because I'm from Taiwan, Taipei, so it's also like the city area. So, yeah, I think it's alright for me, I quite like Brisbane when I arrived here." She had enjoyed the relaxed lifestyle of afternoon barbeques with her university friends and heading to Sunnybank, Brisbane's 'Little Asia', for an evening when she craved Taiwanese food. When Anastasia finished her long drive from Brisbane to her new home, which she would come to affectionately refer to as 'Rocky', she unknowingly entered into an entirely different temporal experience of local place:

> 'Well when I first came here I feel really bored. It's nothing here, nothing happening, people just go to bed even earlier than people in Brisbane because there's no night life here. Pretty much people drink. ... Yeah, Taipei is like 24 hours and Brisbane is sort of nearly 24 hours, but probably not. We can still do a lot of things after ten, because there's so many Asian shops in Sunnybank, Sunnybank Hill. So, we still can sort of feel like we're live in kind of like an Asian place. But Rockhampton is totally different in [that] the people here are very nice, very friendly, I find they are actually more friendly than people in Brisbane. They are also a lot more Aussie I would say, so the culture, I actually start to feel I, I thought I knew Australia well before I moved up to Rocky, because I've been in Brisbane for four years, but after I moved up to Rocky I feel like, "Oh, I actually don't know Australia well."'

When I first spoke with Anastasia via Skype, she was in her late twenties, still living in Rockhampton and waiting to fulfil her two-year

Figure 4.1: Anastasia

Anastasia photographed her speedometer after the long drive from Brisbane to Rockhampton as a memento of the journey.

contract at the health food business. When I asked her where she felt most at home in Australia she replied:

> 'This is a very interesting question! Well me and my boyfriend, we've actually been discussing, because like he might go back to Brisbane and we've been discussing where we're going to live in Australia in the long term. I actually feel a lot more connection in Rocky to be honest, although I've only been up here one year, but because it's a very routine life here for me. It's sort of make me have a lot more connection to this place. I feel like this is my life, like every day I work from this time to this time and go back home, do laundry, you know like housework things. But while in Brisbane, the three, four years that I was in Brisbane I was there as a student and maybe sort of like just part-time working and earn some money. But now is really like, I feel like it's really independently I'm doing a lot of things. So, I actually do feel Rocky is kind of like a home to me.'

Anastasia's moves through space are also moves into different experiences of time. Her move to Rocky took place because of the time-regime of migration transification that seeks to filter skilled migrants into regional labour markets for particular durations of time. Anastasia was fixed in place for the duration of her visa sponsorship, but with the promise of PR at the end. PR offers, for migrants like Anastasia, the privilege of permanence (the right to stay in Australia indefinitely, to not have to return) as well as the privilege of unfettered mobility (the right to move within Australia or move back and forth between Australia and other places without visa restrictions). Although living in Rocky was a form of containment or suspension of mobility, and in many ways an 'indentured present', Anastasia gradually found herself more and more 'in sync' with the rhythms of life in her new home.

Anastasia, like many of the young migrants I met, understood time as embedded in place – as inherently local. For Anastasia, multicultural Brisbane, although not a "24 hours" global city like Taipei, still contained localized pockets of time that felt comfortingly familiar. In Sunnybank, for example, a contemporary 'ethnoburb' produced, as Ip (2005) argues, by the sociocultural agency of recent middle-class East Asian migrants like Anastasia, the cluster of plazas and open air markets feel like an "Asian place" not only because of the products they sell but because unlike other retail spaces in Brisbane, they remain open after ten o'clock. Rocky, in contrast, was to Anastasia initially a sleepy place with no night-time economy, a place that closed down after sunset. These local rhythms of life in Rocky were shaped by the daily practices of local people (like early bedtimes) and the infrastructural practices of local institutions (like early closing hours). Yet despite her initial boredom with the slower pace of life in Rocky, Anastasia soon felt a deeper sense of connection to place develop alongside the slower tempo of life.

In terms of a logic of sequence, Anastasia's sense of feeling quickly like Rocky was "kind of like a home" also changed her orientation towards her past life in Brisbane. Despite living, working and studying in Brisbane for nearly four years, Anastasia came to feel she didn't really "know" Australia until she came to Rocky. Her timeline towards belonging in place seemed to reset, to start anew, with the drive up the Bruce Highway, and although she had only been there for a year, she felt "a lot more connection" to Rocky. This sense of attachment to place was shaped by transitions in Anastasia's individual life-stage and daily routine, as well as the place itself. No longer a student, Anastasia's schedule of work and domestic tasks became, in a positive sense, "a very routine life", and she thus felt more independent. Transitioning across the boundary from student to professional moved her towards adulthood, yet also deepened her attachment to place, despite the fact that, quantitatively, she had lived in Brisbane for four years and Rockhampton for only one. Here, we see how mobility can reorder the sequencing of time in ways that are subjective rather quantitative; how rather than a staged and linear life-course, migration can involve reversals and multiple uncertain transitions (Hörschelmann, 2011) in the journey towards belonging. Despite her sense of attachment to Rocky, at the time I first interviewed Anastasia in 2015, the town remained 'home for now' rather than 'home for the future'. Her boyfriend, an Australian permanent resident originally from Japan, was less happy with regional life, and they were contemplating moving on once Anastasia's PR was secured.

By the time of Anastasia's second interview in 2016, she had moved back to Brisbane with her boyfriend. Her sense of routine and synchronization with her local surroundings had been destabilized by the move, especially as she had only been able to find two part-time jobs with irregular hours. Anastasia had been granted her PR before leaving Rockhampton and now had the security, from the perspective of her migration status, to stay or move on from places and jobs as she liked. But despite her permanent migration status and her past connection to Brisbane, Anastasia felt less secure and less grounded after the move. Her relationship floundered, then ended, an experience that made her acutely miss having the proximate support of her family. She struggled to reconnect with her old social networks in Brisbane and missed her more stable work routine and the closeness she had shared with her co-workers in Rockhampton.

Anastasia's story shows how time and place are intimately interwoven and mutually dependent, and how 'times in place' contain complex and evolving layers of meaning as migrants stay, move and dwell translocally and transnationally. In this chapter, I seek to untangle the way migrants' understandings of 'times in place' develop across their journeys. I draw on my interlocutors' understandings of tempo, synchronicity and sequence as they move and dwell across different cities, town and homes to understand the interdependencies between temporality and mobility (Ibañez Tirado, 2019) and how experiences of time are shaped by place at various scales.

I first outline this chapter's positioning in relation to some existing discussions of migration, place and temporality. I then explore middling migrants' 'aspirations of tempo' – that is, how they see migration as enabling a future within place that has a desirable pace of life, and in turn how these desires around tempo are shaped by their understandings of sequential stages in both migration trajectories and life transitions. In the second half of the chapter, I move to an exploration of 'time in place' at the scale of the domestic – how transified migration trajectories reshape temporal experiences of home and homemaking. Here, I focus on how migrants imagine their housing trajectories to parallel their migration trajectories and their accumulation of belonging in Australia over time. I also show, however, how, in practice, the fragmented sequencing of transified migration often suspends investment into the material and embodied practices of making a home.

Migration, temporality and place

Studies of the quotidian experiences of migration abound with analyses of the politics of local place, place attachments and place making (see, for example, Glick Schiller and Çağlar, 2010; Hou, 2013; Jankowski, 2018), yet often with little focus on how places are also constituted through and by multiple forms of time. The ruptures of moving between places mean that migrants become immersed into different temporalities, and particular temporalities in turn develop in particular places around particular life-stages and life transitions (Oliver, 2010; Boccagni, 2017). Work on the cultures of migrant temporality has focused on how migrants bring particular cultural temporal orientations and practices with them as they move – in Cwerner's (2001) words, how 'times migrate with people' – and thus how the times of migrants and local populations may 'clash' (Elchardus et al, 1987). Yet, how migrants aspire towards particular 'times in place', how they adapt and respond to local temporal rhythms, or how they develop a sense of home that is particular to the temporal logics of mobile lives are issues that are rarely examined in migration sociologies.

Temporal gaps exist between different places in migrants' transnational and translocal networks, because 'prevalent ways of constructing time, and its rhythm, in everyday life' (Boccagni, 2017: 66) vary across the different local nodes in these networks. It is important to understand how migrants, especially under the conditions of hegemonic flexibility and transification, exist within and between these gaps, making their own lives, plans and routines within the often-divergent temporal rhythms of different places. Migration is, as Coe (2016) importantly notes, transtemporal as well as transnational, and a focus on 'time in place' allows migration trajectories to be understood to be as much about immobility as mobility (Baas and Yeoh, 2019) and as much about multiple scales of space – local, regional, domestic – as the transnational. This is particularly important to the analysis of middling migrants' experiences, as their visa conditions as well as other aspects of their transification move them between cities, towns and homes, and concurrently and consequently across different future imaginaries of place, settledness and unsettledness.

Migrants often operate reflexively across multiple 'time-worlds' (Farrar, 2003; Rogaly and Thieme, 2012), and indeed, the conditions of flexible modernity have made many modern subjects, whether mobile or immobile, ever-more reflexive in relation to the temporalities of different cultures and places. I argue that middling, 'transified' migrants display more complex orientations towards time perhaps than secure settler migrants or highly precarious undocumented migrants. They are the temporally reflexive subjects of modernity, closely attuned to the multiplicities of temporal lifestyles, cultures and values; they are active in seeking out specific local temporalities that align with their desires and identities, but they also often have limited control over the temporal orders they find themselves inhabiting. As such, their experiences show how migrants move or aspire towards desirable temporal possibilities as much as towards places, and how they negotiate these aspirations within local lived realities as their migration trajectories unfold.

Rogaly and Thieme (2012) and Sharma (2014) importantly critique the universality of concepts like acceleration and time-space compression, exploring how different experiences of time are shaped by differentiated positions in terms of class, age, occupation and gender. I develop these critiques further with my focus on middling and transified migrants, arguing that an analysis of hegemonic flexibility must look not only to the global dominance of time-space compression and acceleration, but also to how these temporal conditions are actually negotiated in differentiated ways in everyday life. Such an analysis hinges on exploring the agencies of different individuals who seek to reshape or resist these conditions, aspire to different temporal ways of being and consider alternative framings of temporal social value.

Local temporalities: aspirations of life-stage and lifestyle

When I asked my interlocutors about their first impressions of Australia, or how Australia compared to where they had come from – cities like Seoul, Taipei, Kuala Lumpur, Mumbai and Shanghai – the usual observations about Australia's comparatively temperate climate, lack of pollution, and low population density were common. But just as common were responses that highlighted temporal divergences in how life was lived in these different places. Most often, these responses involved observations of how Australia seems somehow 'backward' and 'decelerated' – how internet connectivity is incredibly slow; how retailers, restaurants and entertainment venues close far too early in the

Figure 4.2: Anastasia

Anastasia's photo of her favourite local beach in Rockhampton. Her weekend ritual to unwind after the working week became a trip to the beach rather than a late night out.

evenings; and how, as Anastasia was not alone in noting, Australians go to bed at unreasonably early hours.

These impressions reflect a set of temporal distinctions around place that are in many senses indicative of the middling migration experience, an experience more complex than the 'rural' versus 'industrial' contrast of global time-orientations often suggested in traditional studies of South–North migration (Farrar, 2003). These young migrants do not move from a Global South village life into a more modern, dynamic or accelerated urban Global North, but rather 'sideways' across more subtly differentiated 'times of place'. They come from rapidly transforming 'fast cities' (Datta, 2016) where lifestyles, urban rhythms and consumption cultures often reflect a 'hypermodern' sense of constant activity and acceleration. For these migrants, Australia still symbolizes 'the West' as an aspirational destination that can take their lives in new directions. But Australia is associated not with hypermodern speed, but rather a comparatively decelerated tempo – encapsulated in imaginaries of less technological advancement, diminished night-time economies, and more regularized, segmented and 'balanced' rhythms of work, socializing and leisure.

In terms of the unevenness of the temporalities of place globally, the moves of middling migrants into and within Australia are thus moves not from 'temporal periphery' to 'temporal metropole' but through highly differentiated local time-scapes – especially as middling migrants often, like Anastasia, move not only from their countries of origin to Australia but also between urban and regional locations within Australia as part of their migration trajectories. This speaks to Australia's ambivalent positioning as a migration destination that sits somewhat 'outside' teleological and hierarchical narratives of nation states and 'progress' in the Asia–Pacific. Cheng's (2014) Southeast Asian student migrant respondents in Singapore, for example, positioned their home countries as 'inefficient' and 'lagging behind' the aspirational destination of Singapore in a teleological hierarchy of place in relation to 'progress' and 'modernity'. For the migrants I met, in contrast, although Australia was an aspirational destination, aspiration was not always oriented towards an accelerated and 'more modern' future. I thus explore aspirations around 'decelerated' versus 'accelerated' places in more detail in the following sections of this chapter.

Australia as the 'relaxed and comfortable nation' (Noble, 2005) is, for many middling migrants, synonymous with a slowed-down pace of living, and this imagined logic of tempo as a lifestyle is a central driver of their migration aspirations and imaginaries of their futures of settlement. Behind this overarching imaginary that Australia is a 'slow place', however, sit the lived realities of the daily temporalities they encounter as migrants under a time-regime of transification. As outlined in the previous chapter, the everyday schedules that middling migrants must balance as they negotiate 'contingent careers' often sit paradoxically between frenzy and monotony, as they are pushed into intense or fragmented work schedules and worry about uncertain migration outcomes. Yet, the desire for slowness still motivates their ongoing aspirations, despite their frenzied presents, which they hope are a transitory temporal state. Like the first-generation Chinese migrants in New Zealand studied by Wang and Collins (2020) my interlocutors continued to imagine their destination as 'a place where a relaxed lifestyle could be lived' even when 'actual experiences of daily life undermined this possibility' (9).

Carolyn and David, for example, whose journey I explored in the Introduction, were attracted to Australia, and Queensland specifically, as a place that could provide more leisure time and more time with family in comparison to their frantic work schedules in Seoul. Such desires were prevalent in my discussions with many other migrants especially for those with children or actively planning for children.

Long working hours (often beyond what employees are paid for) have long been considered by labour scholars as characteristic of employment in many contexts in Asia (Welford, 2005; Ogura, 2009; Chandra, 2012). Certainly, my interlocutors saw working far beyond standard nine to five hours as normatively embedded into professional middle-class careers in the Asian metropolises they had left. Australia could, they believed, in terms of both cultural and economic local structures, provide a more balanced life routine – if not immediately, then at least in the future.

Ji-Min, an international and community development practitioner from Korea who was in her mid-thirties when interviewed, described her imaginaries of the local temporal order in Australia. More so than any other economic or lifestyle opportunity, this imaginary had been the impetus for her and her husband to stay in Australia and seek PR after the birth of their daughter:

> 'I gave birth in here and so I thought it would be good to apply for PR because I don't know if you know but Korea is a very, like I said, we work very hard so more than 15 hours per day. So my husband and I feel blessed to be here because I can spend a lot of quality time with my baby. Yeah so, I think that was that main thing that yeah, led me to apply for the PR. Back in Korea, yes you're very busy. If there's like, we go, we went home just to restore our strength to work again because we came home around 10 pm. So yes it's very, yes it's the biggest difference I think. Here my husband has no overwork or. ... And if he worked more than the scheduled time then he's paid and it's such a difference. It's such a different type thing. ... [Time off] is not quite common concepts for Korean workers because we thought it's just natural to lots of work. ... And my husband, he's a family man but when he was in Korea he had to go to work even during the weekends. And when he didn't go he was disadvantaged.'

Anik, an Indian engineer in his late twenties, had lived and worked in Dubai prior to coming to Australia to study aerospace engineering. He had gone back and forth between Dubai and Australia after graduating, finally settling in Melbourne, at least for the present, when he found a desirable job, although he harboured a desire to one day work in the US. Anik had initially wanted to work in Australia to 'accelerate' his career, and was at first somewhat frustrated by the slower rates of

Figure 4.3: Ji-Min

Ji-Min shared some photos of "relaxed times" in Brisbane, including this leisurely waterfront bike ride.

workplace productivity. After several years, however, he came to value being able to spend more time on interests outside of work and, like Ji-Min, similarly equated the lower expectations of working hours in Australia with a more desirable lifestyle. Anik spoke of the temporalities of Australia and Dubai as radically divergent, as "two extreme ends of the clock":

> 'These are two extreme ends of the clock. If one is six, the other one is 12 o'clock. So let's put things in perspective, when I talk about working hours I'm looking at nine to five in Melbourne, no more than eight-and-a-half, if you go more than eight-and-a-half that's double time or overtime.

Figure 4.4: Ji-Min

Another picture from Ji-Min showing a coffee break when her baby was small, also emblematic of a slower pace of life.

> Back in Dubai some of my colleagues they would start work at about nine in the morning, they will finish at about eight o'clock at night. In saying that there is a time when you start work in Dubai, but there is no time when you stop working. ... But out here no matter what, eight-and-a-half out you go ... a lot more healthy lifestyle.'

Anik had also established an after-work "laughter club" – an endeavour based entirely on an embodied 'presentism', on being absorbed within the moment and having time out from the productive and achievement-driven rhythms of engineering work. Such an endeavour was only possible for him to pursue in Australia, where a decelerated work-life allowed for the construction of spaces where one could, in pursuit of physical and mental wellbeing, immerse oneself in the moment.

Slowing down was seen as even more important for children than adults, which was why it was often a strong focus in the narratives of migrants like Ji-Min or David and Carolyn, who were in their thirties and had already arrived at the life-stage transition of entering parenthood for the first time. Many mentioned Asian schooling as highly competitive and children as overly scheduled with study and extra-curricular activities compared with the Australian school system, reflecting work by Watkins and colleagues (2017) on how specific perceptions of educational cultures drive both the anxieties and aspirations of middle-class parents in the context of new forms of Asian migration to the West. Kun Woo, also in his thirties, whose first child, a daughter, was born in Australia, criticized the future-focused nature of parenting in Korea, noting that children are pushed into intense schedules of study, particularly English-language study, from increasingly young ages:

'After school they have to go to a private academy to study and they have to learn extracurricular activities such as playing instruments, do some martial arts and do some paintings and that sort of thing for the future. Because Korean parents are very enthusiastic about their children's education and also they have their prior experience like at this stage if my kids do these things then she will be more competitive in the future. They knew that so they try to force them to do it and because of their competition things goes on the age. Before when I was a student studying English was not a thing of elementary thing but now it becomes five-year or six-year-old kids they are sent to the English-speaking kindergartens to learn English. So they're kids, but they're not like kids.'

In addition to being too fast and too busy in terms of the tempo of everyday routines, migrants like Ji-Min, Kun Woo and Anik also positioned the places they came from through a time-logic that was aggressively and undesirably future-focused rather than centred on a 'healthier' immersion in the present moment. Further, these places were understood as privileging synchronicity with the demands of careers and capitalist production rather than the togetherness of time with family or community. Attention to the values these middling migrants constructed around these translocal temporalities reveals a contrast to the classic intercultural narrative in migration research in which 'Asia' and 'Asian culture' often symbolize collectivism and familial obligation, whereas 'the West' symbolizes individualistic orientations (see, for example, Hyun, 2001; Pyke, 2005).

The discourses of seeking out temporal 'balance' between work time and family or leisure time that dominated my participants' narratives reflect wider cultural trends in middle-class and elite milieus globally in which slowness is positioned as 'an antidote to the fast-paced imperatives of global capitalism' (Fullagar et al, 2012: 1) and comes to be symbolic of a more meaningful life (Osbaldiston, 2013). These temporal desires 'of the middle' are also highlighted in the emergent field of 'lifestyle migration' literature as a constitutive element of middle-class (and often White) aspirations to move towards an escapist project of 'the good life' (O'Reilly and Benson, 2016).

In alignment with existing work that focuses on power and inequality in relation to temporality (Rogaly and Thieme, 2012; Sharma, 2014), it is important to note, however, that my interlocutors lack the agency of more secure and privileged lifestyle migrants to frame their mobility entirely in terms of lifestyle choice. Young, middling migrants often cannot fluidly and immediately transition into a 'slowed-down' temporality by moving to Australia. As seen in Chapter 3, as they try to build careers and achieve migration security in Australia, their working lives involve everyday intensity, periods of indenture and long-term contingency. As such, finding a slow life is an aspiration that often takes time, and struggle, to be realized. It is these uneven and evolving conditions of temporality that contribute to positioning these migrant experiences as middling. The privilege of a slower lifestyle was often aligned with securing one's migration future. As seen in Chapter 3, transification often prevents migrants from slowing down or taking a break; the benefits of a decelerated Australian life can often only be accessed once migration security is assured. 'Slowness' here is thus about sequencing as well as tempo – it is a future desire, and a destination that many interviewees were yet to arrive at.

Slow lives were not, however, desirable for all migrants at all stages of life. Some were often less enthusiastic about the slowness of Australian places, especially urban centres. These were often migrants who were not necessarily biologically younger than the individuals, described earlier, who were seeking slowness, but in an earlier stage of a conventional 'transition to adulthood' timeline – that is, not married or considering children. Kalu, for example, a chemistry graduate from India in his mid-twenties who had recently finished his master's degree in Melbourne, found the slower pace of life in Australia's second largest city, especially the lack of a vibrant night-time economy of leisure and consumption, somewhat frustrating:

'Melbourne is way slower compared to Bombay. Bombay is full on, all the time. When people talk about cities in the first world, expecting things that will be available at all times of the day, nonsensical! Things close here at nine in the evenings. It's just wrong! I mean in Bombay you can go out at three in the morning and there'd be some guy with a tea stand and food. Here, not so much. ... Bombay is very concentrated. Go through your schedule every day. Melbourne, although has the same thing, it's still got those aspects of very bohemian, very easy going.'

Concurrent to his critique of Melbourne's slowness, however, Kalu appreciated its more "bohemian" pace. The disadvantage of the city's "nonsensical" approach to opening hours was somewhat balanced by the fact that Kalu had far more time in Melbourne than in Bombay to pursue interests outside of his chemistry career. He spent time working on creative writing projects and performing at slam poetry events. The opening up of time to dedicate to these interests, however, related not just to Kalu's spatial location within Melbourne with its more "easy going" tempo. The freeing up of time was also constructed by the sequencing of Kalu's migration trajectory that placed him within a period of transition after the completion of his graduate study as he waited for his temporary work visa to be approved. Uncertain at this stage if he would be able to stay, Kalu felt he was afforded a unique period of learning and reflection in Melbourne – a chance to live in the present and enjoy every second as well as to reflect on the growth and personal development he had experienced since leaving Bombay:

'Since I've realized that my time may be fleeting, I've become a lot more open to new experiences. I've become a lot more ... I'm enjoying every second essentially because I know it might be my last year. ... I got these many years to really understand myself and to grow as a person. I'll be eternally grateful for that. So for that, I think I'll never get jaded with Melbourne for what the city has taught me. ... I take time to smell the flowers growing which is great.'

Here, local temporalities of place (and their desirability) are structured by particular tempos of lifestyle intersecting with the sequence of life-stages as well as with the temporal uncertainties of transified migration pathways. Sometimes, as for Kalu, the uncertainty of migration futures creates a 'presentism' in place, an immersion into and appreciation of the 'here and now', even if the overall tempo of local life is not as vibrant as a young person living in an urban centre might desire. In other cases, as for Anastasia, the temporal conditions of visas fix people into place, and subsequently into specific local temporal orders that require gradual lifestyle adjustments as migrants seek to attach and belong in their present lives, even if they will soon move on.

Katie, a junior pharmacist from Malaysia in her mid-twenties, provides another case that illustrates the entanglement of the time-regime of transification with temporalities of both place and life-stage. I first interviewed Katie at the home she shared with her long-term boyfriend in a town called Narangba on the very outskirts of the Brisbane metropolitan area. She was relieved to take a break from studying for a final pharmacy board exam for the interview. Although technically a suburb of Brisbane, Narangba has rural origins and has only recently been redeveloped as a residential area. As such, the area retains the sleepy feel of Australian regional life. There is a small community shopping village opposite the train station and a great deal of green space throughout the suburb, but amenities and consumption spaces are minimal compared with inner-city areas. It takes over an hour to travel from Narangba to 'downtown' Brisbane by train.

Much like Anastasia in Rockhampton, Katie was located in Narangba for a fixed period due to the local pharmacy sponsoring her work visa; she thus experienced the 'indentured present' described in Chapter 3. Katie's sense of suspension, however, was related not to the work itself (she enjoyed her job and pharmacy was her chosen career, not a decision of contingency), but much more to the place she was temporarily tied to. When I asked Katie if she enjoyed living in Narangba, she immediately related the pace of her present life to other places in her past and future mobility trajectory – Kuala Lumpar (her hometown), Brisbane's inner city (where she lived before taking up the job in Narangba), and Sydney (a frequent destination for holiday travel and the place where Katie wanted to live in the future):

> 'Well to be honest not really, it's too quiet for me. ... We have actually talked about moving to Sydney because that's our favourite place, we go to Sydney four times a year just for the sake of having fun I guess. ... It's just so lively all the time, unlike here there's nothing here after five. I guess that's partly because of where I came from as well, I'm from Kuala Lumpur [KL] and it's a really big city and I'm used to that kind of environment. ... I guess I grew up more when I was back at home and my mum is at home all the time so usually we have this impromptu day, "Oh let's go out, go to coffee" and things like that. But as for here I don't have many friends living in this area and I don't have family members here either so most of the time I'll just be

staying at home. ... KL is definitely livelier, Brisbane is a lot more laid back and slower pace. But when I went to Sydney it's completely different to how it's like in Brisbane, it's comparable to KL that's why I like it there a lot better. But I think if I have something to do like if I had to go to uni or if I'm having a full-time job like now it wouldn't make much difference anyway because just go to work and come back, it's the same routine every day. Unless when I'm having a holiday that's when you start feeling the boredom.'

In Katie's experiences we see that the tempos of the local are also connected to social relationships – to logics of synchronicity surrounding how time is shared and passed with others in place. Experiences of time are not just structured by the local social and cultural rhythms of place, but also by migrants' daily routines and the presence and absence of people to spend time with across these routines. Thus, although Katie saw Sydney as livelier and faster paced, and in many ways a better place to live than Narangba, she also acknowledges that her experiences of Sydney are based on a fleeting holiday mode of temporality. If she moved to Sydney permanently and into a full-time work routine, the city's lively tempo might matter less to the realities of her lived experience in place. Katie also saw her boredom with Narangba as related to her lack of local social connections and the suburb's lack of social spaces. She contrasted her routine in Narangba of just working and staying at home to her spontaneous ability to have days out with her mother and friends in KL, to weave time with others seamlessly into the fabric of her days because of the proximity of her friends and family as well as the proximity of leisure spaces where they could easily share time.

Camilla, from Taiwan and in her mid-twenties, similarly positioned the different tempos of place as relational. When asked her about the main differences between her life in Sydney and her life in Taipei, she said:

'I think the way we use time is very different. ... Here, of course it depends on individual, but we would agree, like most of the people in Australia we can finish work on time. ... But in Taiwan, you know, like most of the Asian countries it's hard, like always long hours working, like even I text my sister and I say, "Hi, what are you doing?" She's still working in the office. I say, "Come on, it's already eight. You've got to go home. You have your own life." Like that.

And I almost forgot like how life is in Taiwan. I always text friends and family and say like, "Oh, I'm in the gym" and "I'm looking for something, go window shopping." And they just say they're still working. I just feel sad for that. So time management is very different, because I have spare time here, but I'm alone. So I do hope that friends, family, they can come over here so I can use the time to spend with them. But in Taiwan, even with them together, we don't have much time to spend with each other, because always like under with work, and the living quality is very low.'

Camilla's experience highlights not only divergent tempos across the two places that make up her transnational social field, but also the sequential experience of her own absorption into local tempos over time. The longer she stays in Australia, she can almost forget the accelerated pace of life in Taiwan. Her different orientations towards time in her day-to-day life – spending less time in the office, and more time in the gym or window shopping – have become themselves sequential markers of her own progression into a life elsewhere and as such also markers of the desynchronization of her life from the lives of her loved ones in Taiwan. The lifestyle benefit of free time thus holds some sense of sadness for Camilla. Much like Katie, although she has more free time in Australia, she cannot spend this time with her family. The valuing of slow time in individual mobile lives can thus also contain the rupturing of social relations across transnational space. Camilla cannot reap the real benefits of her decelerated lifestyle in Australia, when she remains separated from her family.

Participants' narrations of logics of synchronicity in relation to place also went beyond the way relationships with friends and family were shaped by the tempos of different places and the stretching and syncing of lives across transnational space. Synchronic understandings of time in place, of migrants feeling 'synced' or 'desynced' to local temporalities, also related to larger collectives – to ideas that there are overarching ways of understanding time and relationality in different cultures or societies. These logics of synchronicity were about far more than daily routines or the pace of life and their impact on social relationships – they were rather about particular modes of collective temporality becoming imbued with social value and understood as an implicit part of the social contract in different local contexts. Carolyn, for example, described how every process in Australia is 'slow', but how this shapes, in her view, more positive modes of relating to others than the hyper-efficiency of Korean society:

'Every process [in Australia] is slow, internet service and I get moved to another house and had to wait almost two weeks [to get connected to the internet]. ... But in Korea just apply one day, next day is everything finished and complete, but here still in the process, so I had to be patient and not complaining much. ... When I went back to Korea I was in a restaurant and I was waiting for 30 minutes and my old friends got upset and I said, "It's fine you know, in Australia people are waiting one hour." So my friends, old friends they say, "You've become really relaxed and patient." And you say it's just a slow procedure but things, people respect each other like they respect the customer and the waitress, between the relationship; in Korea, too much stress. Clients or customers expect everything is given, like the people who are giving service; they look down actually to the other workers who are giving the service to them. But here they appreciate and I get the bus, you know people say, "Hello" and "How are you?", and it's an equal relationship. ... And nurses have more time to get conversation with the patients and there is no hierarchy between the doctors, nurses and patients here I found.'

Like many transnational migrants, Carolyn negotiated an asynchrony between 'here' and 'there', with distinctive forms of daily rhythms, time management, and meaningfulness of time (Levitt and Lamba-Nieves, 2013) existing across her old home and her new. Carolyn, like the majority of my interlocutors, was initially very frustrated about how long everyday services, such as having the internet connected, take in Australia. But her transnational mobility over time between Korea and Australia eventually began to shape a new way of understanding slowness and delay. Slowed-down customer service interactions, the possibility of longer engagements with patients in her work in nursing, and unhurried daily encounters in public spaces started to represent, for Carolyn, a collective and more equal way of relating to others. In her interactions with her friends on visits home to Korea, they noted that Carolyn now embodied this different temporality as she had become more "relaxed and patient". 'Lifestyle temporalities', then, are more than just the desires for the individualized schedules made possible by different places but are also relational and collective. These temporalities not only slow life down, but in the process construct different ways of 'being together' and 'being with one another' and become embodied within the affective and performative dimensions of the self.

In this section, I have sought to show how a focus on the middling experiences of migrant mobility provides a space of analysis that can draw out the unevenness of 'time in place' for people on the move. The middling Asian subjects whose lives I explore here are neither the global elites 'cushioned' from the destructive tendencies of speed, nor the marginalized workers eroded by them. As middling subjects, who have the privilege of moving between differentiated temporalities of place, they are explicitly conscious of both the benefits and challenges of accelerated and decelerated local times. They have the agency to move and to seek out places where time-logics match their preferred ways of living for particular stages in their lives. They are conscious and reflective on how they personally value time and how it is spent. The privilege of middling migrants enables this active pursuit of desirable lifestyle tempos in different places. At the same time, however, the hegemonic flexibilities of both labour markets and migration governance delay, sometimes indefinitely, their capacities to realize these aspirations of 'making time their own'. Further, moving to recalibrate temporal lifestyles also often involves the sacrifice of desynchronization with social networks, both locally and transnationally.

Domestic temporalities: dwelling under transification

Thus far in this chapter I have explored the temporalities of place in relation to particular cities, suburbs and towns that migrants live in and move between, as well as their understandings of larger-scale national cultural temporalities, and how they value and aspire to these temporalities of place in different ways. But migrants also often understand time in place through the scale of the domestic – the different homes they reside in across their migration journeys. Housing is, for middling migrants, imagined as having its own ordered sequential logic – a biography of housing mobility that sits alongside both migration timelines and progress towards stable adult lives. Many migrants in this study started off in student accommodation, cheap shared flats or suburban homestays when they first arrived. Making a life in Australia over time meant gradually moving into higher-quality private rentals in more desirable locales, and the ultimate goal of a secure future in Australia was often envisioned through home ownership.

For many, home ownership signified both a key milestone towards adulthood and, concurrently, the arrival of 'legitimate' belonging in Australia. This reflects Brun's (2016) work on the more marginalized mobilities of internally displaced people, in which home ownership is valued as changing one's status and providing a form of social recognition. As Brun (2016) argues, migrants with insecure statuses 'dwell in the temporary' and migration and residential insecurity often go hand in hand. The (imagined) sequencings of housing mobilities of my participants also, however, reflect global middle-class desires and imaginaries of home ownership as a key part of the transition to adult life.

Percy, for example, whose career narrative was explored in some detail in Chapter 3, was very explicit in seeing the housing pathways of young middling migrants as intimately connected to their passage towards greater personal independence and autonomy as well as towards a form of 'authentic' belonging in Australia. Like many who had arrived in Australia as students, Percy initially lived in a 'homestay' – a room in the home of a local family. Although relatively expensive, this is often the accommodation type encouraged by parents and education agents when students first arrive as a supportive introduction to Australian culture, and a transition experience for young people who are not only moving overseas but also often out of the family home for the first time. Homestay families are vetted by universities or more often private homestay agencies, and students are provided with a single room and meals. Percy felt the homestay was beneficial, but only as a transition space, not as a long-term home. Independent adult life only became possible when he moved on to sharing rental accommodation with peers:

> 'What I believe is, at the beginning for the first couple of months, yeah for sure, the homestay family actually is beneficial. While, to be honest, as time goes on, after a couple of months' time, because we have been in Australia for a short while, actually we have gained a better understanding about the basics about everything, like living, studying, accommodation, transportations here. So, I think it should be better if we move to a house sharing with others, because in that space we could handle like these more daily things in the real life. Because, if I still live in the homestay family, I don't need to cook, so I am an adult, but that's not really independent. We always needed to do everything ourselves, to make decisions ourselves, rather than relying on others. And, also from an economic perspective, it's much cheaper to share a house with others.'

Percy was also extremely keen, like many of the migrants I spoke with, to own his own home in Australia, once his career was underway and his PR secured. This was not, he said, about purchasing property as a financial investment, but rather about the innate sense of stability home ownership would provide, and the way it would attach him to Australia:

> 'It's for the stability itself. Also, because as a traditional Chinese I believe without my own house I'm not really stabilized. So, if I have my own house, which means officially Australia becomes my second home besides my one in my hometown, so I know no matter what happens, this is always my home. So, yeah which like mentally it will just comfort me.'

As Noble (2002: 55) notes, 'making ourselves "at home"' situates the physical architecture of the house within a sense of 'locale', of being '"at home" in the wider social landscape: and especially the spatial environment of the nation'. For Percy, as for many migrants, to have security of residential tenure as a homeowner would enable deeper belonging to the nation state, and allow Australia to become, indefinitely, a 'second home'. At the same time, for Percy, home ownership was about stable and mutual attachment across transnational space, of having 'two homes', rather than about a linear assimilation away from his hometown in China. In fact, his desires to be 'stabilized' in Australia in his own home were equally about both the Chinese cultural values of his upbringing and the localized attachments of his present life in Perth.

Such interweavings of domestic and wider spatial belonging are understood by migrants via the time-logics that constitute them. Sequential logics of movement across different types of housing arrangements over time (arrangements that ideally become progressively more independent and more stable) synchronize with both the temporal progression through migration from 'arrival' to 'belonging' and through the life-course from youthful identities into independent adult life. Such experiences reflect how both the materiality and the meaning of homes 'should be understood as connected with the changing life course of each individual' (Boccagni, 2017: 66) and that further, for migrants in particular, becoming 'at home' in the nation 'should be analysed as parallel to their housing and integration trajectories, in light of the variety of underlying physical locations, and of the tension between the long-term aspiration to an inclusive stability, and a prevalent sense of dwelling temporariness at present' (Boccagni, 2017: 65).

As with the career pathways discussed in Chapter 3, the desires and imaginaries of sequence and linearity in housing trajectories were seldom actualized in my interlocutors' lived realities. A lack of residential continuity was often part and parcel of the migration experience, not only because of the expected rupture of one-time international mobility that characterizes all international migrations (Boccagni, 2017), but also because residential mobility continued after arrival and often not, as Percy imagined, in the ordered and linear sense of 'moving up' a residential trajectory. Middling migrants moved often, like Anastasia, to access work and visa opportunities in different cities or regions. But other structural conditions around housing that reflect a broader hegemonic flexibility also created discontinuity and ongoing transit in housing pathways. For example, rental agreements in Australia usually have a maximum lease of 12 months, and many properties affordable to middling migrants offer shorter terms or month-by-month arrangements that landlords can cancel at any time (Robertson, 2017). Migrants often lived, even many years after their arrival, in shared accommodation under informal leasing arrangements with other transient residents. Such arrangements, although affordable, also made housing precarious – a housemate moving out would often result in the remaining tenants being unable to cover rental costs, or conflicts with housemates or landlords would make living situations untenable.

The disruptive sequential logics of transified migration, with their unforeseeable reroutings and suspensions, as well as the dominance of flexibility in the housing markets available to these migrants, thus frequently reconfigured how individuals understood the temporalities of dwelling and homemaking in place. The complex mobility pathways wrought by transification shaped the everyday, material ways people felt 'at home' in the domestic spaces they inhabited and the ways they reflected on residential pasts, present and futures. In contrast to Nowicka's (2007) transnational professionals, who, although 'chronically mobile' had little difficulty in constructing homes, middling mobiles often developed reflexively ambivalent attachments to their domestic spaces.

Sima, introduced in Chapter 3, had experienced a zig-zagging mobility pathway that strongly affected her material sense of home. She and her husband had tried unsuccessfully to gain PR after studying in Australia and working in low-paid jobs in Sydney for several years. They returned to India with a sense that their migration aspirations had 'failed'. They remained in India for three years, during which their son was born. Sima's husband, however, was unhappy with running his business in India and wanted to try again for a permanent visa in Australia. They moved again to Melbourne, leading to the situation described in Chapter 3, in which Sima had to work full-time for a year to be eligible for PR, and their son had to return temporarily to India to be cared for by his grandparents.

Sima talked at length in her interview about her sadness of having set up her first home with her husband as a married couple in Sydney and then leaving involuntarily. This reframed the way she thought about the space of her home when they relocated yet again to Melbourne. In Melbourne she wanted to limit her investment into the domestic space, both emotionally and materially, until after her family's future there was made certain by PR:

> 'As soon as I put my [permanent residency] application through and then I was like feeling very much relaxed about it. But you know like now even I will tell you very frankly whatever I have to buy just to survive in here like if you buy bed or if you buy the furniture whatever, it was in terms of PR. Because I had my home settled in Sydney, you know it was like very much homely feeling, we got married, we bought the things and then we decided not to stay there anymore, so we have to put everything on a road side. Whenever you go and buy something it's not about the money but you got your emotions attached with the things and you have to leave the things there you know, it's like very sad part you know. Even a cup of tea, even a mug, it will make a big difference to you. So I thought like, "This time I'm not going to buy expensive stuff and I'm not going to really spend my time in shopping around, I will just stay with my minimum requirements." And then when I will have my mind status that "Okay I'm now going to stay in this country permanently", then only will I buy the things. So recently I bought like whole lot of things, and until that time I was like, "No not sure."'

Sima's experience of 'dwelling in the temporary' (Brun, 2016) by consciously limiting her attachment to her domestic world was a common one, even for migrants who had not had to leave Australia and come back. Vera, for example, in her early twenties, had lived in Sydney continuously during her five years in Australia, yet had cycled through a series of homestays and shared rentals, forced to move often by rent increases, exploitative landlords or housemates moving out.

Vera had grown to love Sydney as a city, enjoyed a great sense of independence in Australia, and hoped to be able to stay in the long term. Like the migrants discussed earlier in this chapter, the lifestyle temporalities were a major part of Sydney's appeal:

'I just think people are nice and relaxed and carefree which I love. I love the way that people can have a barbeque, have some beers and have a nice talk. Just not get up and go, go, go all the time, which was common in China.'

Yet, the ongoing discontinuity Vera experienced in her housing trajectory constituted a sharp rupture to her developing sense of belonging. The constant, involuntary residential mobility made Vera feel, she said, like a "drifting bottle" who "belonged nowhere". She had been forced to let go of attachment to material things, including the household and personal items that her parents had lovingly packed for her when she first left home: "My lovely parents packed up half of China for me. But within a month I came to Australia, I moved three times, always packing stuff. I always say this. I will never be materialistic [again] [it] is a burden." The often-fraught relations with other tenants and landlords also exacerbated for Vera a deeply embodied sense of insecurity that was directly related to her accumulation of past experiences of residential rupture:

'[I'm] just scared, always scared here by myself. I just feel like sometimes I have no power, feel like, "Oh my God, did I say something to upset someone? Will the landlord be upset? Did I use too much electricity?" They complain if you use too much. Somehow I always feel insecure, whereas in China I just don't care.'

A sense of security in the space of the home was thus deeply temporal – investments (both psychic and material) into the present space of the home were only possible when migrants felt that their futures were secure and they would not be faced with future involuntary mobility, whether having to move out of a residence, like Vera, or having to leave the country, like Sima. Sima said of her present living situation:

'Because if you see your house is just bricks, you don't feel like it's house, it's your home, it's a place to stay. But now it's like more family type of feeling, you are attached with the things and it's like when you come home after your

137

work you feel so relaxed. It's not that much worried what I use to have before, it was like I wasn't secure about my work, whether I will have work next week or not so in that type of thing. Like I've got full-time permanent work now so I'm pretty much secure with that, but no matter what will happen I will get my 76 hours in 15 days. So work-wise, money-wise, mental satisfaction-wise I feel much very better.'

The time-regime of transification positions migrants within a logic of the sequencing of mobility in which they are often highly mobile (both within Australia and transnationally) yet often have limited agency over both past and future mobility. As such, 'settledness' into the present home and the present moment becomes impossible until migration futures are concrete. Such chronomobilities create reluctance to commit to the material objects and practices of making a home, reflecting how the stability of social identities is grounded in the objects that surround us and the spaces we reside in (Silverstone, 1994, as cited in Noble, 2002). Subsequently, as Sima notes, spaces of dwelling can be "just bricks" rather than homes, and even small affordable items, like teacups or mugs, become potentially imbued with emotion, attachment and futurity.

The impact of transification and hegemonic flexibility on practices of dwelling form part of why the lives of these migrants, despite their mostly middle-class backgrounds, don't always reflect middle-class consumption patterns or lifestyles in Australia. The homes I visited during fieldwork, particularly those of migrants who were yet to achieve PR, were often austere spaces, sparsely furnished or decorated, and home goods and furniture were mostly second- and third-hand. Migrants were often seeking to save money with this minimalist homemaking, but even more so seeking to compartmentalize investment into the materiality of home, to remain 'detached' from the space and from material possessions in anticipation of future moves.

As Boccagni (2017: 72) states, one of the key social functions of the home is 'the provision of a sense of continuity, or even of permanency, embedded in a place which is subject to routines of security, familiarity and control'. Continuity, here, is associated with security and control of tenure as well as of material possessions. While the potential instability of migrant homes is often understood in relation to the highly liminal temporal zones of asylum shelters, camps and squats (Villegas, 2014; Boccagni, 2017; Lilja et al, 2018), the experiences of

Figure 4.5: Anastasia

A picture provided by Anastasia of deep cleaning rental accommodation before moving out – a common experience for middling migrants who often move frequently during their early years in Australia due to short-term leasing arrangements, financial pressures or needing to be close to changing work and study opportunities. Spending at least a day cleaning thoroughly is important, otherwise the significant bond payment made at the beginning of the lease to secure the tenancy might not be returned by the landlord.

my more 'middling' interlocutors, operating under the conditions of the time-regime of transification, add another layer of meaning to the significance of the materiality of home to the temporal security that interweaves residential and migration continuity. The sense of lack of control over the present and future created by previous sequences of disrupted settlement (whether migration settlement or domestic settlement) creates a lack of investment in the present, even if, as is the case with middling migrants, mobile subjects have the legal right to reside and the material resources to invest in their dwellings.

The chronomobilities of middling migrants who build and rebuild lives on the move under the conditions of hegemonic flexibility and transification challenge the chronologic sequencing of settler migration paradigms, which assume that place attachments and senses of home intensify as the years between arrival and the present accumulate. Within the chronomobilities of the middle, even if migrants have accumulated a past in Australia that stretches over most of their adult lives, presence in place remain unsettled, often indefinitely. The unpredictability of future mobility means that homemaking and place attachments remain, consciously, somewhat on hold.

Figure 4.6: Kun Woo

Another image of deep cleaning before moving provided by Kun Woo. He even hired an industrial carpet cleaner, after his landlord had threatened to charge him for stains on the carpeting.

Conclusion

The focus in this chapter on migrants' experience of 'time in place' reveals that, for middling migrants, serial mobility is not experienced as fluidity, but is constituted through multiple and often unanticipated sequences and cycles of upheaval and starting again. Transified migration is seldom about a single temporal rupture of departure and arrival across an international border, nor about a movement between and adjustment across binary East/West or North/South cultural temporalities. Rather, the chronomobilities of the middle are constituted through an ongoing series of moves between locales and homes that each have their own specific experience of time embedded within them. Local temporalities emerge through the intersections of the dominant tempos of place, as well as the temporal practices of migrants who inhabit them, which relate in turn to their stage in the sequencing of a life or migration trajectory. Further, migrants' sense of time in place is relational, that is, it is made meaningful through how places enable time to be synchronous with others, either via daily routines of encounter with friends and family, or via the larger scale and collective social valuing of time.

It is significant that these localized temporalities are an imaginary and an aspiration, a driver of migration, not merely a by-product. Middling mobile subjects become consciously attuned to the multiplicities of time (especially the paces and rhythms that make up logics of tempo) in different local places. Migrants understand present, localized times in relation to the other places that are linked in sequence across the dual trajectories of their geographic mobility and their mobility across the different stages and transitions of their lives. Their positioning as middling migrant shapes the imaginaries and realities of these trajectories across, places, times and indeed, times within places. Middle-class values and resources enable them to imagine and to seek out specific 'lifestyle temporalities' at different life-stages. Yet at the same time, the transification of migration limits their agency over where they can go, how long they can stay, and how much they can plan for the future.

Sequential imaginaries of upwardly linear housing trajectories align with feelings of both 'settling' into adulthood and 'settlement' into belonging in and to place. Yet, the continuous temporal rupture of residential mobility structured by the hegemonic flexibility of migrants' housing options and their pathways to visa permanence fractures these imaginaries of an ordered progress towards 'home', leaving migrants consciously ambivalent and detached from the materiality of the homes they move into and out of.

Across this chapter, as in the two preceding chapters, we have seen how the life-course is made malleable by mobility, how mobility can be strategically used to reroute and reshape normative progression towards adult life, but also how it can have unmappable and unknowable consequences of suspension, delay, reversal and rerouting, as migrants forge new directions, 'start again' and reimagine their pasts, present and futures. In this chapter, I have explored how these chronomobilities affect the experience of time in place, and in turn destabilize notions of settlement that posit linear, accumulative place attachment over time, or limit the experience of migrant temporalities to binary understandings of the cultural times of 'here' and of 'there', of 'then' and of 'now'. In Chapter 5, I extend this discussion of the complexity of temporality in highly mobile lives, and in particular the tensions of 'settling' and 'unsettling', by showing how they unfold in relation to migrants' romantic partnerships. This moves the analysis from concerns of migrants' experience as workers and their relationships to place to an understanding of the chronomobilities of intimate lives.

Times of the Heart: Reconfiguring Intimacy

Saji, from India, introduced in Chapter 3, was an outgoing and energetic character. When we spoke on Skype, I could see a large world map pinned to the wall behind him in his home in a regional centre not far from Melbourne. When I asked Saji about the map, he said that he and his girlfriend Victoria placed pins in the map to mark the different places around the world they had each visited. At present, Victoria's pins far outnumbered Saji's, but he had lots of plans to add to this map over the coming years, and to increase the number of places that he and Victoria visited together. Saji, whose career travails were outlined in some detail in Chapter 3, initially came to Australia, like many of the young migrants in this book, to obtain a tertiary qualification, leaving Hyderabad at the age of 17 for aviation school in the suburban outskirts of Melbourne. Education, and education that would lead to social mobility and financial security, was the driver, Saji explained, for his own mobility decisions, as well as those of most of his peers. For young Indians like him, from middle-class but not wealthy families, the journey was, according to Saji, about 'return on investment' for the family as well as the individual: "Education is probably like the primary reason why people think of, you know, going overseas, probably because it is a huge return investment. Because my family we were not in a situation at that time where I could think of just holidaying to go to Australia."

Financial return and economic mobility were ultimately, however, of little consequence to many of Saji's future mobility decisions. Instead, such decisions were largely driven by one factor – a relationship Saji ended up forming with an Australian woman. Saji and Victoria met as co-workers at the fast-food franchise where Saji found his first job

Figure 5.1: Saji

Saji and Victoria's world map, showing the different places they have each visited.

in Australia. Saji had not been abroad before and was initially crippled by homesickness and loneliness. The fast-food job was an important avenue to starting to feel settled. Saji started going to pubs with his work mates, 'hanging out', smoking his first cigarettes. He and Victoria became especially close friends. Despite strong romantic feelings, Saji didn't try to pursue anything further because he knew he was going back to India when he finished his course. His transience, driven by his pre-determined goals to return to India and work as a pilot, prevented him from 'going in that direction' with Victoria:

> 'I thought it was really nice and she was very nice. She thought the same too, I think, as well at that time. But one of our biggest problems, so we used to, you know, hang out and all that sort of stuff, but we couldn't really go further at the time with the sense because we were both thinking that I'm leaving in a month or so, or next year, or whenever, how are we even supposed to go in that direction when we don't know what's happening? But I don't know why I did, somewhere I was like, "Oh, I don't know how, this is

not going to happen." But I really liked her and I couldn't really say anything at that time.'

Saji and Victoria kept in touch over email and Skype for two years after he left Australia. When Victoria planned a trip to India with friends, they spent a good part of the trip in Hyderabad visiting Saji. The old feelings were still there for Saji. In fact, they were tenfold. He still had no sense of how a relationship could work across the divides of both space and culture, but this time he did not want to leave things unsaid. This was a moment of intense emotion for Saji, as he grappled with his first serious experience of romance alongside the apparent 'impossibility' of a shared future:

> 'I don't know how this is going to work, how is this, you know, even possible ... but this time I really wanted to [tell her], because I hadn't done this before, like I have not been in the relationship before, all of this was a very alien thing for me ... so I was very, very nervous and I didn't know how I was going to do it, but my plan was to actually just start out and tell her!'

For Saji, a future with Victoria was unknowable and unmappable. The only plan could be, then, to "start out" in the moment of the present and tell her how he felt. Victoria returned his feelings, and despite having no firm plans yet for how they could make a relationship work, they both held on to a sense that a future together was possible – that they could, together, 'make it happen': "And both of us were like, we don't know how this is going to happen, but we if want to make this happen, it will happen. So we continued with the trip just hoping that somehow things would work out and we would do what we can." A few months after Victoria's Hyderabad visit, the couple arranged to meet up again in Singapore – a trip that cemented for them both that they wanted to find a way to live in the same place and start a life together. Some concrete planning then began to take shape. The relative present security and future opportunities that each were facing as young graduates were key factors the couple considered. Victoria was finishing off her engineering degree in Australia and considering graduate positions locally. Saji had been, as described in Chapter 3, underemployed for much of the two years he had been back in India. He was living with his parents, and although they had met Victoria during her visit, they were not party to the blossoming romance.

Victoria was willing to try living in India, but when she secured a good graduate job in a regional town not far from Melbourne it made more sense to settle in Australia, where one of them had secure work. Saji returned to Australia on a visitor visa, initially planning to investigate study options and secure another student visa. It became soon apparent, however, that it would be less expensive and more secure to apply for a partner visa with Victoria as his sponsor.

Saji and Victoria moved in together and applied to the immigration authorities for Saji to be sponsored for a visa as Victoria's *de facto* partner. Saji's fragmented work schedule of evening and weekend shifts, described in Chapter 3, clashed with Victoria's more regularized nine-to-five office hours at her engineering job and limited their leisure time together to a few evenings a week. Yet they were in the same place, and working towards a future, which made the struggles of the present meaningful. "I mean we couldn't complain," Saji reflected about their first year as an official couple, "to see each other for even an hour to actually not being able to see each other at all. And we knew that this was something which was a part of the struggle and if we did that there was great things for us to come."

Underneath this optimism about their future, however, Saji was concerned about following the partner visa path, hyper-aware of how their relationship might "look" to outsiders, how "these sort of relationships" – that is, relationships that are entangled with a visa sponsorship – are perceived, both in India and in Australia. For Saji, the timing mattered to these questions of social legitimacy; he felt that the newness of their official relationship, his recent return to Australia and his temporary visa status combined to position their relationship as potentially suspect in the eyes of others. He was especially concerned about Victoria's parents:

> 'It shouldn't look … as if I'm just coming here to actually just marry her to get a visa, do you know what I mean? Even now I think that people will be thinking that. That's something that I, I mean, any parent would think that. … Because it's an average thing that anybody would get if you see these, sort of, weddings or these sort of relationships, an average person I think, maybe that's my perception, an average person would think that that's probably why, you know, you're sort of doing that. So that was a big concern to me at that time as well.'

Another simmering tension was the fact that Saji had still not told his own parents about the nature of his relationship with Victoria, describing her to them as a platonic "housemate" rather than an intimate partner. This caused periodic conflict in their otherwise happy relationship and was a constant source of stress for Saji. Telling his mum and dad, he thought, was all about the timing – but how to know when the time was right?

> 'And this will be one of those things that will be always hiding at the back, like my head will be always filled with that thing of "How do I get this out of my parents? How am I going to do it?" "It's about the timing, right?", that's what I used to say as well, but how do we get this timing? When do we find the right time, know it, how do we do this stuff?'

Saji tried to explain to Victoria that despite changing social mores about pre-marital cohabitation in India, telling his parents was still a difficult process, and one that needed, for their sake, to happen gradually:

> 'Because we all discussed about the point that, you know, in India things are a bit different, you don't just directly this girlfriend, boyfriend business, you know, relationships and before we were married. I mean it's even happening in India now like, you know, live in relationships ... but still it's very, very hard for parents to accept, finally to accept ... we had to do it in stages, not shock people and how are we going to do this, something that we all had to work together. And everybody was very cooperative of that.'

I will return to Saji's story in more detail, including the ultimate revealing of the relationship to his parents, in the latter half of this chapter. But this transnational romance does have a 'happy ending' in the conventional sense. The last email I received from Saji reported that he and Victoria were engaged, with his parents' blessing, and planning two weddings, one in India and one in Australia.

Saji and Victoria's journey to a life together reflects the key concerns of this chapter: how intimate relationships are one of the most significant yet unacknowledged referents in migrants' motivations to move (Gorman-Murray, 2009) as well as narratives of their belonging (Walsh, 2018). Saji's experiences also reflect the intersections of youthful mobilities with the intimate transitions of 'becoming adult' – falling in love for the first time, planning a future as a couple, introducing partners to families, moving towards marriage – and how proximity, distance and transience (and the governance structures through which these are mediated) complicate these processes and their temporalities.

For many of the young middling migrants I met in the course of my research, intimate relationships[1] played a pivotal role in their decisions and experiences of mobility. For nearly all the migrants interviewed, the lived and imagined timelines and timings of intimate partnerships were highly significant to defining, structuring and in different contexts both enabling and constraining their mobilities. Relationships unfolded alongside and became intertwined with im/mobility in complex ways, becoming part of the multiplicity of considerations and motivations that young and mobile migrants had to weigh up as they made decisions about when to move, when to stay and how to structure their relationships and their obligations to partners and families across transnational space.

In this chapter, I sort through some of the varied ways that the temporalities of intimate partnerships develop through, transform and are transformed by mobility under the time-regimes of hegemonic flexibility and the transification of migration. While other kinds of intimate relations are highly relevant to these young migrants' lives – for example, parents, siblings, kin and friendships – the focus on romantic relationships in this chapter reflects the middling position of these migrants in terms of their temporal transitioning in between dependence on the natal family and the formation of their own independent coupled lives, single lives or nuclear families. Their life-stage in between youth and adulthood means that specific and significant romantic relationship formations are central to their narratives of movement through time and their embodied experience of time.

In the preceding chapters, I have argued that transformations to life-course temporalities are often made possible by transnational mobility, such as a stretching of the period of youth and subsequent delaying of 'settled' forms of adulthood. A chronomobilities perspective can further reveal how intimate lives intertwine with this 'flexibilized' passaging towards adulthood – committed adult relationships are, after all, known as 'settling down', implying both an arrival at an endpoint and a transition to fixity in time and space after a delimited phase of youthful mobility and flexibility. But how does such an intimate settling take place, or not take place, within the open-ended, insecure and unmappable mobility pathways of transification? Furthermore, in the Australian context, settling into certain forms of committed intimate partnership can also constitute pathways to legal settlement through partner visas. The chapter focuses first on the general reconfigurations of intimate timelines and timings under transification, discussing mobility decisions in relation to intimate lives, including how transnational mobility can extend periods of youthful singlehood. It then moves on to a discussion of the specific implications of partner visas and how the governance conditions of 'sponsored love' reshape the time-logics of intimate lives.

Intimate relationships, mobility and temporality

It is a critical task of this book to foreground the link between intimate relationships, temporality and mobility, not only because such relationships loomed large in my interlocutors' narratives but also because this intersection is often sidelined in analyses of Asian middle-class transnationalism. The field of migration studies has generally focused heavily on transnational families and traditional marriage migration and has too often ignored how more complex and varied forms of emotional entanglements and personal relationships factor into experiences of being on the move, how 'distinct intimate practices interweave transnational mobility' (Bloch, 2011: 503). Further, as Tu (2016) notes, research on young middle-class migrants from Asia has tended to focus on education, career aspirations and transnational family strategies for capital accumulation and flexible citizenship. Such narratives have sidelined issues of romantic encounters and relationships and leave unacknowledged forms of migration in which the emotional and economic can be intertwined (Lauser, 2008; Yea, 2008).

Also significant to my arguments in this chapter is that personal experiences of 'intimate chronomobilities' are emblematic of wider sociological connection between temporality and intimate life. The logics of sequence that shape progress through young adulthood are often discursively and affectively marked by 'intimate' milestones – serious romantic relationships are markers of transition to adulthood, and even break-ups and heartbreaks are supposed to form part of the 'rite of passage' to emotional maturity. Marriage and family formation symbolize, across many places and cultures, the 'ending' of youthful autonomy and the 'arrival' of adult responsibility. While cultural norms about 'when' and 'how long' differ, ideas of the 'right time' to form adult relationships and for these relationships to develop are pervasive directives in young adults' lives. Under the time-regimes of hegemonic flexibility and transification, young adults navigate these intimate transitions and milestones in entanglement with the precarities and opportunities of mobility, as 'flexibilization is something which not only characterizes production but also the reproductive sphere' (Yeoh, 2009: 2). In addition, as Saji's experiences suggest, young people's mobilities can transform and challenge familial and cultural norms of the timelines and timings of intimate relationships.

Alongside increasing interest in the emotional, affective and embodied consequences of mobilities more generally (Mai and King, 2009), the intimate lives and loves of migrants have become emergent concerns of migration research. Scholarship has begun to grapple with how migrants' intimacies are often co-constitutive of their desires for im/mobility and how intimate bonds become bound up, both legally and emotionally, in capacities to stay and to move (Lyons and Ford, 2008; Mahdavi, 2016). Much of the literature on intimacy and mobility focuses on the stretching or reconfiguring of intimacy across space (see, for example, Kumsa, 2002; Thien, 2007; Frohlick, 2009; Mai and King, 2009). The temporalities of intimacy in migration contexts have received far less attention. The specifically temporal dimensions of intimate life – its timelines, timings, rhythms and velocities – remain largely uninterrogated in the sociological literature on migration.

Conceptually, then, I draw in this chapter on recent work in migration and mobilities studies that links intimacy and im/mobility (see, for example, Gorman-Murray, 2009; Mahdavi, 2016; Vogel, 2016; Walsh, 2018). However, I expand this thinking into the explicitly temporal perspective of the chronomobilities framework in order to describe the relational, reflexive and governance processes surrounding how intimate partnerships intertwine with migration desires and migration possibilities in my interlocutors' lives.

Suspending and settling: reconfiguring intimate timelines and timings

In this section, I explore how participants understood the timings of intimate lives – periods of singlehood, relationship formations and breakdowns, marriage – in relation to their mobility trajectories and choices under a transified migration time-regime. First, relationship timings and timelines affect mobility decisions, particularly decisions about when to stay and when to leave, revealing that such decisions are often driven by emergent emotions and desires rather than pre-planned goals. Second, mobility often enables or enforces a suspension or delay of culturally normative transitions towards marriage and family formation. This sometimes (most often for women) enables new forms of autonomy and reconfigured periods of singlehood or pre-marital intimacies but sometimes also (most often for men), creates anxieties about delays to reaching the 'arrival point' of secure intimate adult life. Here, disruptions to imagined sequential timelines of intimate settling down parallel in many ways the fragmented careers described in Chapter 3. Third, I argue that 'settling down' (the endpoint of youthful intimate lives and the commencement of adult commitment) and 'settlement' (the imagined endpoint of migrant belonging) are closely intertwined in migrants' understandings of their futures. Fourth, marriage marks new demands on women's time for forms of largely symbolic transnational care.

"That's why I didn't go": staying and leaving

As described in Chapter 3, Abigail, from Malaysia, had initially only planned to finish her study in Australia and then return, as her older sisters had done and as her parents expected her to do. But her timeline for return and concurrently for settling down became indefinitely stretched when she decided to apply for an 18-month post-study visa so she could continue a relationship she had started at university. The eventual breakdown of this relationship temporarily suspended Abigail's decision making about her mobility. The relationship, her reason for staying, had evaporated, but the embodied emotional inertia of the breakup prevented her from deciding about going back:

> 'I just went into a slump for ages because that didn't work out, the boyfriend didn't work out. ... So, when the relationship ended, I just, I don't know, I didn't want to do anything. I didn't even want to look for a job. I just wanted to just stay at home and just cry, like such a loser. And, yeah, I just wanted to stay home and do nothing or even get out ... I actually did date someone in between that, and when I started dating him is when I actually got the real estate job. So maybe that helped pick me up. And I was like, "Okay, fine, I'll look for a job." And, literally, I applied for three jobs and one of them called me, which was this one. Yeah, but it was, what, a good ten months that I did nothing. Yeah. It was wasting my time.'

Abigail's experiences reflect Gorman-Murray's (2009) observation that relationship breakdowns, as well as formations, can have significant implications for mobility as well as immobility. The emotional stasis that followed her break-up was an embodied experience that affected the tempo of Abigail's daily routine as she stopped going out and avoided applying for jobs, an inertia that is familiar in many narratives of recovery from heartbreak. However, under a transified migration time-regime, this 'wasted time' also constituted a risky ten-month suspension of the expected sequence of Abigail's post-study transitions. Her post-break-up inertia used up a significant chunk of her 485 visa time period, a stage during which most young migrants intend to build up employment experience and save money before they either return 'home' or seek employer sponsorship for permanent visas. A brief new relationship was the trigger out of this state of suspension and Abigail found the real estate position described in Chapter 3. Abigail, in her mid-twenties when interviewed, was reflective about the crucial role that the timings of intimate partnerships, their beginnings, endings and possible futures had played in her mobility decisions. The indentured time at work that she experienced was something she endured primarily for the sake of the continuation of her current relationship:

'But I think the things that affected me the most was my romantic relationships. I think they're the ones that made me stay. Even this one that I'm in now. Remember how I said before that I was in a job role that I didn't want to stay? I could have easily just picked up my stuff and gone, but ... I was in a relationship with him. That's why I didn't go, yeah. ... Touch wood if anything did happen, like if my parents at home were sick. I think, yes, I would pack up my stuff and go, and that would definitely affect, you know – if anything happened right now, being so close to getting my permanent residency, that would be a real struggle, figuring out should I go back and look after my mum or, you know [stay with my boyfriend]?'

For Abigail, as for many of the young migrants in the study, emplacement within Australia for specific time periods – their immobility – is crucial to achieving migration security. Yet the time-regime that requires staying put for certain periods to achieve permanent legal status often cannot synchronize with the unplannable events of intimate lives, whether falling in and out of love, or parents getting sick and requiring care. As relatively well-resourced, middle-class young people, my interlocutors all had the privilege of being able to pack up and go relatively instantaneously if their circumstances changed. Such decisions, however, although possible, were rarely easy.

Hyon-Woo, whose story is described in Chapter 1, experienced the very situation Abigail feared – her mother's cancer diagnosis coincided with the processing of her PR, a period in which she was meant to remain in Australia. Hyon-Woo's temporary return to Korea to care for her mother put her application in jeopardy, which in turn placed her future in Australia with her partner Peter at risk. Intimate relationships under a transified migration time-regime become a constant series of 'what ifs' and 'touch woods', a process of complex shuffling of the sequence between pasts, present and futures as migrants try to plan around the unplannable events of intimate lives and the precarities of their legal capacities to stay.

"Not now, maybe later": extended singlehood

As illustrated in the previous section, intimate partnerships affect the timings of mobility, but mobility also conversely transforms the possibilities of intimate timelines. The most common narrative among my interlocuters of mobility reconfiguring intimate temporalities involved moving to Australia becoming a suspension of the timeline towards marriage, and thus a stretching out of periods of singlehood and relative autonomy. While individualized or 'do-it-yourself' biographies of intimacy, family and sexuality, described in the work of Giddens (1991), reflect the social condition of hegemonic flexibility, for most of my middle-class Asian interlocutors such 're-doings' of intimate sequencing and transitions occurred only around the edges of relatively fixed senses of the 'acceptable' intimate life-course. Marriage, for example, remained largely perceived by migrants and their families as a natural part of the life-course, an end goal of youthful endeavours and necessary to achieve adulthood. These sequential imaginaries embed marriage and family formation as unavoidable milestones in the life-course. Such imaginaries remain particularly unmalleable for young women, for whom normative life-course temporalities dictate singlehood as 'waiting' or 'being late' (Leccardi, 2005), a transitional state that awaits a future 'completeness' only possible through marrying and having children (Ramdas, 2012).

In this context, many of the young migrants in this study, particularly but not exclusively women, felt that time spent in Australia offered what Martin (2018) has identified as 'zones of suspension' – liminal space-times that can function to delay marriage and family formation, but also, at least temporarily, rescript some of the norms of intimate (and gendered) behaviours and practices.

Many of the young women I met during this research were consciously reflective of how distance from familial and cultural norms allowed for decelerations of tempo in the pathway towards the inevitability of married life. Participants often pointed out during our discussions how their lives had, intentionally or unintentionally, deviated from expected schedules around marriage due to coming to or staying in Australia. Abigail, for example, described herself as having "deviated" from what is "supposed to be" by remaining in Australia, but sees the rerouting of her life as temporary; despite the lack of clarity around her future, she believes she will eventually return to the prescribed path, both in terms of returning to her home country and in terms of marrying and having children:

> 'Usually you'd stay until the 18-month visa is done and then you go back, but it's – it had deviated a little bit. Like, my sister, she did that. She came here, she studied, she went back, got married, had the kid. You know, that's what it's supposed to be. But I'm still going back and I'm still going to have the kid. That's my plan. I don't know what happens, but yeah, so I'm still going along those lines, and that's my story!'

Colleen and Vera, both from China and in their late twenties, enjoyed their single lives in Australia but noted that their ongoing singlehood was a rupture from a normative life sequence – a rupture made possible by their distance from families and peers. Colleen was certain that if she had stayed in China she would already have married and started a family. She could envision this alternative, immobile present through the life of her cousin in China:

> 'I can see that from my cousin. She's only one year younger than me. Yeah, like she – I know if I didn't come to Australia then I would be like her. Kids, and with work, several jobs. … Yeah, compared to what I am now, yeah. It would be different. There would be pressure to get married [in China]. … It can be as earlier as 22, 23 now. The general assumption is by 27, 28, get married. …] [I'm] still looking but you just don't want to be pressured to get married with the wrong person. At my own pace.'

Vera similarly compared her single life with the lives of her friends of the same age back in China, from whom she felt she was growing increasingly distanced over time as their life-courses diverged:

> 'But most of [my friends in China] have already married or have kids. Because in China you do what everybody else is doing. By my age, I'm 26-and-a-half, some of my friends have already got babies. Because in China you have to otherwise you're strange, you're "left-out woman". "What's wrong with you? You don't love boys, are you lesbian?" My parents would be worried.'

For these young women, being in Australia suspends the pressure to marry at the 'right' time. Unlike Hyon-Woo, for whom staying in Australia enabled the choice not to marry or have children at all (see Chapter 1), these women still plan to eventually marry and have families. But their mobility has enabled a temporary rupture, a suspension from the norm, and a chance to extend their singlehood and delay the transition to married life – a chance to live, as Colleen notes, a different tempo of the life-course, setting their own pace for their intimate lives. While this has desynchronized their lives from those of their immobile relatives and peers, and from the expectations of their parents, the social pressure from family and community is somewhat diffused by their mobility. While in China, for example, Vera would be a "left-out woman", living in Australia affords a liminal space-time where her extended singlehood is, if not entirely legitimized, at least somewhat destigmatized.

As Martin (2018) and Ramdas (2012) have noted, for transnationally mobile young women such experiences are not just about an extended period of singlehood but also about different ways to be single and to explore intimate relationships before marriage. This seemed to be an experience most prevalent in the interviews conducted with migrants from China and India, who were more likely to specifically mention taboos around cohabitation and pre-marital relationships "back home". Casual dating or living with a partner before marriage became possibilities that could be explored with mobility. Many, like Saji, chose not to disclose the nature of their intimate lives to their parents until the time was right. Most agreed, however, that whenever they disclosed their relationships, the distance ameliorated some of the social repercussions. Shukti, for example, in her early thirties when we spoke, said:

'So when I was in India, say for example having a boyfriend is probably – I'm sorry, that's how it was. But these days it's changing. … My cousins have boyfriends. … But you [still] can't go to your parents, "I have a boyfriend." As opposed to in Australia, I can do whatever I like and tell my parents [when I want to]. Whether they agree or not, it's not going to affect me because I'm so far away. Freedom. Actually I forgot to mention, it's all about freedom and you can use it in a good or bad way. So I think I have this freedom and I think I've used it in the right way, the right path. For positive changes. But I wouldn't say I'd be having that much freedom back home.'

For many of my interlocutors, like Shukti, it was seldom a simplistic duality of one culture of appropriate pre-marital intimacy back home and another away. Instead, they tended to note that attitudes to pre-marital dating or cohabitation were already slowly changing in their home cultures. They see themselves not just as individuals but as a generation, part of a larger transformation of social norms, a transition to different ways of thinking about intimate lives within their cultures and families. What being in Australia allows is a speeding up of this transition, especially within their own families – distance ameliorates the friction of social acceleration in the sense that it cushions both the migrant and their families from the direct social repercussions of young people exploring more flexible pre-marital intimate lives. For some of my interlocutors, this was not simply 'time out' or a time-delimited period of exploration, but a way to transform their lives and practices around intimacy in the long term.

Increased autonomy was not the only outcome of these chronomobilities of suspending rather than settling. Mobility's often disruptive logics of sequence (particularly the contingent careers described in Chapter 3) also wrought unwanted frictions or delays to intimate transitions to adulthood. For example, several men I spoke with mentioned the difficulty of synchronizing career security (understood as a precursor for men to marriage) with 'appropriate' marriage timings.

Kun Woo, for example, who had been in a relationship with his long-term partner since high school, explained how he had to navigate the temporal 'age limits' for marriage in Korean society alongside his insecure employment. Having left Korea to do his master's degree in Australia, he was yet to have a stable career, and although he and his partner both wanted to settle in Australia, they were still on temporary visas. While Kun Woo, in his early thirties when we met, felt that the time pressure to be married by a specific age was more pressing for his partner, as a woman, the pressure was on him to have achieved the transition to a stable career as a breadwinner prior to asking her to marry him.

> 'We met first time when we were high school students so we continue maintaining our relationship for nearly ten years. It was about a time that we need to get married. In Korea there is a kind of age limit, invisible age limit, that you have to get married at this age. That's 30 for women. So once you go over 30s that is a kind of perception, you have a bad perception about the woman. Because we are the same age the time when I complete my master's we'd come to 30. But the one problem was that when Koreans get married they must have a job. That's also a kind of invisible requirement. The one reason that I was reluctant was that I was a student and I cannot really ask my wife to go with me in this uncertain future. At least I want to show her what would happen next year but at the time of our marriage I could not even say what will happen within a few months. But she was okay with that. She said for the last ten years it was not different at all. So now is the time we can get together to make this uncertain future. We go together for the future.'

It was Kun Woo's partner who encouraged him to rethink what the temporality of settling down as a married couple could mean in the context of hegemonic flexibility, particularly the "uncertain future" of both their employment prospects and migration goals. Her response was that they had tackled such uncertainty in the past, as an unmarried couple, and that they should "go together" into an uncertain future. She understood their sequential progress through intimate milestones as a couple as not contingent on economic security or spatial fixity, seeing the future instead as something they could make together.

Percy, whose career ups and downs opened Chapter 3, similarly felt pressure to have financial and job security before he felt he could form a serious relationship. He recounted that he was, in fact, delaying 'acting' on some interest in women he knew, feeling like life events needed to be sequenced in a specific way – career first, then the chance to buy a home and settle down with a woman with a similar level of education and a good career. The delays to his career pathway

Figure 5.2: Kun Woo

Kun Woo walked past this street sign in Brisbane on his way to work. He found the name memorable. The image also resonated with his story because his relationship with his wife and the birth of his baby daughter had been so significant to his sense of direction in life.

described in Chapter 3 meant, for Percy, a synchronous delay in acting on goals for a relationship, adjourning his romantic interests into an indefinite future time:

> 'Even though I have the girls actually I'm interested into, but I still worry about some other factors, so I really don't want to act now; maybe later ... because I think personally what I believe is like career is always the first and foremost for a gentleman, right. So, without an appropriate career or a job, it's rather difficult for you, first of all to buy a decent house, because your income couldn't be increased if your work is not good enough. Secondly, definitely it's difficult to find the girl who's in the same level as you.'

For young men like Percy, the delay of intimate transitions to adulthood and the extension of single life was not framed by autonomy of pace as it was for his female counterparts like Colleen and Vera. Rather, 'settling down' in terms of a committed intimate partnership was intrinsically a logic of synchronicity as well as of sequence, existing in parallel not only with 'settling' into adult life but also with 'settlement' in terms of reaching secure belonging as a migrant.

Delays in one trajectory through time, such as career building, cascaded into indefinite suspension of other areas of adult 'arrival' such as relationship formation. Percy also felt that his extended singlehood delayed becoming truly 'at home' in Perth. Although he had accumulated many memories and formative experiences in the West Australian capital, planned to remain living there into the future, and had achieved PR, Percy stated that only a relationship and a family could make the city truly become his "second home":

> 'Perth has been bringing me many unforgettable and memorable experiences, but I'm still alone here. Probably if I have a girlfriend or get married and I established my own family maybe I would regard Perth as my second home, but anyway all in all my real home is still back in China.'

Anastasia, who features in Chapters 3 and 4, had a similar sense that settling down into an intimate partnership was inextricably intertwined with settling into place. Despite her relative migration security via her employer sponsorship for PR and her sense of local belonging in her daily life in Rockhampton, her relationship with her boyfriend, which was facing some difficulties at the time of her first interview, left her feeling still unsettled and uncertain overall about her future in Australia:

> 'Even now I still feel a bit uncertain about what's going to happen in the future. Yeah, I think that this is a very big thing, for not just me but I believe for a lot of other people who come to Australia, they have this feeling all the time, they're always moving. We enjoy living here in Australia, but like actually settling down is a very, like it's another level for us. ... I think work-wise is okay, but for me personally I would say it's because, like, me and my boyfriend were not looking, we're not talking about like getting married. So I think that is also one thing affect me. I would say probably other people, if they have a very stable relationship and they already have a plan in the future of getting married, probably will help them to settle down a bit more. But for me just sort of affect a little bit.'

Settling, then (imagined as the temporal and spatial stabilization of 'flexible' and 'mobile' lives), represents multiple and interrelated endpoints for many of these young migrants – the establishment of a committed relationship or marriage, the arrival of adulthood, and a transition into established emotional belonging in place. Settling down into a relationship marks not only adulthood but also belonging as a migrant, the end of youthful, open-ended mobility and ambivalence, and is thus a symbolic, if not actual, process of settling into place. When such intimate settling down is delayed, belonging remains elusive, regardless of the official temporal security of migration status.

"I took it as my duty": transnational symbolic care as time investment

Despite reconfigurations around the timings and meanings of settling down into marriage, and despite the fact that most married couples were separated from natal families, after marriage the formalization of spouse positions into transnational families meant new demands on women's time. Practices and performances of desirable 'daughter-in-law-hood' were discussed in many of the interviews and were described as extremely important for women to establish and demonstrate their position in their husband's families. These practices involved dedicating time to symbolic care that often had to be orchestrated across transnational space. As members of the middle class, my interlocutors' parents and parents-in-law were mostly financially secure, and as my interlocutors were young adults, their parents were also relatively young and mostly in good health. Traditional practices of filial care from children to parents – such as sending remittances or providing materially in other ways – were seldom required, reflecting, as Tu (2016) suggests, that in middle-class Asian transnational families, there are changing dynamics of intergenerational care in the context of modernization and globalization that often circulate around symbolic or affective care practices, rather than material ones. Transnational, symbolic care practices were highly gendered in my discussions with participants, firmly seen to be the duty of women rather than men, and especially in terms of a woman's relationship with her husband's parents. What mattered most here was 'investing time' in various 'duties' that, rather than providing practical forms of care, demonstrated symbolically that women were 'good' daughters-in-law.

Because of physical separation from families, symbolic care had to be performed transnationally, or conducted intensely over the fixed period of the visit home. Anik's parents, for example, were unhappy with his engagement to his fiancée whom he had met in Australia. Although she was also Indian, she was from a different caste and a family that they did not know. Anik's parents would not give their blessing until his fiancée, Priya, flew from Australia to his family's home in Dubai and lived with his parents for a month, performing daily mundane duties of making tea and snacks and chatting with his mother, and helping to run the household. There was no practical need for Priya to perform these tasks. Rather, her symbolic investment of time into performing daughter-in-law-hood, even for this transient period, was required for Anik's parents to support the marriage.

Carolyn and Ji-Min, both from Korea, also spoke extensively about the difficulties of sustaining filial duties as daughters-in-law at a distance, and how they had to invest time into performative acts of care both in Australia and when they visit Korea. Carolyn said she seldom enjoys visits back to Korea when they stay with her husband's family, especially during festivals, when she is confined to the house all day with traditional domestic duties, barely able to go to the toilet because she is given so much to do:

> 'I couldn't have much chance to meet my friends, because I had to stay in my parents-in-law's house because maybe you can't understand like our culture but in-laws it's a bit too much rules, lots of pressure on me, the woman who marry. ... Like New Year's Day or occasions, I'm going to work from morning to night. There is not much break, right. ... My parents-in-law, they don't need [this help], but [I have] much obligations. ... So one week I couldn't use the bath that much stress, yeah I couldn't. [Although they are] very kind and friendly to me and I think they're much better than the others ... but still they own the culture, so I want to help, because we only visit sometimes. ... So when I get there home just myself from morning half past five I had to get up and start with the cooking and altogether with the woman. Guys, boys don't have to. Many people around house like big families he has, so aunties, and uncles and all the cousins around, I can't go to the toilet!'

While Carolyn's in-laws do not require care in a practical sense most of the time, when Carolyn is in Korea for special events such as significant holidays and festivals, she must perform care through highly gendered domestic duties that take up her entire day. Carolyn's sense of duty and obligation is heightened by the fact that she is not often there – because she and her partner only visit "sometimes" she had a limited and intense period of time in which to fulfil her obligations.

Ji-Min's experiences similarly outline a sense of reconfigured temporalities of care that stretch beyond both the practical and the tangible and across space. Ceremonial duties in honouring her husband's family's ancestors (*jesa*) fall to Ji-Min under traditional Korean kinship traditions, and, as Ji-Min explains, she has had to reconfigure these duties in terms of both proximity and spatiality, but also in terms of her own sense of their meaning as an investment of her time:

> 'I think I need to mention the duty as a family member, I mean as a daughter-in-law. Yes because I don't know if you know but in Korea we have some family, like in the memory of the ancestors and it's a really big duty of the in-law and I'm the only one. I mean, yes because my husband has only two sisters. So it really goes out of the duties, the only son is the duty bearer, and not the son, the daughter-in-law. So I always feel like, I don't know I feel sorry to my husband's family because. ... Anyway the moving to Australia it was because of me, not my husband, so they had to be apart for a long time and I cannot fully do my duties as daughter-in-law. ... So actually took the duty so I can do it in Australia now but still, but it's the thing because possibly I don't think it's a very important thing. I mean, spending time to prepare the all luxury food which should be wasted later. So I don't quite feel it's very important but it's important for my husband and my family-in-law. So I took it as my duty, yes. [But] I think one of the meaningful in that is gathering family. But here there is no point, it's just us, so it's just to, just I suppose a formality thing, but yes. So if I think of the family and family-in-law, yes I feel sometimes guilty.'

Ji-Min still performs her duties at a distance while in Australia. Yet, her relationship to these performative and ritualistic types of care (which involve preparing and displaying food for ancestors) is ambivalent; she finds it hard to reconcile the time spent on these duties with the fact there is no proximate family to 'gather'. While Ji-Min feels that without the actual co-present shared time with family there is "no point" in spending time on these ceremonies and they are merely "a formality thing", they remain an important part of the mediation of her relationship with her in-laws and the amelioration of her guilt at living away from them. This is a particularly acute and distinctly gendered set of negotiations for Ji-Min because the decision to come to Australia was in the interests of her own career, rather than that of her husband, who travelled with her as a dependent spouse. She

Figure 5.3: Ji-Min

The food laid out for Ji-Min's *jesa* ceremony to honour family ancestors.

feels guilt that her husband and his family "had to be apart for a long time", and so time spent on symbolic care is invested to try to make up for the desynchronization of intergenerational family life caused by their migration.

Sponsored love: unmappable intimacy and transforming families

In the Australian context, as in several settler nations globally, migrants' intimate partnerships intertwine with settlement in distinctly material as well as symbolic ways. Capacities for im/mobility (arriving, staying, leaving, returning) are often legally embedded into intimate partnerships. While other migration regimes globally directly prohibit temporary migrants from forming relationships, reunifying with partners or having reproductive autonomy (see, for example, Huang and Yeoh's [1996, 2003] work on Singapore or Mahdavi's [2016] work on the United Arab Emirates), the relative privilege that middling migrants in Australia experience includes legal provisions that generally allow couples and families to remain together. With the exception of working holiday visas, most temporary visas in Australia, including student visas, allow dependent spouses and children to enter Australia and remain temporarily on the basis of their relationship with a primary visa holder. These policy arrangements allowed David and Carolyn, as described in the Introduction, to 'take turns' studying as the primary visa holder and working as the dependent spouse. Partner category visas within the family migration stream also allow partners of Australian citizens and permanent residents (married or *de facto*) to enter and remain permanently in Australia and are inclusive of non-heterosexual couples. Initially, partners are granted a temporary visa, and then a permanent visa following an eligibility period. The couple must demonstrate that they have been in a *de facto* relationship for at least 12 months before the visa application is made. Domestic im/ mobilities are often crucially shaped by this policy, as living together and joint household responsibility is a key criterion that defines a *de facto* relationship for immigration purposes. In 2016/17, 47,825 permanent visas were granted in the partner category, making up 85.1% of the total family stream, and comprising 43,896 spouse and 3,929 fiancé visas. This is a 7% increase on the previous year. Furthermore, the application pipeline as at 30 June 2017 was 71,523 clients (DHA, 2017). As such, partner visas make up a significant segment of the overall migration intake and have been rising in recent years with the increasing circulation of young people both into and out of Australia.

Obtaining partner visas was a reality faced by many of my interlocutors, when, as in Saji's case, they formed a partnership with an Australian resident or citizen or when they themselves achieved residency and could then act as a sponsor for a partner. Of the migrants I interviewed, nearly half had either stayed in Australia via a partner visa, or sponsored a partner once they got PR. In these cases, couples' intimate timelines and timings had to align with the requirements of migration governance as 'couple rhythms of lives and livelihoods' had to be 'synchronized with bureaucratic typologies' (Wagner, 2014: 89) as well as with familial and cultural expectations. Various intimate dependencies and contingencies develop in these cases of 'sponsored love', as the securing of a migration future becomes deeply relational and both legally and symbolically dependent on the future continuation of an intimate partnership. In the second half of this chapter, I focus on the chronomobilities of 'sponsored love', revealing how partner visa sponsorships transform participants' understandings of synchronicity, tempo and sequence. Here, I show how the negotiated, relational nature of temporality encircles not only migrants and their partners but also their families, in particular their parents, as couples navigate the decisions and consequences of partner visa sponsorship.

"They want to cling on to whatever you've got": aligning intimate futures and mobility futures

For many middling migrants, the very possibility of sponsored love transforms the temporal experience of the romantic encounter or relationship under the time-regime of transification. Living within and embodying the temporal state of transification – being transient, in transition, and in transit – creates a logic of sequence around intimacy that is unable to place a relationship, or even a first date, entirely in the present. Colleen, for example, who was single and dating but not in a relationship, reflected on how temporary visa statuses complicate the formation of relationships, as romantic futures via commitment become entangled with migration uncertainties and consequent anxieties about dependency or hidden agendas:

> 'On the one hand, I just feel like the residency's like a passport. If you don't get it, then it will restrict you in a lot of ways: employment and in relationships as well, because it's hard for you to meet someone and then they would assume that you approach them for some purpose. [If you have PR] yeah, you just feel like you're on the equal ground, not rely on them to be here and it's just equal. ... I met someone who is here on a working holiday visa, and he was scared to commit, to be committed, because how to put it ... I just think if both ... it's better to be with someone that they're both permanent resident or citizen. It's more equal.'

Abigail also noted how transification radically transforms the immediacy of meeting someone and starting a new relationship from a set of open future possibilities to a set of anxieties about mobility dependence, a situation that a citizen or permanent resident would never have to consider:

> 'I think being on a visa, a lot of the times, when you meet someone else from a different visa situation, you always think, "Oh my God, they're going to be with you because they want to cling on to whatever you've got." And that's so crazy, because any Australian would not – that's not the first – you meet someone and you go, "Oh my God, you want my visa." Like, you don't think that.'

Most of my interlocutors were, like Saji, very wary of the pathway of sponsored love as a means to permanence. Partner visas were often considered only as a "last resort" if other options to stay did not work out or were prohibitively expensive. For example, despite Abigail's narrative of her mobility decisions as driven primarily by her love life, she was extremely reluctant for her current relationship to become formally implicated in immigration bureaucracy. Once her PR was approved, Abigail would be in a position to sponsor her boyfriend, who was also a temporary migrant. But she was thoroughly relieved when he was instead able to independently find sponsorship through his work:

> 'He's [my boyfriend] also being sponsored by his work now, and yeah, he's lucky he got that. It was very close to his end date, but yeah, he got it on his own, so we didn't have to do that [a partner visa] which I definitely did not want. I didn't say that, but yeah, it would have been, like, the last, last resort. ... That's, like, pretty much committing to someone for as long as they get their visa, but it's scary to know that – I guess knowing that you've got someone else's life based on you, you know, if we ended up breaking up or I left or suddenly we had this fight and, okay, well what happens to this visa? You know, we're breaking up and, yeah, that's why I didn't want it. I didn't want to have that in my mind, you know, "I can't break up with him because he's still got that visa." And I'm like that, so I know that I didn't want to do that, yeah.'

As Abigail notes, sponsoring can affect the sponsoring partner's autonomy to leave a relationship when they wish, because you come to have 'someone else's life based on you.' In Chapters 3 and 4, sponsored work visas 'fixed' migrants in space and in a state of suspended time in relation to where they worked and where they lived. Similarly, sponsored love has the risky future potential to 'fix' the time period of an intimate relationship and reduce autonomy over its temporal boundaries.

Future dependency can be equally concerning for sponsored as well as sponsoring partners, and couples may have to radically reframe the pace of their intimate commitments to align with migration timings. Camilla, for example, had met her boyfriend Ted when they were high school classmates in Taiwan, and they started dating when they were at university. They had not been together long when Ted's family migrated permanently to Australia. Camilla had always planned to study overseas anyway, so although the relationship was not yet very serious, she decided to "give it a try" by coming to Australia for graduate studies, deferring the question of staying (in terms of both Australia and the relationship) for the future. Camilla described the open-endedness of this initial decision to come to Australia, where the timelines of the relationship and the mobility were both still provisional and ambivalent:

> 'It's kind of just, "Give it a try", because we start our relationship in 2010, but since then I already knew he would come over there. At that time, I thought it's no point if we're going to have a distance relationship, so I just thought, "Oh, okay. Since I planned to study abroad, why not give it a try, like try Australia? Maybe it's a good choice; you never know." Yeah, so that's how I think about, yeah.'

Camilla's graduate programme was only one-and-a-half years long. She was, therefore, unlike some of the interviewees who arrived as students, not eligible for a temporary graduate visa, which requires a minimum of two years of prior study in Australia. With her student visa expiring at graduation, Camilla and Ted's romance could not simply continue to unfold at an uncontrolled pace. Decisions about how serious they were could not be deferred if they did not want to become an indefinitely long-distance couple. The looming 'paper border' (Rajkumar et al, 2012) of Camilla's student visa expiry brought the discussion of their future as a couple abruptly into the present, and the pace of their commitment was accelerated as they discussed the possibility of applying for a partner visa so she could stay. Camilla wanted to continue their relationship, but was uncomfortable about what the intimate acceleration of visa sponsorship might symbolize – a commitment to a future for which she wasn't sure they were ready:

> 'Kind of like we have to review our relationship and then to justify like how deep we want or how long we want to keep going … I feel like I don't really know what to do. I do want to stay and also keep the relationship, and so me and my boyfriend – we've discussed about this for several times. Just want to make sure, I say, "Hey, what if? What if? We have to think about it." And when we applied [for the visa], when I applied that, I was only 24. It was quite young, and I just told him, "Listen, like we don't have to be the only one for each other, so what if we broke up one day?"'

Migration governance pulled multiple potential futures – of staying together, of breaking up, of other possible relationships – into Camilla and Ted's present, and Camilla was forced to choose between pre-emptively accelerating her commitment to Ted or pre-emptively ending the relationship and returning to Taiwan. The emotional complexity of sponsored love thus circulates around the potentially asynchronous time-logics of intimate futures and mobility futures in the lives of transnationally mobile young people. The ongoing dependence and fixed futures that partner visa sponsorship embodies sit in an uneasy relation to the unmappability of youthful intimate relationships, which cannot always be determined in the present moment as either transient or ongoing.

"They had all of their concerns": negotiating parents, partners and visas

As Saji's story at the opening of this chapter suggests, decision making on sponsored love involves not only couples, but their families, in particular their parents, who often provide both emotional care (in the form of advice and support) as well as financial assistance for their young adult children as they negotiate these relationships. Many of my interlocutors spoke frequently about the influence of their parents and parents-in-law when narrating the stories of their intimate partnerships, reflecting the middling position of these migrants as temporally transitioning in between dependence on the natal family and the formation of their own independent lives and potentially their own nuclear families. As 'emergent adults', they remain still connected to natal families in two-way intergenerational patterns of reciprocity. They are often dependent to some extent on practical and symbolic support from their parents in managing their life transitions while on the move, but are also aware of the shifting sequencing of intergenerational dependency – the ways in which their parents could now or in the near future be dependent on them or require their care, due to ageing or illness.

At the same time as maintaining these relations of intergenerational reciprocity across space and time, these migrants were also moving through processes of forming adult households and relationships, sometimes across multiple spaces and cultures. My framing of middling mobility as encapsulating a life-course position in between different sets of current and future familial relations and roles seeks to counter the tendency to separate discussions of parent–child relations from discussions of intimate partner relations under conditions of transnationalism and mobility. Parent–child relations and intimate partner relations are, I argue, deeply and temporally entangled. Marriage or other serious romantic attachments are not only about entering adulthood and deciding on one's future, but also constitute a 'process where notions of identity and belonging are negotiated within local and transnational family' (Rytter, 2012: 572). I thus explore here how the reconfiguring of temporalities of intimacy within situations of sponsored love is a process negotiated around the relations of young migrants with both partners and parents. While Rytter (2012) argues that transnational young people often decide to marry against the preferences of their parents as an act of 'symbolic mobility' that orients their futures towards the host country, my middling migrant participants instead walked a more complicated path of mediating and reconciling their parents' concerns and wishes with their own anxieties about their romantic settlings in Australia.

In Camilla's case, for example, her concerns about the acceleration of her relationship timeline were not just about her and Ted as a couple. Both her parents in Taipei and Ted's parents in Melbourne featured in her worries about the visa sponsorship and what it would mean. Camilla's mother was concerned that the young couple could be moving too fast and that it was risky for Camilla to tie her future in Australia to her relationship with Ted. Camilla recounted her mother telling her, "You don't need to rely on men to stay in Australia Camilla!" To which Camilla replied, "Yeah, of course. I don't want to – I'm not that kind of person." Ted's parents' attitudes to the visa sponsorship were also a concern for Camilla, because she felt the visa tied her future not only to Ted, but also to his family:

'And even one day if we broke up, I don't want them to feel I'm using them. Even his parents. But it's really hard to … to say, like in the future. I mean, you can't really control other people's thought, you know, so it's a bit hard for me at that time. … But I said, "How about your parents? You are not the one who start to move to Australia. That was your father, and we couldn't really control what they said [if we broke up]." And he said he's sure his parents say something really bad. If they did, he said, we already broke up and we won't listen to each other, then that's fine.'

Much like Saji, Camilla's worries circulated around the stigma of visa sponsorship, of the bad things Ted's parents might think of her if the relationship broke up in the future, of how they could assume they had been 'used' by Camilla for the visa. The concern not to be "that kind of person" – the kind of person who uses romance instrumentally for a migration outcome – is a concern that, for middling migrants, is implicitly classed. In Taiwan, as in other parts of wealthy East Asia like South Korea and Japan, 'foreign brides' are primarily poorly educated, rural women from Southeast Asia, seeking economic security through transnational marriage. Such forms of migration sit outside the expected life trajectory for middle-class, educated, urban women like Camilla, whose transnational mobility is supposed to centre around the accumulation of capital via educational and career success rather than dependence on a spouse. Camilla was especially concerned that Ted's father, who had initiated his own family's migration to Australia, would see Camilla's visa as tied to his own history and future, not just his son's. Anchoring her own future migration security into Ted's family's migration past creates, for Camilla, potential patterns of indebtedness and obligation, and shapes her future relationship as a daughter-in-law as well as a spouse. Here, the sequencing logic of Camilla's own mobility biography becomes relational and entangled with multiple future relationships – with Ted, with his parents, and with her own parents.

Negotiating these relationships was further complicated by the fact that, after they had decided to go ahead with the partner visa, Camilla lived with Ted and his family in Australia for three years. Despite a shared Taiwanese background, Camilla found living with Ted's family difficult, as their cultural and religious practices were different from those of her own family: "I think in general my family is very open-minded and his family is very conservative. His father is very religious – Buddhist. So the first year was pretty hard." Camilla's migration status within a transified migration regime structured her domestic immobility during this period. She had to live with Ted for one year to meet requirements for a partner visa, as Australian immigration criteria classify *de facto* relationships for immigration purposes through modern Western norms of intimate cohabitation – that is, sleeping together in the same room within a shared residence. But Camilla's temporary visa made finding full-time employment difficult, which meant that financially she and Ted could not afford to live independently. Camilla described how she and Ted thus had to negotiate their own ideas of domestic intimacy, Ted's parents' expectations, and their anxieties about immigration criteria, which were all based on radically different norms of domestic intimacy for their relationship stage as a committed but unmarried couple:

'I was worried. ... We were thinking maybe they [immigration authorities] will visit our house and check, "Where do you sleep" and something like that, yep. But one of the difficulty for us is seeing as we live with his parents – yeah, and we are not married. For them, we are not married. We still think we are not married, but you know, like for us we are very younger and we don't mind like sleep together and something like that. But there's no – it doesn't work like that.'

Q: 'So you were in separate rooms at his parents' house?'

A: 'Yes. And even like the closet and everything was separate. And until one of the friend, he told us, "Come on guys. It's not like that here in Australia. You guys – yeah, yeah, of course. It's all right for you, for your family, but it doesn't work here. You have to let the [immigration] officer know you guys are together." So one of the trick things we did is I moved all my closet with his closet together. ... So we just put everything in a smaller room to make it [look] like we sleep like that.'

A number of logics of lived time come in to play in such experiences. The first is how Camilla's position within a transified time-regime of migration affected the sequential progression of her and Ted's domestic lives as a young couple. Migration conditions and requirements structured a 'stuckness' as Camilla and Ted spent three years in a less-than-ideal living situation, experiencing a delay in their progress towards autonomy as a couple with their own home. In some ways, such compromises of intimate and domestic life reflect the indentured times described in Chapter 3 in relation to migrants' careers. Second, there is an intergenerational friction or asynchronicity at play, as the expectations of Ted's father as part of an older and more conservative generation clashed with Camilla and Ted's own attitudes as younger people of the same cultural background. Third, specific temporalities of governance structured Camilla's anxieties about their living arrangements. The criteria of long-term cohabitation established by the state (and the cultural norm that defines this as 'sleeping together') combined in Camilla's mind with the state's capacity for constant and immediate surveillance. This surveillance was embodied, for Camilla, in the fear that immigration agents could visit the house at any time to check where they were sleeping and that this could lead to Camilla's instantaneous deportation.

Such frictions of family, governance and autonomy in the making of adult futures mattered considerably to couples, whether, like Ted and Camilla, they were currently in Australia together, or whether they were living separately and waiting to reunite. Diana, from India, was in her early twenties and working as a nurse in Melbourne on a temporary work visa after finishing her nursing degree. She was in a long-distance relationship with her boyfriend, whom she had met during a return visit to India. Diana's future mobility plans were heavily influenced by her boyfriend's own mobility intentions and desires. He wanted to join her in Australia, and if Diana achieved PR she could sponsor him on a partner visa. Yet, their options for a future together were constrained not only by the uncertainty of Diana's PR outcome, but also by gendered family ideologies. In our interview, Diana spoke at length about the problems she and her female friends faced from their parents if they wanted to 'lead' couple migration by sponsoring their male partners:

> 'I'll just be happy if I get my PR. I'll be at ease like I don't know. With my boyfriend he keeps saying that he's not going to like come into the country through me, he wants to prove to my parents that he can do it by himself. Like I don't really care, it's like I [would] bring [him] in through marriage but we don't plan to any time soon that's maybe in another four, five years. That's not a priority. ... I have another friend she's been in long relationship for maybe six years now, and her boyfriend's back in Delhi, they got engaged this year when she went back, she goes back. She's so lucky she has dual citizenships, and her dad's like, "You can't get married till he gets a full-time job", it's so hard because in his field, he's doing engineering but the type of engineering he's doing they don't really need that in Australia, so he doesn't know what he's going to do, and her dad's like, "He can't come through you."'
>
> Q: 'Why is that?'
> A: 'I don't know, I feel dads are really protective, possessive. I think they feel that the guy's trying to use the girl to get in and that's the first thing when I told my dad about my boyfriend, he said, "Oh he wants to get to Australia." I'm like, "Dad can you relax. He's not." Like and when I told my boyfriend he was so upset but he's always said, "I won't come through you then."'

Q: 'So how long do you think you'll be waiting until he's here?'

A: 'So he has two more years of his one and half year's actually, let's say two years of his bachelor's. I want him to come in December but he doesn't really get a long break, and there's no point paying all that money to come for a week. So I'll probably see him next year in June which is annoying, and also I can't go back, because they [immigration authorities] always see like how long you've stayed and I don't want to keep going back, like I want to show them that I'm serious about getting PR here, they can clearly see I've only been back like twice in seven years kind of thing, so I can't really go back. Also with my new job I don't want to just take leave, I don't think it would be good, because I work shift, I get 25 days [annual leave], not 20 but I rather just keep that for next year. If they say, "Use it up", I don't want to just use it up now, and he understands that, he's not pressuring me even though I have two big weddings in the family at the end of the year, so it's annoying I can't go back.'

Diana's narrative highlights a number of ways in which sponsored love's temporalities are reconfigured by mobility decisions that have to be negotiated across the desires and norms of partners, parents and governance, particularly the heavily gendered notions that delegitimize young women's desires to sponsor and therefore reunite with their male partners. While Diana is not planning to get married for another four or five years, she projects to the future via the discussion of her friend, who has recently become engaged after a six-year relationship. Despite being "lucky" to have the privileged flexibility of dual citizenship, Diana's friend remains constrained by gendered familial expectations that she should not sponsor her future husband's migration, thus delaying, and perhaps permanently rupturing, their marriage plans as well as their plans of settlement in Australia. The same gendered expectations drastically affect the sequential timings of Diana's own relationship with her boyfriend. Diana's boyfriend 'not coming through her' via partner sponsorship means that the couple's separation is likely to be significantly extended, as her boyfriend will have to finish his study and then try to qualify for independent skilled migration. The constraints of Diana's present temporary status and her desires for PR in the future also effect patterns of synchronous, proximate time for the couple, their very capacity to share time, over the immediate future. Diana felt limited in how often she could visit her boyfriend, reluctant to make too many trips while her PR outcome was still tenuous. She described her immobility as a way to demonstrate to the state that she is "serious" and committed to PR. Alongside these concerns are the negotiations of other timings – when is it the right time to use up annual leave allocations, for example, or when co-presence at significant family events like weddings can feasibly occur.

Diana and her peers have a series of choices around intimate relationships that are far more expansive than those of previous generations of young, middle-class Indian women – the choice to live independently and study overseas, the choice to spend time building a career before marriage, and the choice to engage in more flexible forms of pre-martial intimacy by having boyfriends. Yet, increasing flexibility combined with the transification of their migration pathways creates a set of dependencies and contingencies that remain heavily gendered and often serve to suspend or delay the movement towards autonomy in their 'coupled futures'.

Intimate timings were also implicated in when and how parents were introduced to partners or indeed even informed about the relationships their children had formed in Australia. Saji's experiences, for example, which opened this chapter, were all about the 'right time' to tell his parents about his relationship. This important revelation became, however, less about a rupture or an event in time and more about a gradual negotiation over time.

When Saji's parents came to visit him, a year after he had moved in with Victoria, the couple unveiled their relationship with a deliberate tempo of slowness, as means to smooth his parents' transition into new understandings of intimacy and of family. An obviously pivotal event in Saji's life, he described his parents' visit to me in some detail:

> 'It was their first trip as well. ... Yeah, but I was really excited about the fact that I was getting that chance to be that child through whom they got to do their first overseas trip, and that was a very proud thing for me. ... And, yeah, so when I picked them up at the airport, picked them up, I was feeling very nervous of how this is all going to happen, but we just went about it so normally. ...
>
> We were just being both nice as good friends would do to them, to my, you know, friends' parents and stuff. We decided that we wouldn't sleep in the same room when the parents were here. ... And we did that pretty much

throughout the whole stay, they stayed here for about a month. It was almost about a week since nobody asked the question of what's happening. ... One day, I think it was dad, he was like ... "So what is happening here? I understand that, you know, this [relationship] is happening, I mean, what are you guys' plans? What are you thinking? What are you doing? How are you going to do it?" So they had all of their concerns, mum was like really sad, a lot sadder than my dad. Sad in the sense of, you know, the whole Indian system of mum and dad getting to choose their son and daughter-in-law for them, choosing a wife for me sort of a thing. ... They feel that that's one of the big responsibilities of their life and then sort of being taken away from them.

But because they'd seen us, the way we had sort of hosted them, had them, I mean, we had like a mix of the Indian hospitality and the things that Victoria could do from the Australian way of things. And they just loved that, they thought it was just an amazing combination of how with they were sort of getting both the worlds that they probably wouldn't get even an Indian wife is the ideal Indian *bahu* as they call it. They probably wouldn't get that over there they were thinking. So that really made them think differently. ...

But by just keeping things normal in terms of, you know, being as hospitable to them as possible, and seeing to it that it's the right food that they eat is being cooked, or that sort of things that we get, that's the thing that we showed them. Victoria makes all these itinerary of things that they are going to see and how she looks after them and all that sort of stuff, is something that they noticed and think like, you know, what world were we living in. ...

I mean we had so many arguments and fights in front of them!... They've seen it all, like when they were here as well. And still they think that, you know, they were quite happy with the way they saw things.'

Saji's parents ultimately accepted his relationship, something he felt could not have occurred if they had not been able to physically visit and to share proximate time over several weeks with him and Victoria as a couple. The timings of the visit were significant across multiple layers of relational temporality. The visit was a significant life event for his parents, their first time outside of India, and Saji demonstrated his transition to adult life by being able to host and facilitate their mobility. The everyday tempos of shared time during the visit also mattered – the organization of activities and itineraries, the preparing of meals, the witnessing of mundane daily affective demonstrations of Saji and Victoria's 'couple-ness' (including their regular arguments). This temporal smoothing, of trying to keep things normal for Saji's parents in terms of routines and rhythms during the visit, allowed their gradual immersion in Saji and Victoria's shared world – and thus their gradual acceptance of Saji and Victoria's relationship. This did not occur, however, without some initial grief, especially from Saji's mother, at being denied the important cultural life event of choosing a wife for her son. In addition, despite a carefully calibrated performance of 'normal time' for his parents' benefit, the month-long visit was, for Saji and Victoria, very much an 'exceptional time' in their lives as a couple. His parents' presence in their home temporarily suspended their ordinary intimate life, as they remained in separate rooms for the duration of the visit, even after the relationship had been revealed and accepted by Saji's mother and father.

Conclusion

Youthful and middle-class transnational mobility is often framed by individualized narratives of self-actualization, capital accumulation or social mobility (Robertson et al, 2018). Yet, intimate relationships, their distinctive temporalities, and the ways these are reconfigured within mobile lives are central to the way young and middling Asian migrants to Australia narrate their experiences of 'becoming adult' under the time-regimes of transification and hegemonic flexibility. Young migrants understand themselves as reflexive subjects who grapple simultaneously with changing social norms across time and space, their own expectations of the sequence and timings of their first adult relationships, and the interplay of both cultural and legal systems that dictate the 'right' kinds of relationship timings and practices for cultural and state legitimacy.

In the previous chapters, migrants' experiences with both work and local place attachments have already highlighted how 'the middle' often comprises a space of oscillation between the freedom to plot new and autonomous futures and the creation of complex patterns of dependence and contingency. This experience of middling mobility also permeates intimate lives and relationships. Romantic partnerships inevitably mean one's own mobility timings and futures become inexorably entangled with another person's – in terms of choices and desires, as well as the possibilities afforded through governance structures. Desires for synchronicity in making relationship and mobility trajectories unfold in sequential alignment over time (for example, first I will get a good job, then I will get PR, then I will get married), are problematic to achieve in practice as the futures of intimate relationships and indeed of migration outcomes are often unmappable.

The lives of the migrants I encountered in the course of the research for this book also reveal how transnational mobility has capacity to elasticize the temporalities of the intimate life-course, accelerating, suspending, stretching or rerouting the timings of relationships and transitions. Transnational mobility can create liminal space–times where more flexibility and freedom in intimate lives and choices are at least temporarily possible. This involves a reconfiguring of logics of sequence in terms of the age one gets married as well as the sequencing of marriage with other life transitions, such as studying, buying homes and building careers. Often, what mobility offers is sequential but also synchronic transformations to intimate temporalities – specifically a suspension or desyncing from the normative, and particularly from the lives of peers and the expectations of families back home.

For many of my interlocutors, especially young women, mobility was often a means to obtain freedom and autonomy over intimate timing and timelines – such as delaying marriage and having a more autonomous period of singlehood. But such affordances to stretch and suspend intimate timelines sit in paradoxical relation to that fact that transification can also force relationships into forms of acceleration or into sustainment beyond their natural endpoint. Permanent residency, then, is a passport not just to migration security, but also to the capacity to form and sustain 'equal' relationships, that is, relationships that can begin and end according to one's own emotional timelines and desires, rather than visas dependencies. Autonomy over beginnings and endings, over staying or moving on, is what becomes comprised in relationships under regimes of transification.

Yet the intimate relationships of these young and in-between subjects, and their temporalities, are influenced by far more than governance structures. The life-stage of the middle that these young mobiles inhabit, floating between dependence on the natal family and the launch of their independent single, coupled or familial futures, means that they are often positioned relationally and generationally in between conflicting sets of norms and obligations. Interactions of 'gender ideologies, cultural expectations and filial obligations' (Yeoh et al, 2018: 416) thus continue to shape the timelines and timings of young migrants' intimate lives, even as they consciously seek to transform such ideologies, expectations and obligations across generations and across distances. The process of such transformations constitutes 'different topological smoothings and frictions' (Wagner, 2014: 83) within lived time as migrants seek to negotiate synchronicity between the desires and expectations of partners, families and the state.

Conclusion

I'm finishing this book in Sydney, just as the celebrations of the 2019 Lunar New Year, the Year of the Pig, are winding down. There have been night noodle markets, dragon boats on the harbour, lion dances in the squares, red lanterns gleaming from the trees in the parks. The airports and train stations have also been crowded. Thousands of Australian residents of East Asian descent travel out of Australia during the festival to celebrate with families and friends elsewhere in the world, but thousands of travellers also arrive in Sydney for the largest celebration of the lunisolar new year outside of China. The buzz of the festival used to be largely confined to Sydney's historic downtown Chinatown, but in recent years it has spread, with events held in outer suburbs and emerging inner-city hubs where East Asian migrants have increasingly settled since the turn of the century. Just as Lunar New Year has come to mark the beginning of the final month of Australian summer, in October, Deepavali, the Hindu festival of lights, will herald the beginning of our southern hemisphere spring. Although less ubiquitous (and perhaps, for now, less commodified) than Sydney's Lunar New Year, the South Asian festival is also increasingly celebrated in pockets across the city with food stalls, Bollywood-style and classical entertainment, and the traditional coloured lights, including in Martin Place, the 'civic heart' of the downtown business district. While Australia has a long history of celebrations of migrant culture, patterned by changing migration demographics since the Second World War, these 21st-century festivals are no longer contained within bounded ethnic communities. Rather, they are enmeshed into a cacophonous and complex urban diversity, celebrated to differing extents and with different layers of meaning by both visitors and locals, whose identities sit within, beyond and between the conventional boundaries of ethnic and diasporic community.

Sydney's Lunar New Year and Deepavali celebrations are gradually becoming engrained into the collective and cyclical temporality of the year, part of the evolving cultural calendar of an Asia–Pacific 'global city'. They involve significant annual collective mobilities of people into, out of and across Sydney to take part in the festivities. Such events represent the synchronicity and multiplicity of temporalities that have emerged in Australia, as in other settler nations globally, through many decades of evolving migration flows. They are emblematic of the possibilities for wider social transformation that emerge from the everyday temporalities and mobilities of the individual lives that have knitted together new transnational networks between Asia and Australia over the past 20 years. Many of the Asian young people who celebrate these festivals across Sydney are, like my interlocutors, often simultaneously both visitors and locals, transients and residents, migrants and 'not yet' or 'not quite' migrants – mobile subjects who move through various temporal stages and transitions as they arrive, settle, uproot and return multiple times across their lives. It is the temporalities of these lives – of young, largely middle-class and highly mobile migrants from Asia to Australia who experience increasingly complex and non-linear migration trajectories – that I have sought to understand in this book through the concept of chronomobilities.

I have drawn on this concept to show how my interlocutors' imaginaries and lived realities are ordered by time-regimes of hegemonic flexibility and transification, and how they understand and experience these imaginaries and realities through differing logics of time: of tempo, synchronicity and sequence. I have used this framework to explore young migrants' experiences with the intersecting velocities, trajectories and rhythms that exist in and across different places, life-stages and relationships. I have shown in particular how mobility patterns the temporalities of working lives, of place attachments and of intimate relationships in terms of movements through the life-course and in terms of everyday embodied experiences of time.

Through this engagement with the lives of these young and distinctly 21st-century migrants, I suggest that a renewed focus on the temporal is critical to the sociology of contemporary migration. Contemporary migration globally is often distinctly non-linear, multidirectional and open-ended. In the Australian context, as I have argued, this is shaped by the specific time-regime of transification. But uneven, circuitous and ongoing routes and trajectories increasingly categorize migration in many other contexts globally. The 'times of migration' (Cwerner, 2001) are no longer neatly divided, chronologically, into binaries of past/home and present/host or 'before-migration' and 'after-migration'.

Temporal analysis becomes important here, as the lives of my interlocutors reveal, to understand the multiplicity of migration as an open-ended process rather than an event; to understand how migration reshapes the temporal horizons of individual lives and the embodied temporalities of the everyday; and to destabilize traditional political understandings of migration, which, in 'settler' societies in particular, remain often predicated on a linear temporal journey from alien to citizen, and from arrival to belonging.

Contemporary temporal conditions of migration are in turn shaped by wider socio-temporal conditions. Twenty-first-century global social conditions, driven by 'just-in-time' capitalism, involve increasing fragmentation and desequentialization of the life-course, insecure futures and subsequently a demand for ongoing flexibilization in many arenas of social life. Migration can be a strategy to respond to these conditions. People seek to move towards a slower or a faster pace of life, move to escape crisis times such as a recession cycle, or move to purposefully disrupt present stasis or predetermined, socially normative futures. Despite this linking of migration with desires to 'make time one's own', the actual consequences of migration remain increasingly unknowable in advance, leaving migrants to grapple with the disjunctures that develop between their imagined futures of the past and their present realities. Beyond the chronological sequencing of the individual life-course, time is also a relational process of synchronization with others. It is a social commodity that becomes distributed in different ways by migration, as maintaining social relations across space often involves a reconfiguring of social time and how it is shared and passed with others, both proximate and distant. Intersections of age, gender, class, race and ethnicity have bearing on the ways time interweaves into daily life, and the tensions it produces for individual migrant subjects.

My approach emerges at an important juncture for the field of migration studies as it develops new ways of thinking about migration under these 21st-century conditions. The emergent temporal turn, which I have sought to contribute to in this book, draws on the established turns toward spatial, transnational and mobilities perspectives that have shaped the study of migration since the 1990s. These interrelated lenses have done much to break down assumptions of linearity, uni-directionality, settlement and push–pull rationality, and to position migration as one form of mobility within broader frames of spatio-temporal transformation in the contemporary world. The chronomobilities approach to migration that I have employed here does not represent any kind of radical break with these established ways of thinking about contemporary migrant mobilities. Rather, a chronomobilities perspective highlights, synthesizes and systematizes, through the explicit analysis of temporality in relation to mobility, a set of ideas that are very much already present in extant thinking. Transnationalism has broken down ideas of the linearity of migration in positioning migrant lives as constituted by ongoing bonds with homelands and social fields that exist across multiple spaces (see, for example, Basch et al, 1994; Vertovec, 2009). Spatial analysis within migration geography has shown the mutually constitutive relationship between migration and structures of space-time (Samers, 2010), particularly relationships between urban spaces and migrants' lives (Glick Schiller and Çağlar, 2010; Hou, 2013; Wong and Rigg, 2010). The more recent turn towards mobilities perspectives has also played a crucial role in positioning the 'event' of international migration as merely one part of a series ongoing and diverse mobilities, which are local and transnational, virtual and embodied (Hannam et al, 2006). Mobilities research has also crucially highlighted the importance of immobility and stasis (Blunt, 2007; Conlon, 2011) as well as velocity and pace (Martin 2011) to migration processes, and a number of critical recent interventions have explicitly foregrounded the importance of temporality to 21st-century migration studies (Mavroudi et al, 2017; Barber and Lem, 2018).

What I have demonstrated throughout this book, following in particular from the pioneering work of Cwerner (2001), is simply that by making an analysis of the temporal in migration more explicit through the study of time in everyday lives, we can highlight with more nuance some of the ambivalence, hybridity, displacement and uncertainty of migrant experience within contemporary, globalized social formations. Just as Samers (2010) has argued that all migration research is essentially geographic, since it takes place in and across space and always involves spatial categories, all migration research is inherently temporal, always involving ruptures, transits, beginnings and endings, pasts and futures. Focusing empirically on the lived experience of migration, I have also sought, rather than an abstract, metaphysical or philosophical approach to time and the social, a sense of 'how time is understood, discussed and negotiated in practice' (Griffiths, 2013: 2–3) in an increasingly mobile world. This approach allows a number of crucial questions to come to the fore, including: how experiences of time change as people move across space; the roles time plays in the governance of mobile bodies, both when they are on the move and when they are securely or insecurely emplaced; how transnational, multidirectional and continuous migrant mobilities shape everyday temporal practices and experiences; and the salience of timelines and timings to the structuring of migrants' social relations across spaces and cultures.

It is not only, however, that understandings of migration experiences are richer through the application of a temporal lens. The approach I have taken throughout this book also has, in a small way, the capacity to renew understandings of the sociology of time. In engaging with migrant lives through the idea of chronomobilities, I have demonstrated how time is multiple in a mobile world, how multiple experiences of time exist contemporaneously but also intertwine with and inflect each other as people move through space. The sociology of time often begins from genealogies of social time that are constituted by a distinctly Western standpoint. Time is positioned as a social construct that became increasingly standardized and institutionalized with industrialization (Zerubavel, 1982), and then spread through economic globalization from the Global North to the rest of the world, allowing for the sedimentation of hegemonic and global constructions of clock time and Gregorian calendar time into different places and cultures.

However, divergent ontologies and experiences of time continue to exist contemporaneously with standardized global time, and indeed to move around the globe. The cosmological and lunisolar temporalities of the Lunar New Year and Deepavali are one example of such layering and mobility of divergent collective times; similarly, my interlocutors' experiences convey how everyday time exists in diverse and ever-evolving layers for individual subjects, as they are both submerged within and resistant to hegemonic forms of time and operate between and across different cultures of time. Importantly, then, as various cultural and social practices of time move with people (Cwerner, 2001), migration throws into sharp relief the multiplicities of time, and the alternative ways of 'doing' time that exist within hegemonic global time-regimes. Migration reveals what happens when different practices of time rub up against each other in different spaces. The study of migrants' lives through a temporal lens thus highlights specific relations between time and place as transnational and translocal. Different local places have different orientations towards time. The relentless pace and myriad uncertainties of global modernity do not touch all places with the same degree of intensity, and the conditions of individuals' mobility and emplacement can shape differentiated experiences of accelerated, risky or compressed times. Migration highlights how temporality is the product of both everyday social and cultural practices and the structures and systems that such practices exist within and move between (Baas and Yeoh, 2019).

While a chronomobilities approach opens up possibilities for new insights in a broad range of empirical contexts of migration, in this book, my focus has been on 'middling' migrants, whose experiences are often less visible in migration sociology. The lives of migrants 'of the middle' represent a rich empirical vein to understand the multiplicities of time-in-mobility, as they constitute a specific form of migration marked by ambiguity, in-betweenness and transition. Nuances in the interrelationships between temporality and mobility, and spatial mobility and social mobility, thus become visible in the analysis of the uneven 'middling' experiences that exist in between the liminality of the migrant precariat and the fluidity of the mobile elite. The middle presents an important site of rethinking 21st-century migration globally in a context where a growing global middle class increasingly imagines and creates lives on the move, and where middling migrants now constitute the majority of documented migration to post-industrial countries (Mar, 2005).

For the young and Asian middling subjects of this book, like many of their compatriots in other global contexts, complex desires around leisure, labour, education, lifestyle and identity co-mingle within migration projects that have indeterminate outcomes. Migration governance creates both friction and possibility as it comes up against migrants' own desires to use mobility strategically to create new pathways, new lives and new ways of being. Such desires are linked, culturally, to the life-stage in between youth and adulthood in Asian middle-class imaginaries. The negotiation of mobility thus takes place in intertwinement with the negotiation of both normative and emergent social and cultural imaginaries of 'becoming adult' and the timings and milestones that this entails.

As Conradson and Latham (2005b) have argued, a focus on middling experience draws attention to the more mundane, everyday and 'ordinary' practices of migrant lives. There is perhaps a politics of this 'mundane-ness' of the middle that is significant to discursive understandings of the migrant subject in a time of intensified bordering and politicization of migration. My interlocutors struggled with complex and often constrictive time-regimes, yet they also made, and lived, 'ordinary' lives within and in spite of them. They had babies, learnt to drive, fell in and out of love, made and lost friends, started businesses, changed careers, moved houses, adopted dogs, lost parents, left, returned, and left again. They took part in collective forms of solidarity within and outside their identities as migrants – they participated in poetry slams, founded laughter clubs, volunteered for local charities, marched in street protests for national and global causes, and organized cultural festivals, traditional music groups, and migrant mothers' support groups. All of these experiences were coloured by the hegemonic flexibility of their mobility – questions of how long they could stay, when and where they would move on, and what they had to do in the 'here and now' to make their lives work whether their future was 'here', 'there' or 'somewhere else altogether'. In many ways, the stories in this book are stories of how life happens alongside, because of and sometimes in spite of migration uncertainty. A temporal perspective allows everyday events, the milestones and the rhythms of the mundane stuff of social life (work, love, home) to come to the fore, positioning these mobile subjects as both more than 'transients' in the nation state and more than 'victims' of exploitative border policies. This perspective also importantly reveals that lives of the middle are not wholly spaces of fluidity, flexibility and hypermobility. The temporalities of settling and staying, of sedentariness and belonging, still very much matter, particularly to ideas of 'achieving' the imagined stability of adult life.

What applying a chronomobilities approach allows, then, in this rather contradictory space of the middle, is a lens that can capture continuity and transition, redirection and multiplicity, standing still and moving forward. It is an approach that pays attention to multiple spatio-temporal and socioeconomic (re)positionings, transformations and transitions. Such an approach can work to unpack the nuances of experience that sit at the edges, intersections and crossings between conventional understandings of migrant experience, particularly in relation to migrants who are relatively educated and resourced, but not elite, whose lives unveil the unevenness and ambiguity of lived experience within the time-regimes of global modernity. Exploring middling mobilities reveals how migration can simultaneously and paradoxically embody freedom and constraint, closure and openness, anxiety and opportunity.

The stories of work, place and love explored across Chapters 3 to 5 have sought to illuminate the realities of how these contradictions touch down in migrants' lives. These are migration stories that are not bracketed by fixed points of departure and settlement, but instead involve an open-ended series of mobilities, ruptures and transitions, and create multiple experiences and understandings of 'time-in-mobility' or chronomobilities. Middling migrants are, as subjects often 'interrupted' (Robertson, 2019), inherently reflexive about time, attuned to its multiplicities and responsive to its possibilities. The lives of my interlocutors – their engagements with work, their experiences of place, their intimate relationships and their fractured transitions to adulthood while on the move – speak to how individuals craft ways of being that resist fragmentation, acceleration, uncertainty and risk. There are negotiations and resistance to hegemonic regimes of time, ways of finding slowness, certainty, belonging and the accumulation of meaning within the often turbulent chronomobilities of their lives.

Notes

Introduction
[1] The Working Holiday Maker Visa Program in Australia consists of two subclasses, the Work and Holiday visa (subclass 462) and the Working Holiday visa (subclass 417). The two subclasses relate to the different reciprocal arrangements with specific partner countries. Both visas require migrants to be between 18 and 31 years of age on application and do not allow dependent children to stay in Australia. Both visas allow a one-year stay with six months of work with any one employer. Both subclasses also allow extension to a second one-year visa if specified work is undertaken in regional Australia during the first year. Subclass 462 visas are available to passport holders of Argentina, Bangladesh, Chile, China, Hungary, Indonesia, Israel, Luxembourg, Malaysia, Poland, Portugal, San Marino, Slovak Republic, Slovenia, Spain, Thailand, Turkey, the US, Uruguay and Vietnam, while subclass 417 visas are available to passport holders of Belgium, Canada, the Republic of Cyprus, Denmark, Estonia, Finland, France, Germany, Hong Kong, Ireland, Italy, Japan, South Korea, Malta, Netherlands, Norway, Sweden, Taiwan and the United Kingdom. Applicants for subclass 462 visas are subject to more criteria than 417 applicants, including educational requirements, government letters of support, and minimum English standards.

Chapter 2
[1] K-pop is a form of popular music originating in South Korea.
[2] 'Specified work' currently includes work in plant and animal cultivation, fishing and pearling, or mining and construction. 'Regional Australia' encompasses a broad geographic space, including capital cities and suburban areas in some states.

Chapter 3
[1] In Australian employment law and lay discourse, work without guaranteed hours and hourly pay on a per-shift basis is usually referred to as 'casual work'. I use this term throughout this chapter to describe these working arrangements. Casual workers do not receive the same benefits as full-time or part-time workers, such as paid leave. Casual work can be formal, or it can be 'cash-in- hand', which signifies informal arrangements in which cash payments are used so employers can bypass paying legal wages and entitlements and employees do not pay tax.

2   It is, of course, possible that, in a national context where direct racial discrimination in recruitment is illegal, visa statuses could function as a proxy identifier for racial difference. Yet the migrants I interviewed seldom saw their experiences in this light – often because they knew Asian-Australian citizens who did not have the same problems they experienced in finding work. Transification in this sense is likely to intersect with other forms of difference (racial, ethnic and gendered) in the labour market to place transified migrants at a further disadvantage (Robertson, 2015a).

3   457 skilled work visas were a common step in transified pathways when I conducted interviews in 2015 and 2016, but were replaced by a new (albeit similar) scheme in 2017.

Chapter 5

1   In this chapter, I use the general terms 'intimate partnerships' or 'intimate relationships' to describe the wide range of 'couple' relationships that were discussed in the interviews, and generally describe members of these couples as 'intimate partners'. These terms inclusively cover both married couples and unmarried but committed relationships. They also align with both the legal and colloquial norm in Australia, adopted by many of the participants, to describe *de facto* couples (who under Australian law have largely the same rights are married couples) as 'partners'. In discussing specific participants' relationships, however, I use that participant's own terms and pronouns to describe their significant others, for example 'boyfriend' or 'girlfriend'.

References

ABS (Australian Bureau of Statistics) (2016) 2024.0 – Census of Population and Housing: Australia Revealed. https://www.abs.gov.au/ausstats/abs@.nsf/mf/2024.0

AEI (Australia Education International) (2016) Research Snapshot. International Student Numbers 2015. https://internationaleducation.gov.au/research/Research-Snapshots/Documents/Student%20Numbers%202015.pdf

Acedera, Kristel A.F. and Brenda S.A. Yeoh (2019) '"Making time": long-distance marriages and the temporalities of the transnational family.' *Current Sociology*, 67(2): 250–72.

Adam, Barbara (1995) *Timewatch: The Social Analysis of Time*. Cambridge: Polity Press.

Ahmad, Ali Nobil (2008) 'Dead men working: time and space in London's (illegal) migrant economy.' *Work, Employment & Society*, 22(2): 301–18.

Amin, Ash (1994) *Post-Fordism: A Reader*. Oxford: Blackwell.

Anderson, Bridget (2007) *Battles in Time: The Relation Between Global and Labour Mobilities*, COMPAS Working Paper No.55. Oxford: Centre on Migration, Policy and Society, University of Oxford.

Andersson, Ruben (2014) 'Time and the migrant other: European border controls and the temporal economics of illegality.' *American Anthropologist*, 116 (4): 795–809.

Aneesh, Aneesh (2001) 'Rethinking migration: on-line labour flows from India to the United States.' In *The International Migration of the Highly Skilled*, edited by W.A. Cornelius, T.J. Espenshade and I. Salehyan. San Diego, CA: Center for Comparative Immigration Studies, University of California, pp 351–70.

Arnado, Janet M. (2010) 'Performances across time and space: drama in the global households of Filipina transmigrant workers.' *International Migration*, 48(6): 132–54.

Arnett, Jeffrey Jensen (2000) 'Emerging adulthood: A theory of development from the late teens through the twenties.' *American Psychologist*, 55(5): 469–80.

Arnett, Jeffrey Jenson (2001) 'Conceptions of the transition to adulthood: perspectives from adolescence through midlife.' *Journal of Adult Development*, 8(2): 133–43.

Axelsson, Linn (2017) 'Living within temporally thick borders: IT professionals' experiences of Swedish immigration policy and practice.' *Journal of Ethnic and Migration Studies*, 43(6): 974–90.

Baas, Michiel (2012) *Imagined Mobility: Migration and Transnationalism among Indian Students in Australia.* London: Anthem Press.

Baas, Michiel (2017) 'The mobile middle: Indian skilled migrants in Singapore and the "middling" space between migration categories.' *Transitions: Journal of Transient Migration* no. 1 (1):47–63.

Baas, Michiel and Brenda S.A. Yeoh (2019) 'Introduction: migration studies and critical temporalities.' *Current Sociology*, 67(2): 161–8.

Baey, Grace and Brenda S.A. Yeoh (2018) '"The lottery of my life": migration trajectories and the production of precarity among Bangladeshi migrant workers in Singapore's construction industry.' *Asian and Pacific Migration Journal*, 27(3): 249–72.

Bailey, Adrian J. (2009) 'Population geography: lifecourse matters.' *Progress in Human Geography*, 33(3): 407–18.

Baldassar, Loretta (2008) 'Missing kin and longing to be together: emotions and the construction of co-presence in transnational relationships.' *Journal of Intercultural Studies*, 29(3): 247–66.

Baldassar, Loretta (2016) 'De-demonizing distance in mobile family lives: co-presence, care circulation and polymedia as vibrant matter.' *Global Networks*, 16(2): 145–63.

Barber, Pauline Gardiner and Winnie Lem (eds) (2018) *Migration, Temporality, and Capitalism.* Basingstoke: Palgrave Macmillan.

Basch, Linda, Nina Glick Schiller and Cristina Szanton Blanc (1994) *Nations Unbound: Transnational Projects, Postcolonial Predicaments and Deterritorialized Nation-States.* Langhorne: Pennsylvania.

Bastia, Tanja and Siobhan McGrath (2011) *Temporality, Migration and Unfree Labour: Migrant Garment Workers*, Manchester Papers in Political Economy No. 6. Manchester: University of Manchester.

Batnitzky, Adina, Linda McDowell and Sarah Dyer (2012) 'Remittances and the maintenance of dual social worlds: the transnational working lives of migrants in greater London.' *International Migration*, 50(4): 140–56.

Bauman, Zygmunt. (1998) 'Parvenu and Pariah: Heroes and victims of modernity.' In *The Politics of Postmodernity*, edited by J. Good, and I. Velody. Cambridge: Cambridge University Press, pp 23–35.

Bauman, Zygmunt (2013) *Liquid Modernity*. Chichester: John Wiley & Sons.

Beck, Ulrich (1992) *Risk Society: Towards a New Modernity*. London: Sage Publications.

Beck, Ulrich (2009) *World at Risk*. Cambridge: Polity Press.

Benson, Michaela and Karen B. O'Reilly (2009) *Lifestyle Migration: Expectations, Aspirations and Experiences*. Burlington, VT: Ashgate Publishing.

Bergmann, Werner (1992) 'The problem of time in sociology: an overview of the literature on the state of theory and research on the "sociology of time", 1900–82.' *Time & Society*, 1(1): 81–134.

Bloch, Alexia (2011) 'Intimate circuits: modernity, migration and marriage among post-Soviet women in Turkey.' *Global Networks*, 11(4): 502–21.

Blunt, Alison (2007) 'Cultural geographies of migration: mobility, transnationality and diaspora.' *Progress in Human Geography*, 31 (5): 684–94.

Boccagni, Paolo (2017) *Migration and the Search for Home: Mapping Domestic Space in Migrants' Everyday Lives*. New York, NY: Palgrave Macmillan.

Brickell, Katherine and Ayona Datta (2011) *Translocal Geographies: Spaces, Places, Connections*. Farnham: Ashgate Publishing.

Brosius, Christiane (2012) *India's Middle Class: New Forms of Urban Leisure, Consumption and Prosperity*. London: Routledge India.

Brown, Trent, Timothy J. Scrase and Ruchira Ganguly-Scrase (2017) 'Globalised dreams, local constraints: migration and youth aspirations in an Indian regional town.' *Children's Geographies*, 15(5): 531–44.

Brun, Cathrine (2015) 'Active waiting and changing hopes: toward a time perspective on protracted displacement.' *Social Analysis*, 59(1): 19–37.

Brun, Cathrine (2016) 'Dwelling in the temporary: the involuntary mobility of displaced Georgians in rented accommodation.' *Cultural Studies*, 30(3): 421–40.

Brun, Cathrine and Anita Fábos (2015) 'Making homes in limbo? A conceptual framework.' *Refuge: Canada's Journal on Refugees*, 31(1): 5–17.

Carling, Jørgen (2017) 'On conjunctures in transnational lives: linear time, relative mobility and individual experience.' In *Timespace and International Migration*, edited by Elizabeth Mavroudi, Ben Page and Anastasia Christou. Cheltenham: Edward Elgar Publishing, pp 33–47.

Carling, Jørgen and Francis Collins (2018) 'Aspiration, desire and drivers of migration.' *Journal of Ethnic and Migration Studies* no. 44(6): 909–26.

Chandra, V. (2012) 'Work–life balance: eastern and western perspectives.' *The International Journal of Human Resource Management*, 23(5): 1040–56.

Cheng, Yi'En (2014) 'Time protagonists: student migrants, practices of time and cultural construction of the Singapore-educated person.' *Social & Cultural Geography*, 15(4): 385–405.

Chiang, Lan-Hung Nora (2008) '"Astronaut families": transnational lives of middle-class Taiwanese married women in Canada.' *Social & Cultural Geography*, 9(5): 505–18.

Clarke, Nick (2005) 'Detailing transnational lives of the middle: British working holiday makers in Australia.' *Journal of Ethnic and Migration Studies*, 31(2): 307–22.

Clausen, John A. (1993) *American Lives: Looking Back at the Children of the Great Depression*. New York, NY: The Free Press.

Coe, Cati (2015) 'The temporality of care: gender, migration, and the entrainment of life-courses.' In *Anthropological Perspectives on Care*, edited by Erdmute Alber and Heike Drotbohm. New York, NY: Palgrave Macmillan, pp 181–205.

Coe, Cati (2016) 'Orchestrating care in time: Ghanaian migrant women, family, and reciprocity.' *American Anthropologist*, 118(1): 37–48.

Collins, Francis L. (2014) 'Teaching English in South Korea: mobility norms and higher education outcomes in youth migration.' *Children's Geographies*, 12(1): 40–55.

Collins, Francis L. (2018) 'Desire as a theory for migration studies: temporality, assemblage and becoming in the narratives of migrants.' *Journal of Ethnic and Migration Studies*, 44(6): 964–80.

Collins, Francis L. and Sergei Shubin (2015) 'Migrant times beyond the life course: the temporalities of foreign English teachers in south Korea.' *Geoforum*, 62: 96–104.

Collins, Francis L. and Sergei Shubin (2017) 'The temporal complexity of international student mobilities.' In *Timespace and International Migration*, edited by E. Mavroudi, B. Page and A. Christou. Cheltenham: Edward Elgar, pp 17–32.

Conlon, Deirdre (2011) 'Waiting: feminist perspectives on the spacings/timings of migrant (im)mobility.' *Gender, Place & Culture*, 18(3): 353–60.

Conradson, David and Alan Latham (2005a) 'Friendship, networks and transnationality in a world city: Antipodean transmigrants in London.' *Journal of Ethnic and Migration Studies*, 31(2): 287–305.

Conradson, David and Alan Latham (2005b) 'Ordinary and "middling" transnationalism.' *Journal of Ethnic and Migration Studies*, 31(2): 227–33.

Conradson, David and Alan Latham (2005c) 'Transnational urbanism: attending to everyday practices and mobilities.' *Journal of Ethnic and Migration Studies*, 31(2): 227–33.

Constable, Nicole (2007) *Maid to Order in Hong Kong: Stories of Migrant Workers*. Ithaca, NY: Cornell University Press.

Crivello, Gina (2015) "There's no future here': the time and place of children's migration aspirations in Peru.' *Geoforum*, 62: 38–46.

Cuervo, Hernan and Johanna Wyn (2011) *Rethinking Youth Transitions in Australia: A Historical and Multidimensional Approach*. Melbourne: Youth Research Centre, Melbourne Graduate School of Education.

Cwerner, Saulo B. (2001) 'The times of migration.' *Journal of Ethnic and Migration Studies*, 27(1): 7–36.

D'Andrea, Anthony (2006) 'Neo-nomadism: a theory of post-identitarian mobility in the global age.' *Mobilities*, 1(1): 95–119.

Datta, Ayona (2016) 'Introduction: fast cities in an urban age.' In *Mega-Urbanization in the Global South*, edited by Ayona Datta and Abdul Shaban, Abingdon: Routledge, pp 13–40.

DHA (Department of Home Affairs) (2015) 'Australia's migration trends 2014–15 at a glance.' www.homeaffairs.gov.au/research-and-stats/files/migration-trends-14-15-glance.pdf

DHA (2017) '2016–17 Migration Programme Report.' www.homeaffairs.gov.au/research-and-stats/files/report-on-migration-program-2016-17.pdf

DHA (2018) 'Country profiles – Philippines.' DHA [Online]. www.homeaffairs.gov.au/research-and-statistics/statistics/country-profiles/profiles/philippines

DIBP (Department of Immigration and Border Protection) (2016a) 'Temporary entrants and New Zealand citizens in Australia as at 30 September 2016.' www.homeaffairs.gov.au/research-and-stats/files/temp-entrants-newzealand-30-sept-2016.pdf

DIBP (2016b) 'Subclass 457 Quarterly Report.' www.homeaffairs.gov.au/research-and-stats/files/457-quarterly-report-30-09-2016.pdf

DIBP (2016c) 'Working Holiday Maker Visa Program Report.' www.homeaffairs.gov.au/research-and-stats/files/working-holiday-report-jun16.pdf

DIMIA (Department of Immigration and Multicultural Affairs) (2005) '2004–05 Annual Report.' www.homeaffairs.gov.au/reports-and-pubs/Annualreports/dimia-annual-report-2004-05.pdf

Doherty, Catherine A. and Parlo Singh (2005) 'International student subjectivities: biographical investments for liquid times.' In AARE Education Research Conference, 'Creative Dissent: Constructive Solutions', 2005-11-27-2005-12-01. https://eprints.qut.edu.au/2868/

Durkheim, Emile (1915) *Elementary Forms of the Religious Life*. London: George Allen and Unwin.

Durkheim, Emile (1964) *Rules of the Sociological Method*. New York, NY: Free Press of Glencoe.

Elchardus, Mark, I. Glorieux and M. Scheys (1987) 'Time, cultures, and coexistence.' *Studi emigrazione/Etudes migrations*, 24(86): 138–54.

Elder Jr, Glen H. (1994) 'Time, human agency, and social change: perspectives on the life course.' *Social Psychology Quarterly*, 57(1): 4–15.

Elliot, Alice (2016) 'Paused subjects: Waiting for migration in North Africa.' *Time & Society*, 25(1): 102–16.

Elliott, Anthony and John Urry (2010) *Mobile Lives*. London: Routledge.

Erdal, Marta Bivand and Rojan Ezzati (2015) '"Where are you from" or "When did you come"? Temporal dimensions in migrants' reflections about settlement and return.' *Ethnic and Racial Studies*, 38(7): 1202–17.

Erel, Umut and Louise Ryan (2019) 'Migrant capitals: proposing a multi-level spatio-temporal analytical framework.' *Sociology*, 53(2): 246–63.

Farrar, Max (2003) 'Migrant spaces and settlers' time: forming and de-forming an inner city.' In *Imagining Cities*, edited by Sallie Westwood and John Williams. London: Routledge, pp 111–30.

Fathi, Mastoureh (2017) *Intersectionality, Class and Migration. Narratives of Iranian Women Migrants in the UK*. New York, NY: Springer.

Fernandes, Leela (2000) 'Restructuring the new middle class in liberalizing India.' *Comparative Studies of South Asia, Africa and the Middle East*, 20(1): 88–104.

Flaherty, Michael G. (2011) *The Textures of Time: Agency and Temporal Experience*. Philadelphia: Temple University Press.

Flores, Mikhail (2019) 'Remittances from overseas Filipinos hit record, but growth slows.' *Nikkei Asian Review* [Online]. https://asia.nikkei.com/Economy/Remittances-from-overseas-Filipinos-hit-record-but-growth-slows

Fong, Vanessa (2011) *Paradise Redefined: Transnational Chinese Students and the Quest for Flexible Citizenship in the Developed World*. Stanford, CA: Stanford University Press.

Forsberg, Sara (2017) 'Educated to be global: transnational horizons of middle class students in Kerala, India.' *Environment and Planning A*, 49(9): 2099–115.

Frohlick, Susan (2009) 'Pathos of love in Puerto Viejo, Costa Rica: emotion, travel and migration.' *Mobilities*, 4(3): 389–405.

Fullagar, Simone, Erica Wilson and Kevin Markwell (2012) 'Starting slow: thinking through slow mobilities and experiences.' In *Slow Tourism: Experiences and Mobilities*, edited by Simone Fullagar, Kevin Markwell and Erica Wilson, pp 1–10. Bristol: Channel View Publications.

Giddens, Anthony (1991) *Modernity and Self-Identity: Self and Society in the Late Modern Age*. Stanford, CA: Stanford University Press.

Giles, Wenona, Valerie Preston and Mary Romero (2014) *When Care Work Goes Global: Locating the Social Relations of Domestic Work*. Farnham: Ashgate Publishing.

Glick Schiller, Nina and Ayşe Çağlar (2010) *Locating Migration: Rescaling Cities and Migrants*. Ithaca, NY: Cornell University Press.

Gomes, Catherine (2016) *Transient Mobility and Middle Class Identity: Media and Migration in Australia and Singapore*. Singapore: Macmillan.

Gorman-Murray, Andrew (2009) 'Intimate mobilities: emotional embodiment and queer migration.' *Social & Cultural Geography*, 10(4): 441–60.

Griffiths, Melanie B.E. (2014) 'Out of time: the temporal uncertainties of refused asylum seekers and immigration detainees.' *Journal of Ethnic and Migration Studies*, 40(12): 1991–2009.

Griffiths, Melanie, Ali Rogers and Bridget Anderson (2013) *Migration, Time and Temporalities: Review and Prospect*, COMPAS Research Resources Paper. Oxford: COMPAS, University of Oxford.

Hannam, Kevin, Mimi Sheller and John Urry (2006) 'Mobilities, immobilities and moorings.' *Mobilities*, 1(1): 1–22.

Hao, Jie and Anthony Welch (2012) 'A tale of sea turtles: job-seeking experiences of hai gui (high-skilled returnees) in China.' *Higher Education Policy*, 25(2): 243–60.

Harney, Nicholas Demaria and Loretta Baldassar (2007) 'Tracking transnationalism: migrancy and its futures.' *Journal of Ethnic and Migration Studies*, 33(2): 189–98.

Harris, Anita, Loretta Baldassar and Shanthi Robertson (2020) 'Settling down in time and place? Changing intimacies in mobile young people's migration- and Life-Courses.' *Population, Space and Place*. doi: 10.1002/psp.2357

Harvey, David (1990) 'Between space and time: reflections on the geographical imagination.' *Annals of the Association of American Geographers*, 80(3): 418–34.

Harvey, David (1999) 'Time-space compression and the postmodern condition.' *Modernity: Critical Concepts*, 4: 98–118.

Ho, Elaine Lynn-Ee (2011a) 'Identity politics and cultural asymmetries: Singaporean transmigrants 'fashioning' cosmopolitanism.' *Journal of Ethnic and Migration Studies*, 37(5): 729–46.

Ho, Elaine Lynn-Ee (2011b) 'Migration trajectories of "highly skilled" middling transnationals: Singaporean transmigrants in London.' *Population, Space and Place*, 17(1): 116–29.

Ho, Elaine Lynn-Ee and David Ley (2014) '"Middling" Chinese returnees or immigrants from Canada? The ambiguity of return migration and claims to modernity.' *Asian Studies Review*, 38(1): 36–52.

Hörschelmann, Kathrin (2011) 'Theorising life transitions: geographical perspectives.' *Area*, 43(4): 378–83.

Hou, Jeffrey (2013) *Transcultural Cities: Border Crossing and Placemaking*. Abingdon: Routledge.

Hoy, David Couzens (2012) *The Time of Our Lives: A Critical History of Temporality*. Cambridge, MA: MIT Press.

Huang, Shirlena and Brenda S.A. Yeoh (1996) 'Ties that bind: state policy and migrant female domestic helpers in Singapore.' *Geoforum*, 27(4): 479–93.

Huang, Shirlena and Brenda S.A. Yeoh (2003) 'The difference gender makes: state policy and contract migrant workers in Singapore.' *Asian and Pacific Migration Journal*, 12(1–2): 75–97.

Hugo, Graeme (2008) 'In and out of Australia: rethinking Chinese and Indian skilled migration to Australia.' *Asian Population Studies*, 4(3): 267–91.

Hyndman, Jennifer and Wenona Giles (2011) 'Waiting for what? The feminization of asylum in protracted situations.' *Gender, Place & Culture*, 18(3): 361–79.

Hyun, Kyoung Ja (2001) 'Sociocultural change and traditional values: Confucian values among Koreans and Korean Americans.' *International Journal of Intercultural Relations*, 25(2): 203–29.

Ibañez Tirado, Diana (2019) '"We sit and wait": migration, mobility and temporality in Guliston, southern Tajikistan.' *Current Sociology*, 67(2): 315–33.

Ip, David (2001) 'A decade of Taiwanese migrant settlement in Australia: comparisons with mainland Chinese and Hong Kong settlers.' *Journal of Population Studies*, 23(1): 113–45.

Ip, David (2005) 'Contesting Chinatown: place-making and the emergence of "ethnoburbia" in Brisbane, Australia.' *GeoJournal*, 64(1): 63–74.

Jankowski, Krzysztof Z. (2018) 'The middling mobile: finding place in the liquid city.' *Mobilities*, 13(4): 601–14.

Jeffrey, Craig (2008) '"Generation Nowhere": rethinking youth through the lens of unemployed young men.' *Progress in Human Geography*, 32(6): 739–58.

Jeffrey, Craig (2009) 'Fixing futures: educated unemployment through a north Indian lens.' *Comparative Studies in Society and History*, 51(1): 182–211.

Jeffrey, Craig (2010) *Timepass: Youth, Class, and the Politics of Waiting in India*. Stanford, CA: Stanford University Press.

Kang, Yoonhee (2018) 'A pathway to "constant becoming": time, temporalities and the construction of self among South Korean educational migrants in Singapore.' *Discourse: Studies in the Cultural Politics of Education*, 39(5): 798–813.

Kathiravelu, Laavanya (2016) *Migrant Dubai: Low Wage Workers and the Construction of a Global City*. Basingstoke: Palgrave Macmillan.

Kato, Etsuko (2013) 'Self-searching migrants: youth and adulthood, work and holiday in the lives of Japanese temporary residents in Canada and Australia.' *Asian Anthropology*, 12(1): 20–34.

Kawashima, Kumiko (2010) 'Japanese working holiday makers in Australia and their relationship to the Japanese labour market: before and after.' *Asian Studies Review*, 34(3): 267–86.

Kelly, Melissa (2015) 'Using an intersectional lifecourse approach to understand the migration of the highly skilled.' In *Researching the Lifecourse: Critical Reflections from the Social Sciences*, edited by Nancy Worth and Irene Hardill. Bristol: Policy Press, pp 231–46.

Khoo, Siew-Ean, Graeme Hugo and Peter McDonald (2008) 'Which skilled temporary migrants become permanent residents and why?' *International Migration Review*, 42(1): 193–226.

King, Russell and Enric Ruiz-Gelices (2003) 'International student migration and the European "year abroad": effects on European identity and subsequent migration behaviour.' *Population, Space and Place*, 9(3): 229–52.

Knoblauch, Hubert (2005) 'Focused ethnography.' *Forum Qualitative Sozialforschung/Forum: Qualitative Social Research*, 6(3), Art. 44, http://nbn-resolving.de/urn:nbn:de:0114-fqs0503440

Kobayashi, Audrey and Valerie Preston (2007) 'Transnationalism through the life course: Hong Kong immigrants in Canada.' *Asia Pacific Viewpoint*, 48(2): 151–67.

Koleth, Elsa (2012) 'Temporary migration: stranger politics for a transient time.' Paper presented at Strangers, Aliens and Foreigners Global Conference, Oxford, 21–23 September.

Kõu, Anu and Ajay Bailey (2014). '"Movement is a constant feature in my life": contextualising migration processes of highly skilled Indians.' *Geoforum*, 52: 113–22.

Kõu, Anu, Clara H. Mulder and Ajay Bailey (2017) '"For the sake of the family and future": the linked lives of highly skilled Indian migrants.' *Journal of Ethnic and Migration Studies*, 43(16): 2788-805.

Krivenko, Ekaterina Yahyaoui (2016) 'Considering time in migration and border control practices.' *International Journal of Migration and Border Studies*, 2(4): 329–44.

Kumsa, Martha Kuwee (2002) 'Negotiating intimacies in a globalized space: identity and cohesion in young Oromo refugee women.' *Affilia*, 17(4): 471–96.

Lan, Pei-Chia (2006) *Global Cinderellas: Migrant Domestics and Newly Rich Employers in Taiwan*. Durham, NC: Duke University Press.

Lan, Pei-Chia (2011) 'White privilege, language capital and cultural ghettoisation: Western high-skilled migrants in Taiwan.' *Journal of Ethnic and Migration Studies*, 37(10): 1669–93.

Lan, Shanshan (2020) 'Youth, mobility, and the emotional burdens of youxue (travel and study): a case study of Chinese students in Italy.' *International Migration*, 58(3): 163–76.

Lauser, Andrea (2008) 'Philippine women on the move: marriage across borders.' *International Migration*, 46(4): 85–110.

Leccardi, Carmen (2005) 'Facing uncertainty: temporality and biographies in the new century.' *Young*, 13(2): 123–46.

Leccardi, Carmen (2012) 'Changing time experience, changing biographies and new youth values.' In *Youth Policy in a Changing World: From Theory to Practice*, edited by Marina Hahn-Bleibtreu and Marc Molgat. Leverkusen: Barbara Budrich Publishers, pp 225–38.

Lee, Hwok-Aun (2012) 'Affirmative action in Malaysia: education and employment outcomes since the 1990s.' *Journal of Contemporary Asia*, 42(2): 230–54.

Lee, Michelle and Nicola Piper (2003) 'Reflections on transnational life-course and migratory patterns of middle-class women. Preliminary observations from Malaysia.' In *Wife or Worker? Asian Women and Migration*, edited by Nicola Piper and Mina Roces. Lanham, MA: Rowman & Littlefield, pp 121–36.

Lehmann, Angela (2014) *Transnational Lives in China: Expatriates in a Globalizing City*. Basingstoke: Palgrave Macmillan.

Levitt, Peggy and Deepak Lamba-Nieves (2013) 'Rethinking social remittances and the migration-development nexus from the perspective of time.' *Migration Letters*, 10(1): 11–22.

Lilja, Mona, Andreas Henriksson and Mikael Baaz (2018) '(Re)thinking the precarity of Swedish migrants: governing through decelerations and timescapes.' *Journal of Refugee Studies*, 32(1): 144–61.

Limpangog, Cirila (2013) 'Migration as a strategy for maintaining a middle-class identity: The case of professional Filipino women in Melbourne.' *Austrian Journal of South-East Asian Studies*, 6(2): 307–29.

Lundström, Catrin (2014) *White Migrations: Gender, Whiteness and Privilege in Transnational Migration*. Basingstoke: Palgrave Macmillan.

Lyons, Lenore and Michele Ford (2008) 'Love, sex and the spaces in-between: Kepri wives and their cross-border husbands.' *Citizenship Studies*, 12(1): 55–72.

Madianou, Mirca and Daniel Miller (2013) *Migration and New Media: Transnational Families and Polymedia*. Abingdon: Routledge.

Mahdavi, Pardis (2016) *Crossing the Gulf: Love and Family in Migrant Lives*. Stanford, CA: Stanford University Press.

Mai, Nicola and Russell King (2009) 'Love, sexuality and migration: mapping the issue(s).' *Mobilities*, 4(3): 295–307.

Mapril, José (2014) 'The dreams of middle class: consumption, life-course and migration between Bangladesh and Portugal.' *Modern Asian Studies*, 48(3): 693–719.

Mar, Phillip (2005) 'Unsettling potentialities: topographies of hope in transnational migration.' *Journal of Intercultural Studies*, 26(4): 361–78.

Marcu, Silvia (2012) 'Emotions on the move: belonging, sense of place and feelings identities among young Romanian immigrants in Spain.' *Journal of Youth Studies*, 15(2): 207–23.

Marcu, Silvia (2017) 'Tears of time: a Lefebvrian rhythmanalysis approach to explore the mobility experiences of young Eastern Europeans in Spain.' *Transactions of the Institute of British Geographers*, 42(3): 405–16.

Mares, Peter (2016) *Not Quite Australian: How Temporary Migration is Changing the Nation*. Melbourne: Text Publishing.

Martin, Fran (2018) 'Overseas study as zone of suspension: Chinese students re-negotiating youth, gender, and intimacy.' *Journal of Intercultural Studies*, 39(6): 688–703.

Massey, Doreen (1993) 'Power-geometry and a progressive sense of place.' In *Mapping the Futures: Local Cultures, Global Change*, edited by Jon Bird, Barry Curtis, Tim Putnam, George Robertson and Lisa Tickner. London: Routledge, pp 60–70.

Matthews, Amie (2014) 'Young backpackers and the rite of passage of travel: examining the transformative effects of liminality.' In *Travel and Transformation*, edited by Garth Lean and Russell Staiff. Abingdon: Routledge, pp 157–71.

Matthews, J. and R. Sidhu (2005) 'Desperately seeking the global subject: International education, citizenship and cosmopolitanism.' *Globalisation, Societies and Education*, 3(1): 49–66.

Mavroudi, Elizabeth, Ben Page and Anastasia Christou (2017) *Timespace and International Migration*. Cheltenham: Edward Elgar.

May, Jon and Nigel Thrift (2004) *Timespace: Geographies of Temporality*. London: Routledge.

McHugh, Kevin E. (2000) 'Inside, outside, upside down, backward, forward, round and round: a case for ethnographic studies in migration.' *Progress in Human Geography*, 24(1): 71–89.

Mead, George Herbert (1932) *The Philosophy of the Present*. Chicago, IL: University of Chicago Press.

Mezzadra, Sandro (2011) 'The gaze of autonomy: capitalism, migration and social struggles.' In *The Contested Politics of Mobility: Borderzones and Irregularity*, edited by Vicki Squire. Abingdon: Routledge, pp 121–42.

Mountz, Alison (2011) 'Where asylum-seekers wait: feminist counter-topographies of sites between states.' *Gender, Place & Culture*, 18(3): 381–99.

Naafs, Suzanne and Tracey Skelton (2018) 'Youthful futures? Aspirations, education and employment in Asia.' *Children's Geographies*, 16(1): 1–14.

Neilson, Brett (2009) 'The world seen from a taxi: students-migrants-workers in the global multiplication of labour.' *Subjectivity*, 29(1): 425–44.

Ní Laoire, Caitríona (2008) '"Settling back"? A biographical and life-course perspective on Ireland's recent return migration.' *Irish Geography*, 41(2): 195–210.

Noble, Greg (2002) 'Comfortable and relaxed: furnishing the home and nation.' *Continuum: Journal of Media & Cultural Studies*, 16(1): 53–66.

Noble, Greg (2005) 'The discomfort of strangers: racism, incivility and ontological security in a relaxed and comfortable nation.' *Journal of Intercultural Studies*, 26(1–2): 107–20.

Noble, Greg and Paul Tabar (2017) 'The "career" of the migrant.' In *Critical Reflections on Migration, 'Race' and Multiculturalism: Australia in a Global Context*, edited by Martina Boese and Vince Marotta, Abingdon: Routledge, pp 255–70.

Nowicka, Magdalena (2007) 'Mobile locations: construction of home in a group of mobile transnational professionals.' *Global Networks*, 7(1): 69–86.

O'Rand, Angela M. (2003) 'The future of the life course: late modernity and life course risks?' In *Handbook of the Life Course*, edited by Jeylan T. Mortimer and Michael J. Shanahan. Boston, MA: Springer, pp 693-702.

O'Reilly, Karen and Michaela Benson (2016) 'Lifestyle migration: escaping to the good life?' In *Lifestyle Migration: Expectations, Aspirations and Experiences*, edited by Michaela Benson and Karen O'Reilly. Abingdon: Routledge, pp 11–14.

OECD (2013) 'World migration in figures.' https://www.oecd.org/els/mig/World-Migration-in-Figures.pdf

Ogura, Kazuya (2009) 'Long working hours in Japan: an international comparison and research topics.' *Japanese Economy*, 36(2): 23–45.

Oliver, Caroline (2010) 'Between time not there and time not theirs: temporality in retirement migration to Spain.' *Journal of Aging, Humanities, and the Arts*, 4(2): 110–18.

Ong, Aihwa (1999) *Flexible Citizenship: The Cultural Logics of Transnationality*. Durham, NC: Duke University Press.

Osbaldiston, Nick (2011) 'The authentic place in the amenity migration discourse.' *Space and Culture*, 14(2): 214–26.

Osbaldiston, Nick (ed) (2013) *Culture of the Slow: Social Deceleration in an Accelerated World*. Basingstoke: Palgrave Macmillan.

Papastergiadis, Nikos (2000) *The Turbulence of Migration*. Cambridge: Polity Press.

Parreñas, Rhacel Salazar (2008) *The Force of Domesticity: Filipina Migrants and Globalization*. New York, NY: NYU Press.

Parutis, Violetta (2011) '"Economic migrants" or "middling transnationals"? East European migrants' experiences of work in the UK.' *International Migration*, 52(1): 36–55.

Peck, Jamie and Nik Theodore (2010) 'Mobilizing policy: models, methods, and mutations.' *Geoforum*, 41(2): 169–74.

Pezzini, Mario (2012) 'An emerging middle class.' *OECD Observer* [Online]. http://oecdobserver.org/news/fullstory.php/aid/3681/An_emerging_middle_class.html.

Phillips, Janet (2016) 'Australia's Working Holiday Maker program: a quick guide.' Parliament of Australia [Online]. www.aph.gov.au/About_Parliament/Parliamentary_Departments/Parliamentary_Library/pubs/rp/rp1617/Quick_Guides/WorkingHoliday#_Table_2:_Working

Pieke, Frank N. (2007) 'Editorial Introduction: Community and identity in the new Chinese migration order.' *Population, Space and Place*, 13(2): 81–94.

Pyke, Karen (2005) '"Generational deserters" and "black sheep": acculturative differences among siblings in Asian immigrant families.' *Journal of Family Issues*, 26(4): 491–517.

Radhakrishnan, Smitha (2008) 'Examining the "global" Indian middle class: gender and culture in the Silicon Valley/Bangalore circuit.' *Journal of Intercultural Studies*, 29(1): 7–20.

Rajkumar, Deepa, Laurel Berkowitz, Leah F. Vosko, Valerie Preston and Robert Latham (2012) 'At the temporary–permanent divide: how Canada produces temporariness and makes citizens through its security, work, and settlement policies.' *Citizenship Studies*, 16(3–4): 483–510.

Ramdas, Kamalini (2012) 'Women in waiting? Singlehood, marriage, and family in Singapore.' *Environment and Planning A*, 44(4): 832–48.

Roberts, Rosie (2019) *Ongoing Mobility Trajectories: Lived Experiences of Global Migration*. Singapore: Springer.

Robertson, Shanthi (2013) *Transnational Student-Migrants and the State: The Education–Migration Nexus*. Basingstoke: Palgrave Macmillan.

Robertson, Shanthi (2014) 'Time and temporary migration: the case of temporary graduate workers and working holiday makers in Australia.' *Journal of Ethnic and Migration Studies*, 40(12): 1915–33.

Robertson, Shanthi (2015a) 'Contractualization, depoliticization and the limits of solidarity: noncitizens in contemporary Australia.' *Citizenship Studies*, 19(8): 936–50.

Robertson, Shanthi (2015b) 'The temporalities of international migration: implications for ethnographic research.' In *Social Transformation and Migration: National and Local Experiences in South Korea, Turkey, Mexico and Australia*, edited by Stephen Castles, Derya Ozkul and Magdalena Arias Cubas. Basingstoke: Palgrave Macmillan, pp 45–60.

Robertson, Shanthi (2016) 'Intertwined mobilities of education, tourism and labour: the consequences of 417 and 485 visas in Australia.' In *Unintended Consequences: The Impact of Migration Law and Policy*, edited by Marianne Dickie, Dorota Gozdecka and Sudrishti Reich. Canberra: ANU Press, pp 53–80.

Robertson, Shanthi (2017) 'Infrastructures of insecurity: housing and language testing in Asia-Australia migration.' *Geoforum*, 82: 13–20.

Robertson, Shanthi (2018) 'Status-making: rethinking migrant categorization.' *Journal of Sociology*, 55(2): 219–33.

Robertson, Shanthi (2019) 'Migrant, interrupted: the temporalities of "staggered" migration from Asia to Australia.' *Current Sociology*, 67(2):169–85.

Robertson, Shanthi, Anita Harris and Loretta Baldassar (2018a) 'Mobile transitions: a conceptual framework for researching a generation on the move.' *Journal of Youth Studies*, 21(2): 203–17.

Robertson, Shanthi, Yi'En Cheng and Brenda S.A. Yeoh (2018b) 'Introduction: Mobile Aspirations? Youth im/mobilities in the Asia-Pacific.' *Journal of Intercultural Studies*, 39(6): 613–25.

Rogaly, Ben and Susan Thieme (2012) 'Experiencing space–time: the stretched lifeworlds of migrant workers in India.' *Environment and Planning A*, 44(9): 2086–100.

Rosa, Harmut (2013) *Social Acceleration: A New Theory of Modernity*. NY: Columbia University Press.

Rowe, Francisco, Jonathan Corcoran and Alessandra Faggian (2013) 'Mobility patterns of overseas human capital in Australia: the role of a "new" graduate visa scheme and rural development policy.' *Australian Geographer*, 44(2): 177–95.

Roy, Abhijit (2018) 'The middle class in India: from 1947 to the present and beyond.' *Education about Asia*, 23(1): 32–7.

Ruhs, Martin and Bridget Anderson (2010) 'Semi-compliance and illegality in migrant labour markets: an analysis of migrants, employers and the state in the UK.' *Population, Space and Place*, 16(3): 195–211.

Rutten, Mario and Sanderien Verstappen (2014) 'Middling migration: contradictory mobility experiences of Indian youth in London.' *Journal of Ethnic and Migration Studies*, 40(8): 1217–35.

Ryan, Louise, Amanda Klekowski Von Koppenfels and Jon Mulholland (2015) '"The distance between us": a comparative examination of the technical, spatial and temporal dimensions of the transnational social relationships of highly skilled migrants.' *Global Networks*, 15(2): 198–216.

Rytter, Mikkel (2012) 'Between preferences: marriage and mobility among Danish Pakistani youth.' *Journal of the Royal Anthropological Institute*, 18(3): 572–90.

Sala, Emanuela and Loretta Baldassar (2017) 'Leaving family to return to family: roots migration among second-generation Italian-Australians.' *Ethos*, 45(3): 386–408.

Salazar, Noel B. (2011) 'Tanzanian migration imaginaries.' In *Migration and Culture*, edited by Robin Cohen and Gunvor Jonsson. Cheltenham: Edward Elgar, pp 673–87.

Samers, Michael (2010) *Migration*. New York, NY: Routledge.

Sassen, Saskia (1999) *Guests and Aliens*. New York, NY: The New Press.

Schuster, Liza (2005) 'The continuing mobility of migrants in Italy: shifting between places and statuses.' *Journal of Ethnic and Migration Studies*, 31(4): 757–74.

Scott, Sam (2006) 'The social morphology of skilled migration: the case of the British middle class in Paris.' *Journal of Ethnic and Migration Studies*, 32(7): 1105–29.

Scott, Sam (2019) 'New middle-class labor migrants.' In *The Palgrave Handbook of Ethnicity*, edited by Steven Ratuva. Singapore: Palgrave Macmillan, pp 1–20.

Sennett, Richard (2006) *The Culture of the New Capitalism*. New Haven, CT: Yale University Press.

Seo, Seonyoung (2019) 'Temporalities of class in Nepalese labour migration to South Korea.' *Current Sociology*, 67(2): 186–205.

Sharma, Sarah (2014) *In the Meantime: Temporality and Cultural Politics*. Durham, NC: Duke University Press.

Shields, John (2003) *No Safe Haven: Markets, Welfare, and Migrants*. Toronto: CERIS.

Shubin, Sergei (2015) 'Migration timespaces: A Heideggerian approach to understanding the mobile being of Eastern Europeans in Scotland.' *Transactions of the Institute of British Geographers*, 40(3): 350–61.

Sklair, Leslie (2012) 'Transnational capitalist class.' In: *The Wiley-Blackwell Encyclopedia of Globalization*, edited by George Ritzer. Oxford, UK; Malden MA, USA: Wiley-Blackwell.

Skrbis, Zlatko, Ian Woodward and Clive Bean (2014) 'Seeds of cosmopolitan future? Young people and their aspirations for future mobility.' *Journal of Youth Studies*, 17(5): 614–25.

Smith, Michael Peter (2005) 'Transnational urbanism revisited.' *Journal of Ethnic and Migration Studies*, 31(2): 235–44.

Smith, Vicki (2010) 'Review article: Enhancing employability: human, cultural, and social capital in an era of turbulent unpredictability.' *Human Relations*, 63(2): 279–300.

Standing, Guy (2011) *The Precariat: A New Dangerous Class*. New York, NY: Bloomsbury Academic.

Stevens, Catriona (2017) '"Now I can never go back": the thwarted returns of temporary labour migrants from China in Perth, Western Australia.' *Transitions: Journal of Transient Migration*, 1(1): 65–83.

Stevens, Catriona (2019) 'Temporary work, permanent visas and circular dreams: temporal disjunctures and precarity among Chinese migrants to Australia.' *Current Sociology*, 67(2): 294–314.

Stock, Inka (2019) *Time, Migration and Forced Immobility: Sub-Saharan African Migrants in Morocco*. Bristol: Bristol University Press.

Thien, Deborah (2007) 'Intimate distances: considering questions of "us".' In *Emotional Geographies*, edited by Joyce Davidson, Liz Bondi and Mick Smith. Farnham: Ashgate Publishing, pp 191–204.

Thomas, Ward F. and Ong, Paul M. (2015) 'Ethnic mobilization among Korean dry cleaners.' *Ethnic and Racial Studies*, 38(12): 1105–29.

Thomson, Rachel and Taylor, Rebecca (2005) 'Between cosmopolitanism and the locals: mobility as a resource in the transition to adulthood.' *Young*, 13(4): 327–42.

Tomba, Luigi (2004) 'Creating an urban middle class: social engineering in Beijing.' *China Journal*, 5(1): 1–26.

Tsai, Lisa Lee and Collins, Francis L. (2017) 'Youth and mobility in working holidays: imagined freedoms and lived constraints in lives of Taiwanese working holidaymakers in New Zealand.' *New Zealand Geographer*, 73(2): 129–40.

Tseng, Yen-Fen (2000) 'The mobility of entrepreneurs and capital: Taiwanese capital-linked migration.' *International Migration*, 38(2): 143–68.

Tu, Mengwei (2016) 'Chinese one-child families in the age of migration: middle-class transnational mobility, ageing parents, and the changing role of filial piety.' *The Journal of Chinese Sociology*, 3(1): 15.

Tu, Mengwei (2018) *Education, Migration and Family Relations between China and the UK: The Transnational One-Child Generation.* Bingley: Emerald Publishing.

Tuxen, Nonie (2018) 'Seeking "the foreign stamp": international education and the (re)production of class status in Mumbai, India.' Unpublished PhD Dissertation, Australian National University, Canberra.

UNWTO (World Tourism Organization) (2016) *Tourism Highlights: 2016 Edition.* Madrid: UNWTO.

Urry, John (2000) *Sociology Beyond Societies: Mobilities for the Twenty-First Century.* Abingdon: Taylor & Francis.

Valentine, Gill (2003) 'Boundary crossings: transitions from childhood to adulthood.' *Children's Geographies*, 1(1): 37–52.

Varriale, Simone (2019) 'Unequal youth migrations: exploring the synchrony between social ageing and social mobility among post-crisis European migrants.' *Sociology*, 53(6): 1160–76.

Vertovec, Steven (2009) *Transnationalism.* Abingdon: Routledge.

Villegas, Paloma E. (2014) '"I can't even buy a bed because I don't know if I'll have to leave tomorrow": temporal orientations among Mexican precarious status migrants in Toronto.' *Citizenship Studies*, 18(3–4): 277–91.

Virilio, Paul (2006) *Speed and Politics.* New York, NY: Semiotext(e).

Vogel, Erica (2016) 'Ongoing endings: migration, love, and ethnography.' *Journal of Contemporary Ethnography*, 45(6): 673–91.

Wagner, Lauren (2014) 'Rhythms of a transnational marriage: temporal topologies of borders in a knowledge migrant family.' *Etnofoor*, 26(1): 81–105.

Wallace, Michael and David Brady (2001) 'The next long swing: spatialization, technocratic control, and the restructuring of work at the turn of the century.' In *Sourcebook of Labor Markets: Evolving Structures and Processes*, edited by Ivar Berg and Arne Kalleberg. New York, NY: Kluwar Academic and Plenum, pp 101–34.

Walsh, James (2014) 'From nations of immigrants to states of transience: temporary migration in Canada and Australia.' *International Sociology*, 29(6): 584–606.

Walsh, Katie (2006) 'British expatriate belongings: mobile homes and transnational homing.' *Home Cultures*, 3(2): 123–44.

Walsh, Katie (2018) *Transnational Geographies of the Heart: Intimate Subjectivities in a Globalising City*. Chichester: John Wiley & Sons.

Wang, Bingyu (2020) 'A temporal gaze towards academic migration: Everyday times, lifetimes and temporal strategies amongst early career Chinese academic returnees.' *Time & Society*, 29(1): 166–86.

Wang, Bingyu, and Francis Collins (2020) 'Temporally distributed aspirations: new Chinese migrants to New Zealand and the figuring of migration futures.' *Sociology*, 54(3): 573–90.

Waters, Johanna L. (2006) 'Geographies of cultural capital: education, international migration and family strategies between Hong Kong and Canada.' *Transactions of the Institute of British Geographers*, 31(2): 179–92.

Waters, Johanna (2009) 'Transnational geographies of academic distinction: the role of social capital in the recognition and evaluation of "overseas" credentials.' *Globalization, Societies and Education*, 7(2): 113–29.

Waters, Johanna (2015) 'Educational imperatives and the compulsion for credentials: family migration and children's education in East Asia.' *Children's Geographies*, 13(3): 280–93.

Watkins, Megan, Christina Ho and Rose Butler (2017) *Asian Migration and Education Cultures in the Anglo-Sphere*. Abingdon: Routledge.

Welford, Richard (2005) 'Corporate social responsibility in Europe, North America and Asia.' *The Journal of Corporate Citizenship*, 17 (Spring): 33–52.

White, Allen, Caitriona Ní Laoire, Naomi Tyrell and Fina Carpena-Mendez (2011) 'Children's role in transnational migration.' *Journal of Ethnic and Migration Studies*, 37(8): 1159–70.

Wilson, Jude, David Fisher and Kevin Moore (2009) 'The OE goes "home": cultural aspects of a working holiday experience.' *Tourist Studies*, 9(1): 3–21.

Winson, Anthony and Belinda Leach (2002) *Contingent Work, Disrupted Lives: Labour and Community in the New Rural Economy.* Toronto: University of Toronto Press.

Wong, Tai-Chee and Jonathan Rigg (2010) *Asian Cities, Migrant Labor and Contested Spaces.* Abingdon: Routledge.

Wright, Chris F., Stephen Clibborn, Nicola Piper and Nicole Cini (2016) 'Economic migration and Australia in the 21st century.' Lowy Institute [Online]. www.lowyinstitute.org/publications/economic-migration-and-australia-21st-century

Yea, Sallie (2008) 'Married to the military: Filipinas negotiating transnational families.' *International Migration*, 46 (4): 111–44.

Yeoh, Brenda S.A. (2009) 'Making sense of "Asian" families in the age of migration.' *Asian Population Studies*, 5(1): 1–3.

Yeoh, Brenda S.A. (2017) 'Transient migrations: intersectionalities, mobilities and temporalities.' *Transitions: Journal of Transient Migration*, 1(1): 143–6.

Yeoh, Brenda S.A. and Lai Ah Eng (2008) 'Talent migration in and out of Asia: challenges for policies and places.' *Asian Population Studies*, 4(3): 234–45.

Yeoh, Brenda S.A. and Weiqiang Lin (2013) 'Chinese migration to Singapore: discourses and discontents in a globalizing nation-state.' *Asian and Pacific Migration Journal*, 22(1): 31.

Yeoh, Brenda S.A., Shirlena Huang and Theodora Lam (2018) 'Transnational family dynamic in Asia.' In *Handbook of Migration and Globalisation*, edited by Anna Triandafyllidou. Cheltenham UK: Edward Elgar, pp 413–30.

Yoon, Kyong (2014a) 'The racialised mobility of transnational working holidays.' *Identities*, 21(5): 586–603.

Yoon, Kyong (2014b) 'Transnational youth mobility in the neoliberal economy of experience.' *Journal of Youth Studies*, 17(8): 1014–28.

Yoon, Kyong (2015) 'A national construction of transnational mobility in the "overseas working holiday phenomenon" in Korea.' *Journal of Intercultural Studies*, 36(1): 71–87.

Yu, Wan (2016) 'To stay or to return? Return intentions and return migrations of Chinese students during the transition period in the United States.' *Papers in Applied Geography*, 2(2): 201–15.

Zerubavel, Eviatar (1982) 'The standardization of time: a sociohistorical perspective.' *American Journal of Sociology*, 88(1): 1–23.

Zhou, Yanqiu Rachel (2015) 'Time, space and care: rethinking transnational care from a temporal perspective.' *Time & Society*, 24(2): 163–82.

Index